WHITEY

WHITEY

THE STORY OF
REAR ADMIRAL E. L. FEIGHTNER,
A NAVY FIGHTER ACE

PETER B. MERSKY

Naval Institute Press
Annapolis, Maryland

This book has been brought to publication
with the generous assistance of Marguerite and Gerry Lenfest.

Naval Institute Press
291 Wood Road
Annapolis, MD 21402

Library of Congress Cataloging-in-Publication Data
Mersky, Peter B.
  Whitey : the story of Rear Admiral E. L. Feightner, a Navy fighter ace / Peter B.
Mersky.
     pages cm
  Includes bibliographical references and index.
  ISBN 978-1-61251-791-9 (hbk. : alk. paper) — ISBN 978-0-87021-084-6
(ebook) 1. Feightner, Edward Lewis, 1919– 2. Admirals—United States—
Biography. 3. Fighter pilots—United States—Biography. 4. Test pilots—United
States—Biography. 5. United States. Navy—Officers—Biography. 6. United
States. Navy—Aviation—Biography. 7. World War, 1939–1945—Aerial operations,
American. I. Title.
  V63.F45M47 2014
  359.0092—dc23
  [B]
                                                                2014026234

♾ Print editions meet the requirements of ANSI/NISO z39.48-1992 (Permanence
of Paper).
Printed in the United States of America.

22 21 20 19 18 17 16 15 14   9 8 7 6 5 4 3 2 1
First printing

CONTENTS

MAPS

WHITEY

INTRODUCTION

I have known Whitey Feightner for nearly thirty years. Aviation historian Barrett Tillman introduced us when I began researching the story of one of Whitey's wartime fighter squadrons, VF-10. I immediately realized what a unique individual this easygoing, always smiling person was and how much a part of naval aviation history he represented. Many military aviators are intense personalities. It's how they got through a lot of the terrible combat they experienced, putting their lives on the line every day, often watching their friends and comrades die in terrible ways as they themselves fought to survive. Once while I was interviewing him for the VF-10 history, I was again pushing Whitey for photographs.

He always smiled when I asked him, always saying he didn't have very many. Finally, exasperated at running into the same dead end, I complained that I never knew a naval aviator who didn't have lots of pictures of himself. For once, his smile disappeared.

"We were too busy trying to stay alive," he said. It was a reply that was stunning in its simplicity, something I have never forgotten.

Whitey has had a colorful and exciting life, flying more than a hundred different types of aircraft, large and small, props and jets, fighters and bombers, ranging from the little Piper Cub to the monstrous Lockheed R6O Constitution four-engine transport, as well as helicopters, and everything in between, all the while facing the trials and tribulations of a thirty-year naval career. His quiet, knowing smile and positive, team-oriented attitude endeared him to the people he met, both junior and senior.

This may not be the huge book that many people might expect, but I hope that within these pages, the reader will discover one of the Navy's true quiet treasures, a great aviator and a fine example of what it means to be an officer in the U.S. Navy in war and peace.

Peter B. Mersky
Alexandria, Virginia, 2014

CHAPTER 1
GROWING UP IN OHIO

The so-called Greatest Generation of World War II came from everywhere, every state, every city, every walk of life. They were young, middle-aged, even what we would today call seniors. For nearly the last time in the twentieth century and perhaps for well into the twenty-first century, Americans were united in a common cause: to defeat a triumvirate of nations and dictators and their many minions equally focused on hobbling the rest of the world and bending it to their twisted wills. With the arguable exception of the multination coalition that fought the 1991 Gulf War against Saddam Hussein's Iraq, it is doubtful we will see such a coalition again.

In the United States, we were late to join the hard-pressed Europeans. By the summer of 1940, most countries on the continent had been swallowed by the German juggernaut. Only Great Britain stood valiantly alone, the last great bastion of prewar freedom against an enemy it had beaten twenty years earlier. In Asia, the sleepy giant of China battled within itself, desperately trying to come together into a single entity, ready to face the technologically superior Japanese, who had always cast envious eyes on their gigantic neighbor across the sea. Americans were roughly divided into two camps: isolationist and those who knew they would much sooner than later have to fight. Americans listened every evening to reports from Europe, especially London. In Washington, the president and his cabinet agonized over whether to allow continued shipping of raw materials like steel and rubber to the strange but obviously dangerous Japanese Empire, which was determined to create a hemisphere for Asians under its own harsh, demanding rule.

When the time finally came on a seemingly peaceful, pre-Christmas Sunday in 1941, America was ill-prepared to fight. But fight we did, and within nine months, the huge industrial machine that many Japanese and German leaders feared was working at a fever pitch, turning out every implement of war as well as training the hundreds of thousands of men to use them.

Among these eager, patriotic young men was a handsome Ohioan who wanted to fly. Indeed, he had been flying for some time before he sought out a Navy recruiter. Years of hunting had sharpened his already keen eyesight, and his natural affinity for math and science and equally high self-confidence made him a recruiter's dream . . . and soon a Japanese nightmare.

Edward Lewis Feightner, the son of Amos E. and Mary S. Roth Feightner, was born on October 14, 1919, in Lima, Ohio, about fifty miles north of Dayton. His paternal grandfather, Lewis, was descended from Lutheran immigrants from the German state of Schleswig-Holstein. They had come to America in 1736 and settled in Westmoreland County, Pennsylvania. For some reason, they added a "g" to the original spelling of their last name. They trained and bred race horses, trotters to be exact, and brought their expertise and love for the sport over to their new country. The first Feightner, Edward's great-great-great-great grandfather, was killed during an Indian raid, always a great hazard for these early pioneers. Edward's great-great-great grandfather served under George Washington during the American Revolution. His great-grandfather, Solomon Feightner, had gone farther west, to Wayne County, Ohio, to become a farmer and miller. Young Edward's maternal grandparents were Edward and Nelle Roth, and the young Feightner had been named for both his grandfathers. He also had three sisters, Virginia, Marian, and Eleanor, who died at relatively early ages from illnesses. The girls were taller than their brother and enjoyed playing basketball. Edward grew up in the farm country of Elida, six miles west of Lima, about eighty-five miles south of Toledo and eighty miles north of Dayton.

He enjoyed a busy, active childhood that brought out his natural inclinations in athletics—he excelled in baseball and at one time was under scrutiny by scouts from the St. Louis Browns (the team that moved to Baltimore in the mid-1950s to become the Baltimore Orioles). Small at only five feet, one inch and 102 pounds while in high school, Edward joined his college wrestling team and actually grew seven inches in his first year. His interests in farming and chemistry had also led to a brief try at pickle farming for Heinz.

His grandfather, Lewis, had been a tool maker for the Lima Locomotive Works, one of the three or four largest steam locomotive manufacturers in the country, since he was seventeen, and he worked for the company for thirty-two years before retiring to his dairy farm. He did answer the call for the national emergency when America entered World War I in April 1917. Remaining a civilian, he worked for two years as a tool designer at the East Iron & Machine Company, a subsidiary of Lima Locomotive Works. He had his own well-equipped shop and an assistant producing any tool for any need. Young Edward would spend hours watching his grandfather work, fascinated by all the tools and machines in the older Feightner's shop.

Lewis actually held several patents on the Shay locomotive, a gear-driven engine that worked around hills and is still in use today on the Cass Scenic Railroad in Cass, West Virginia, and the Georgetown Loop in Colorado. During his early years, Edward put in a lot of time in his grandfather's dairy farm. He had been driving tractors since he was ten and actually helped out whenever he could in any one of his family's four farms at the time. He raised dairy cattle, and during summers in college he worked at his father's company as a draftsman.

Both his father and grandfather had a big influence on Ed, imparting their work ethic, curiosity, and mechanical skill, all of which would serve him well throughout his life, but nowhere more than in the cockpit. After graduating from high school in 1937 as class president and valedictorian, he accepted a scholarship to Findlay College in Findlay, Ohio. He had been on a tractor working in the field when a man in a suit appeared. Mr. Beano was a history professor and was authorized to offer a full scholarship. Other schools had only promised partial scholarships, and Edward's dad Amos was delighted at the prospect of his son getting a completely funded college education. The scholarship was for valedictorian in scholastic studies. Edward majored in chemical engineering and graduated with a double bachelor of science degree in chemistry and math. He worked part-time as a chemist at the local sugar beet factory. Sugar beets were a big commodity in the town.

Mike Murphy and First Flights

It was Edward's early interest in flying, however, that finally set him on his true life's path. One day, Edward was in the office of James Donnell, president of Ohio Oil, which had actually put up his scholarship, when a stranger entered dressed in flight clothing. It was Mike Murphy, who was also a captain in the Army Reserves. Murphy was fairly well known at the time and gave a lot of attention to the young student. It was Mike who offered Edward his first flight. He took one look at him and said, "Hey, kid, wanna go flyin'?" Donnell quickly sent his student out with Mike, something of a wild man with, Edward thought, a reputation to match. He thought Mike looked like Charles Lindbergh!

Murphy took Edward up in a big Ford Trimotor, one of the largest civilian aircraft of the time and one that had begun to garner its share of fame with various explorations and expeditions and service in general aviation. After a while, he gave the controls to his new student and Edward flew the Ford for the better part of four hours. Thereafter, his studies and schedule permitting, Edward flew with Murphy every chance he got, usually at night. It was Murphy who taught the neophyte aviator something he took with him for the rest of his flying career: keep the plane properly trimmed and you will never have any trouble.

Arguably one of the most well-known aviators of the period and a top-notch pioneer aerobatic pilot, Murphy ran the airport near Findlay College and was also the chief pilot for Ohio Oil. It owned three of the big corrugated Fords, which featured neon signs on their fuselages. Murphy also had quite a collection of aircraft that included many of the popular trainers of the time.

Murphy was well known for his heart-stopping routines at local air shows, especially the popular Cleveland Air Races, usually set for the Labor Day weekend in September. In one maneuver, Murphy would land on and take off from a moving auto fixed with a platform to the amazement of the crowds. The truck's driver was young Edward L. Feightner.

Murphy won the 1938 and 1940 American Aerobatic Championships flying his German-made Bucker Jungmeister, a two-seat biplane that would also see much service as a primary trainer in the Luftwaffe during World War II. Murphy's spritely little biplane, which Romanian pilot Alex Papana had originally brought over in a crate on board the German Zeppelin *Hindenburg* to fly in the 1937 Cleveland Air Races, now resides in the Stephen F. Udvar-Hazy Center of the National Air and Space Museum near Dulles Airport in Chantilly, Virginia. His protégé, Edward, helped recover its wings. Murphy conceived the Mike Murphy Cup, awarded to each year's U.S. National Aerobatics Champion. Thus, Ed Feightner had one of America's greatest pilots as his early instructor.[1]

Edward took to flying as naturally as the proverbial duck to water. He was definitely in his element. He started flying in 1939 in the Civilian Pilot Training Program, created to produce a large pool of civilian pilots that could serve as a quick-draw source for the military, and he earned his private license in 1940. Dr. Yale K. Roots, head of Findlay's physics and math departments, had started the civilian aviation course. He, too, was to have a big effect on Edward's life. Blessed with exceptional 20/15 eyesight, Edward quickly became convinced he wanted to be a fighter pilot. He once noted, "I'm absolutely convinced fighter pilots are the best pilots on earth, naturally. . . . A fighter pilot has to have something different from the rest of the people. It's an instinct."[2]

Discussing his later success in the Pacific, Feightner observed,

> I found that 90 percent of the time I was the first one who was aware of them. . . . We had people that went out time after time and to this day have never seen an enemy airplane. And I could go up and almost every flight we'd go up, [and] we'd run into enemy airplanes somewhere. . . . I think a lot of that is eyesight. . . . I did a lot of looking. And I think the only fighter pilots who survived in those days were people who looked around.[3]

Graduating from Findlay College in 1941 and facing the draft, which had been instituted in October 1940, as well as what many Americans saw as the imminent involvement of the United States in the war raging in Europe and Asia, Feightner decided to approach military service as long as he could fly. He had been to Dayton to watch the Army pilots perform for air show crowds many times and hoped to fly one of the appealing little P-36s, usually showing off their aluminum finish and colorful squadron insignia. It was something bound to appeal to an adventurous young hopeful of the time.

Participating in the Civilian Pilot Training Program, Feightner graduated with some 250 hours and his private pilot's license. He compared it once with the Navy's elimination training program, where applicants were given primary instruction to see if they had the initial physical coordination and mental understanding to continue to more advanced training. Although he couldn't haul passengers for pay, his private certificate allowed him to take other people up when he flew. It worked out, as people who wanted to sample flying would come to the airport and pay Murphy $5 for a few minutes of flight, with Feightner as the pilot. His hours built up and he eventually entered the Navy's flight program with a considerable number in his logbook.

Originally, with the draft breathing down his neck, he had signed up with the Army; the lure of flying P-36s at nearby Wright Field was a real draw. But there was a pool of applicants in front of him, nearly eight months, and Feightner did not want to wait that long. As luck would have it, one day a Navy SNJ (the Navy version of the Army's T-6 two-seat trainer) landed at Murphy's field and the pilot went into the hangar to change clothes. He came out in his whites and quickly stepped into a convertible driven by a striking redhead. Even Murphy was impressed, and he told his protégé to take one of his planes up to the naval air station at Grosse Ile in Michigan, where the Navy recruiters were, and check out the Navy's program.

When Edward and a friend—Sheldon O. "Red" Hall,[4] who had co-captained the college wrestling team with Edward—got up to Grosse Ile, they were warmly greeted by the Navy recruiter, who showed them films and pressed them into taking a physical, which they passed.

"You know," the recruiter said, "if you come in the Navy, we'll take you right now."[5] Most midwesterners, especially those living near Army airfields, had seen only Army aircraft and thus knew little of aircraft carriers or other aspects of naval aviation. Nevertheless, the two boys signed up that day. It was April 1941.

The recruiter told them to finish getting their college degrees, which was only another couple of months, and then report back to him. He gave them all sorts of folders and brochures, which they dutifully brought back to Mike Murphy, who allowed as how they had not made that bad a decision. As far as the Army was concerned, the waiting list could wait. They were in the Navy. In June, the two young graduates flew back up to Michigan two hours after they got their degrees. Murphy told them to leave the airplane and that he would pick it up later. Ed Feightner had nearly three hundred hours in his logbook and had flown thirty-two different types of aircraft, and now he was to start another kind of flight training.

CHAPTER 2
FLYING THE NAVY WAY

Flight Training Begins

Flight instruction is pretty set, no matter the date—1918, 1941, or 2014. It's like riding a bike. There are certain physics, motions, and mental understandings that form the base of the act of taking off, flying from point A to point B, and landing safely. Everything else in between, such as navigation, learning the importance of weather, aerobatics, use of flight aids such as instruments and electronic dials and indicators, comes and goes with various improvements and local requirements. For instance, flying over unpopulated terrain as opposed to flying over densely crowded areas such as cities and airports, not to mention large expanses of water, varies considerably.

Then there are the aircraft and their individual systems. The front-line types of 1941 were in many ways greatly advanced from their sires of 1918. Retractable landing gear, complex engines with individual sets of controls that helped set a propeller's "position" in the air as it pulled—usually—the aircraft along, and advances in the cockpit as well as in armament and expendable ordnance set a 1941 Grumman Wildcat or Mitsubishi Zero far apart from the 1917 French Nieuport series or the German Albatros or the Fokker D.VII of 1918, arguably the best fighter of World War I.

It still required a certain type of individual to fly a military fighter or bomber. Certainly, physical and mental capabilities hadn't changed that much since 1918. A pilot still had to have a certain amount of strength and mental awareness, not to mention more than his fair share of courage, especially a military pilot and most particularly any aviator whose job was to go into combat.

Among the U.S. military services, the Navy was growing perhaps the most, but none grew as rapidly as naval aviation, which was about to enter its greatest conflict. In its first decade, the Navy had trained 2,834 young aviators. In 1941, another 3,112 had gained their wings of gold. In 1944, 21,067 men had achieved the status of naval aviator. Never would so many new pilots—and this does not include the aircrewmen and people who washed out at various stages—be in training. In 1940,

America had only five aircraft carriers. By the spring of 1945, it had ninety-nine in service with more than thirty under construction.

It was into this huge and growing machine of production that men like twenty-two-year-old Edward L. Feightner chose to go. A young but not inexperienced pilot, like many of his compatriots, he was about to offer himself to ride the tip of his country's spear against a highly capable, often implacable enemy that would ask little quarter in the coming fight.

Now Seaman Second Class Feightner had little trouble going through the month-long ground school, including Morse code and the primary flight syllabus at Grosse Ile, which, incredibly, consisted of only *one* flight, one circuit of the field, after which the instructor got out and sent the student off *solo*. The instructor told him, "That's all you get here. You get the rest when you get to Corpus Christi."

There had been thirty-four students in the class, but only thirteen graduated. The elimination phase was tough and very competitive. "They were really weeding them out," Feightner recalled. "They'd had a lot of people."

Then it was on to Corpus Christi, Texas, in July, Naval Cadet Class 10B-41C, which had a good number of already licensed pilots. There were so many, in fact, that the Navy assigned Feightner duty as plane captain for one of the N2S Stearman biplanes. At this time, the press was on to get through as many flight instructors as possible. Training new student aviators could wait until a large pool of instructors was available to take the strain off the system. The Navy was bringing back aviators from the fleet as well as from the Reserve, besides "requesting" qualified aviators from the Marine Corps. Newly designated naval aviators were also being ordered, "plowed back," to instructor duty instead of going to the fleet. The situation didn't sit well with the new pilots, who quite naturally were anxious to get to an operational squadron. When they did eventually arrive in the fleet, however, they appreciated the several hundred hours of extra flight time.

Although not yet a naval aviator, Seaman Feightner got extra time as weight to properly balance the yellow biplanes when the student instructor went out to practice his maneuvers and teaching technique. Feightner wouldn't start his actual training syllabus until October, so he kept his mouth shut as the instructor-in-training waltzed around the sky usually unmindful of his white-hat student with three hundred hours in the rear cockpit. At least he got to know the tough little Stearman well, and sometimes the instructor would let him fly the trainer. Actually, the instructors under training were under a lot of pressure and worked six days a week from dawn to dusk. The training command also had to contend with a rise in mishaps, especially those involving inverted spins. Specialized instructors traveled the circuit of training bases to show students how to extricate themselves from this frightening situation, and gradually the mishap rate began to decrease.

At Corpus, students received more intense training in navigation as well as in the military side of their new status as members of the U.S. Navy. For the first eight weeks, the students went through ground school classes. The flight training really began in earnest in the last two weeks. Those students who soloed had their planes festooned with red streamers, a warning to other people in the air that the pilot should be given a wide berth.

In Seaman Feightner's case, with all his pre-Navy time in the air, he was bored just flying straight and level for an hour and twenty minutes. He decided to do some aerobatics. Unfortunately, an instructor saw his impromptu air show and was waiting for the overzealous student aviator when Feightner landed. The instructor read him the riot act, reminding Feightner of rules and the requirement of simply flying straight and level at this stage of instruction. Duly chastened, Feightner continued with the syllabus.

Finishing the training in the Stearman, his next aircraft was the Curtiss SNC, "a cute little airplane," as he later described it. The company tried making a single-seat fighter out of the design and actually sent several to China and the Netherlands East Indies, where it had an intense but abortive career in combat during the first months of the Pacific War. Feightner enjoyed the little trainer, of which little more than three hundred were built during the war, and used it for navigation, formation flying, and cross-country flights.

His next trainer was the Vultee SNV Valiant, which the Army flew as the BT-13. The tandem-seated trainer bore a strong resemblance to North American's Harvard/Texan (SNJ in the Navy) trainer but did not include retractable landing gear. A steady aircraft, the SNV was a good instrument trainer, and Feightner went through that phase before changing to the Vought OS2U Kingfisher. This aircraft was an odd choice for a trainer because it served as a front-line floatplane, which saw a lot of action during the war, especially in the Pacific. It saved the lives of many downed Allied airmen as well as providing gunfire spotting services for the many battleships, cruisers, and destroyers pummeling enemy positions ashore. This trainer version, however, used a normal fixed-wheeled landing gear.

He was getting consistently high grades and got his choice of fighters. He had to fight for the fighter slot, though. Edward had gone in hoping to be a Marine fighter pilot alongside his friend Red Hall, who did become a leatherneck fighter ace. It seemed like a done deal at the beginning, and Edward had endured his share of marching and drilling as a member of a display group that performed at official functions. He had become well acquainted with Marine Corps drill instructors and their loving attentions.

The places for new Marine fighter pilots dried up fairly quickly, though, and the Navy had him scheduled to fly Curtiss SBC dive bombers, the Navy's last biplane dive bomber, of which the Marines had a few. It was a muddled situation, and the new ensign would have none of it and demanded to go to Washington. He grabbed an SNJ and flew up to the capital, where he met a senior lieutenant commander (whose name is now lost to the dark recesses of memory). The sympathetic lieutenant commander was head of advanced fighter training, and he agreed that this smiling, aggressive ensign should be in fighters. Edward returned to Pensacola feeling much better about it all. Instead of the Marines, he would fly fighters for the Navy.

Then came what seemed to be a step back. The next aircraft in the lineup was a fighter biplane, the F3F, a tubby but maneuverable plane that ended the Grumman line of fighting biplanes. Feightner would become intimately acquainted with the F3F's monoplane successors, the F4F and F6F. But for now, the young student aviator enjoyed wringing out the powerful biplane. "I loved the F3F," he remarked years later. "It was a short-coupled airplane and was just a natural aerobatic airplane . . . it had a big engine [950 horsepower] . . . the only airplane that really compared with it was the F8F Bearcat later on."[1]

Feightner was moving right along in the trainer, and he took the F3F on the all-important carrier qualification phase. As all naval aviators know, short of combat, the action that separates them from the rest of the military flying community is flying on and off ships, often in rough weather or at night, or both. In 1941, night flying at sea was still in its infancy and usually was done only out of real military necessity. Later in the war, it was much more of a routine, and certainly today is an accepted part of operational requirements. But in the days just before the United States entered the war, making your first carrier landing was the pinnacle of the training schedule, and it remains so today.

Feightner made his first "traps" while on board the USS *Saratoga* (CV 3). The ship was off the West Coast, and he flew out in an F3F, aiming for the big ship's straight flight deck.

> I remember the sensation—the airplane came to a stop but everything was still going by. And boy, I had the brakes on and I still had the sensation I was still moving. [The flight deck crew] were out there trying to get me to release the brakes so they could haul [my aircraft] back and unhook the tailhook [from the cable] . . . that's a real sensation, that first carrier landing.[2]

Typically, he hadn't been apprehensive. His high level of self-confidence had gotten him ready for this important milestone.

Heading for the Fleet

By now, Feightner had received his orders to go to his fleet squadron, just before he received his wings on April 3, 1942. His family could not attend the ceremony designating their son as a naval aviator because of the drastic wartime travel restrictions instituted after Pearl Harbor. His father understood. He had been a radioman in the old battleship USS *Wisconsin* (BB 9) during World War I. In fact, he had kept up his qualifications and enjoyed being a ham radio operator for many years.

The United States was now fighting the war that had enveloped most of the world for more than two years. Although he had several hundred hours of civilian flight time, Feightner actually lacked the required number of Navy flight hours, only 234 hours. But the war shortened a lot of training schedules, including the number of flight hours needed to graduate, and the fleet needed a large infusion of new aviators. Thus, now Ensign Feightner seemed headed for VF-5, on board the USS *Yorktown* (CV 5), which had just returned from heavy action at the Battle of the Coral Sea, May 4–8, 1942.

In this first battle in which the opposing ships did not see each other and which was fought by the air components of the carriers involved, and which was the first true combat test of American carrier aviation, the United States had lost the carrier USS *Lexington* (CV 2), while the Japanese had lost one carrier with another badly damaged. The victory was more strategic for the United States as it stopped the enemy steamroller at the very doorstep of Australia.

During this period, one other American action had also contributed to derailing the Japanese machine and made the leaders in Tokyo stop to reassess their own strategies. On April 18, sixteen Army B-25 Mitchell bombers had left the pitching deck of the USS *Hornet* (CV 8) and bombed cities and production facilities in Japan. Although all but one of the B-25s were lost—one landed in the Soviet Union, its crew interned because the Russians were not at war with Japan at the time—the effect of the so-called Doolittle Raid (named after the leader, Lt. Col. James H. Doolittle) was monumental.

Only one more major action would round out the first six months of the war, the Battle of Midway, June 4–7. This would have a more personal effect on many of the newly winged aviators, including Ensign Feightner. A large-scale naval action, Midway resulted in Japan losing four of its major fleet carriers—all of which had participated in the attack on Pearl Harbor six months earlier—along with many aircraft and experienced flight crews. The U.S. Navy lost the *Yorktown*. The loss of the *Lexington* and then the *Yorktown* at such a critical point in the war left the United States with only four large flattops (*Hornet*, *Wasp*, *Saratoga*, and *Enterprise*) in the Pacific to contest the still-potent Japanese fleet. Indeed, the *Saratoga* would be out of combat for a long time as a result of an enemy submarine's torpedo in January 1942. And it was to the *Enterprise* that Ensign Feightner eventually went.

CHAPTER 3
TRAINING WITH BUTCH AND INTO THE FIGHT

The period after Midway was a busy one for all concerned. No longer so sure of themselves, the Japanese realized they had indeed awakened the sleeping giant that had given Admiral Isoroku Yamamoto so much pause after launching the attack on Pearl Harbor. The Americans were pulling themselves together and preparing to sail and march across the Pacific, right up to Japan's very doorstep, ready to pay the admittedly heavy price in lives and material. And to start that long, bloody trip, they planned to invade and retake the Solomons, a group of nearly a thousand islands east of New Guinea.

One of the largest of the islands was Guadalcanal, and it was here that the Japanese had built a base, complete with an airfield. The Allies, led by America and Great Britain, planned a major amphibious operation for August 7, 1942, landing on Guadalcanal to capture the enemy airfield and another they were also building, as well as Tulagi, another island across the water from Guadalcanal. At one point, Tulagi was supposed to be the major operation, but, meeting little resistance, the Allies quickly turned their concentrated attention to Guadalcanal.

The fighting quickly intensified both on the ground and in the air, and just as quickly Guadalcanal entered the American lexicon. Only a few short weeks earlier, few Americans could have pronounced it or found it on a map. Soon, however, many parents and spouses had sons, brothers, husbands, and fathers fighting for their lives on this sodden bit of South Pacific jungle.

But the newly winged naval aviators were learning their trade, mostly in Hawaii. They were gaining more experience in their aircraft, namely F4F Wildcats and SBD Dauntless dive bombers. They were learning how to fly these aging aircraft off carriers and how to get the most out of their lackluster performance once in the air. Among these eager young men was Ens. Edward L. Feightner of Elida, Ohio.

A Change in Plans and Butch's Story

At first, Feightner had gone to Norfolk to get checked out in the F4F Wildcat before joining VF-5 on board the USS *Yorktown*. Then, with the *Yorktown* actually leaving

Pearl Harbor headed for the Battle of Midway in June, he flew across the United States to San Francisco, where he and his compatriots were held for a while, waiting to get transportation to Hawaii. While there, the young ensign got "shanghaied" into a tour as junior officer on the deck of the USS *Henderson* (AP 1), a transport taking Army troops to Hawaii. The voyage took ten days and Feightner stood many watches as he impatiently made his way over. By the time the *Henderson* made Pearl, the *Yorktown* had been sunk at Midway. All the orders changed, and he was sent to VF-3, now shore-based at Maui under the command of Edward O'Hare, always known as "Butch." Newly promoted to lieutenant commander, O'Hare had enjoyed a meteoric rise to fame because of aerial action the previous February. His story is well known but bears briefly repeating.

Born in St. Louis, Missouri, O'Hare was a member of the U.S. Naval Academy's class of 1937. His father was a lawyer with connections to Al Capone, the infamous gangster. Butch's father was assassinated in November 1939, probably as payment for his role in convicting Capone of tax evasion. Bearing up under the terrible loss, Butch finished his flight training and received his wings of gold in May 1940. In less than two years, he would become America's most famous pilot.

Eventually O'Hare was assigned to VF-3, then flying the Brewster F2A-1, one of the Navy's most debated and unproductive aircraft of the prewar era. It was underpowered and had incredibly weak landing gear that often collapsed right after landing on a carrier, certainly not a good recommendation for a front-line fighter.

Butch was promoted to lieutenant junior grade that August, and by December the squadron XO (executive officer), Lt. John "Jimmie" Thach, one of the Navy's great aerial tacticians, had taken command of the squadron. Thach had been watching Butch and had taken him under his wing to show the new aviator the ropes, teaching him the fine points of aerial combat maneuvers and strategy.

VF-3 spent the early months of 1941 practicing landings and takeoffs on available carriers. The big news was the arrival of Grumman F4F-3 Wildcats in August. A much sturdier aircraft than the F2A, these tubby little fighters would be the best the Navy had to fight the Japanese in the coming months.

By December 7, 1941, with the attack on Pearl Harbor, the squadron was part of the USS *Saratoga*'s air wing, but on January 11, 1942, the *Saratoga* was badly damaged by a Japanese submarine's torpedo and limped back to Pearl for a lengthy repair period. Fully equipped with Wildcats, VF-3 joined the USS *Lexington*'s air group, and sortied to confront the enemy. By February 1942, the *Lexington* and her task force were down in the South Pacific, heading toward Australia, now threatened by a possible Japanese drive to the north coast. On February 20, the task force was nearing the Solomon Islands, the same group of islands that would in six months be the scene of some of the most sustained and bloody action of the Pacific War.

Air operations started early. VF-3 was certainly ready to launch. Ship's radar had detected intruders, and soon the squadron's CAP (combat air patrol) found a Japanese flying boat, a Kawanishi Type 97 that would soon be code named Mavis.

MAP 1

The Pacific Theatre

From Thach Weave: The Life of Jimmie Thach (Annapolis, Md.: Naval Institute Press, 2004), 42.

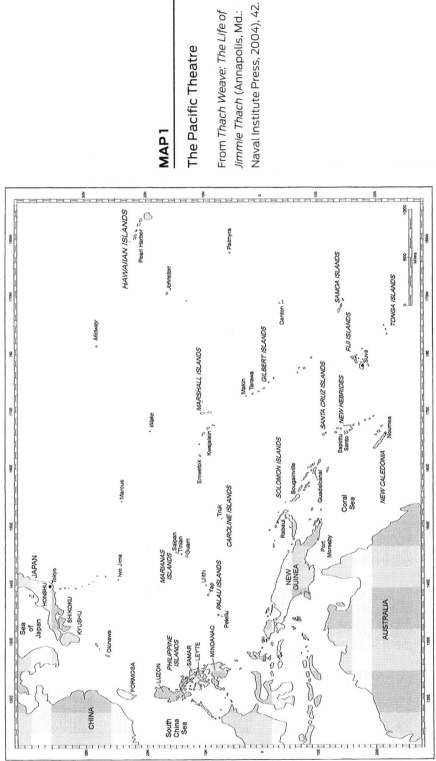

Although the VF-3 fighters splashed the large, parasol-winged "boat," its crew had already alerted enemy headquarters on Rabaul of the approaching American force. Soon, another Wildcat CAP had disposed of a second Mavis. Butch O'Hare had not been in either of these actions, the squadron's first, but he was about to make up for his absence.

As the day wore on, the Japanese sent out a raid to apprehend the U.S. force that had so easily destroyed two valuable assets and to inflict as much damage as possible to ease growing pressure against a Japanese attack on Australia. Land-based Mitsubishi G4M1 bombers—later code named Betty—from the 4th Air Group were launched. A large, rotund twin-engine aircraft, the G4M enjoyed an impressive range and acceptable speed. The G4M's main drawbacks were lack of any appreciable defensive armament and a distinct tendency to catch fire under enemy guns. These two points would play into Butch O'Hare's hands in the late afternoon of February 20.

Seventeen G4Ms lined up to attack the *Lexington*, but were intercepted by VF-3's CAP, resulting in the loss of five of the bombers. Four more went in, but the section of F4Fs led by O'Hare blocked the way. The final numbers of the engagement took years to sort out, but at first the word was that O'Hare had gotten five of the Mitsubishis, thereby saving the carrier from nearly certain heavy damage or worse. In truth, one of the damaged bombers crashed into the ocean and another made it back to base. So his actual confirmed score was four.

The crew of one of the mortally wounded Bettys, its port engine nacelle completely sheared off by O'Hare's four .50-caliber machine guns, had tried to crash into the carrier. Its well-filmed death dive showed the big green bomber veering off at the last moment to crash into the sea off the carrier's port bow. Throughout the encounter, O'Hare's stalwart wingman, Lt. (jg) Marion Dufilho hung onto his lead even though his guns were jammed. O'Hare had signaled for him to leave, but Dufilho refused and stayed in the fight.

In the first flush of action, O'Hare had actually initially claimed *seven* when he recovered on board, all with only one Japanese bullet hole in his port wing. But he is now officially credited with the four. He was nevertheless quickly touted as America's first Navy ace of the war. The original award was written up as the Navy Cross, then third in line in the medal hierarchy, not second as it is today. As the citation went up the endorsement chain, however, it was bumped up to the Medal of Honor. At the time, with the war going badly, America was clamoring for heroes. O'Hare was sent to Washington to receive the Medal of Honor from President Franklin D. Roosevelt.

O'Hare was then sent on war bond drives and public appearances. He had also been promoted to lieutenant commander. Some authors say he jumped lieutenant, but a few pictures show him distinctly wearing the "railroad tracks" of an O-3. The Navy is not given to such rank jumps and the other services do it sparingly, one case being Jimmy Doolittle, who as a lieutenant colonel led the April 1942 raid on Tokyo. Besides receiving the Medal of Honor, he was also raised to a one-star brigadier general, bypassing colonel, over several other men who were approaching promotion to O-6 and O-7. Actually, O'Hare had been made a "temporary lieutenant" until the unusual proceedings to raise him to lieutenant commander were finalized. And it was FDR himself who noted his new permanent rank by pointing to his signature on the paper during the presentation of the Medal of Honor in the Oval Office.

By the time O'Hare returned to Hawaii in June 1942 to take command of VF-3, things were different. Midway was a great victory only a few weeks earlier, and in April, Doolittle and his raiders had shaken Tokyo to its core. New ships and aircraft were on their way to join the fleet as well. But there was a long period ahead of everyone as the American response and drive across the Pacific began gathering steam. And it was into this busy cauldron of activity that several neophyte fighter pilots made their way, including one Ens. E. L. Feightner, fresh from advanced training in the States.

He remembered his impression of his new CO.

> [Butch] was really my first squadron commander. And, of course, he was a big hero in those days . . . one of these [sic] very likable individuals. He was about my size but he was kind of a rotund individual. And, boy, talk about laid back; he was about as relaxed as anybody I'd ever run into in uniform up to that point. But he knew the tactics. And we had just a small group . . . the six of us used to just have a ball.[1]

There was no problem having enough airplanes to fly. O'Hare and his pilots flew from Maui, and they even had a Grumman Duck, a J2F, an old biplane floatplane, as well as an R4D (the Navy designation for the C-47 military version of the DC-3 airliner) and a Vought OS2U observation type that saw great service as an artillery spotter and rescue aircraft during the war. And to round out their aerial menagerie, there were even a few Boeing F4Bs and Culver Cadets that were used in the growing drone program, mainly as controlled, but occasionally piloted, targets for gunnery training. The pilots flew but didn't have a truly organized training syllabus or program. It was actually up to the squadron commanding officer (CO) to train his men, and of course they couldn't have wanted a better or more affable teacher.

Feightner, young, eager and endowed with more than his share of flying skill, hit it off with his new CO. He thought O'Hare was a natural leader who was well liked and respected by his squadron, some of whom had several months of combat experience such as his XO, Lt. Stanley E. Ruehlow. Like many COs, though, O'Hare was energetic and athletic, and, strange for a midwesterner, he loved to swim, especially to skin dive and spear fish for a meal. This was the only area where Feightner didn't measure up to his skipper's standards.

During their almost daily forays into the ocean, the pilots of VF-3 began taking on deep suntans. But where most of them turned a pleasing gold, Ensign Feightner baked to a lobster red at times. Almost inevitably, O'Hare saddled his young pilot with nickname "Whitey." This moniker, bestowed by one of the men Feightner always loved and admired, stayed with Feightner long after the war and into his subsequent career and remained a part of his story.

Whitey remembered Butch's love of swimming and spearfishing. When they weren't flying, O'Hare could be found in one of two places. The first was the water.

"He floated like a cork," Whitey recalled. "He was around 5 feet 9 inches, and probably weighed around 220, 230. He was sort of a rotund individual." O'Hare would go out at 8 a.m. to swim and catch fish.

"The guy was amazing. If he'd get hungry, he would dive down and spear a fish, bring it up, lay on his back just like an otter, and eat the thing raw."[2]

Whitey remembers one of O'Hare's favorite delicacies was octopus, a particular small species of which inhabited the local coast and was only a foot and a half in diameter. After spearing his quarry, O'Hare would come up with the hapless little creature draped over his arm and, adding insult to injury, he would—according to Feightner—bite the octopus on the head behind the eyes, apparently severing a vital nerve and killing it. He would then bring in his catch and proceed to cook them, evidently having learned the many native dishes and methods of preparation. Whitey never did acquire a taste for octopus and considered the flavor "like old rubber tires."

The other place that occupied most of O'Hare's squadron's leisure time was the home of Countess Alexa Von Tempsky Zabriskie, on a large ranch that raised beef cattle. The expansive spread on Maui was on the side of Mount Haleakala, an extinct volcano at a four-thousand-foot elevation. The height always ensured that the temperature was much cooler than at sea level and offered relief from the tropical heat. The countess made her home available to all servicemen, junior and senior alike, counting many flag personalities among her occasional guests, including Adm. Chester Nimitz and Adm. Ernest King.

O'Hare could often be found at the ranch, enjoying the countess's hospitality along with members of his and other squadrons, riding horses on brief excursions out to see the wonderful scenery. Alexa was actually the sister of Robert Von Tempsky and lived near the main house. She had been divorced, and without children she naturally took in many of the visiting young naval aviators as they passed through, coming from and going to the combat zone. Such an arrangement was not unusual. Families or individuals with large houses frequently host servicemen, offering them the comforts of a home and food as well as the attention of a surrogate mother or father. It helps all concerned, on both sides.

Whitey would often make the mail run to Ford Island to pick up the mail as well as supplies. He would use any aircraft available, from the large R4D to the ancient J2F Duck. Maui had a carrier aircraft service unit, or CASU, that kept the various aircraft "up." There was also an Army unit with a few Curtiss P-40s, and Whitey and his friends would occasionally tangle with these fighters in various drill exercises. There was classroom work, including aircraft recognition training, which helped the neophyte fighter pilots to learn and identify their "enemy's" aircraft.

O'Hare's training personality in the air was definitely laid back. Returning from a gunnery hop, he would check the banner along with his pilots. It was plain to everyone he was an excellent shot and had extraordinary eyesight. Whitey himself had 20/15 vision, and he noted that Butch had excellent eyes too. He took advantage of the opportunities to fly against his CO and actually did pretty well.

"Amazingly enough, I could give him a pretty good battle . . . he'd eventually do something and he would win perhaps 60 percent of the time, but I could hold my own with him a lot of the time."

O'Hare would never raise his voice but his men could tell that when the time came he was ready to fight. Certainly, his record to date indicated that aggressive but restrained approach. Whitey noted that he thought O'Hare had great peripheral vision that enabled him to know where everyone was in a dogfight. His fight on February 20 certainly indicated that attribute. Yet, as Whitey noted, his CO said, reflecting the spirit of the times, "Winning is not everything; it's the only thing."[3]

O'Hare even went so far as to demonstrate how distance could play a big role in an engagement. The wing-mounted machine guns of their Wildcats were bore-sighted to converge at 900 feet. To show his pilots, especially the younger less experienced members, just what that meant, he took them out to the flight line where he had had two F4Fs positioned 900 feet apart.

"It looked like you were right in the cockpit with this guy," Feightner recalled. "Nine hundred feet in the air is not very far. Most people early in the war were shooting way out of range; the bullets never even got to the target."

The CO's illustration was striking. He said, "The secret to shooting down airplanes is to try to cut the tail off with the prop before you shoot."

His men took the advice and simple demonstration to heart.

"The first time I shot at an airplane, I shot out of range," Feightner said. "From then on, I had that wing sticking out both sides off [my] windshield before I would shoot. And I don't think I ever missed one after that. You don't waste much ammunition that way."[4]

O'Hare checked Whitey out on the Grumman Duck, and after a short time in the air he let his young pilot alone, satisfied that Whitey knew what he was doing. He was soon sending Whitey on missions, such as the mail run to Ford Island, and he never worried about the ensign's ability to return. They would take the Duck on fishing and hunting excursions, especially to hunt wild goats that lived some two thousand feet down inside the extinct volcano.

Using the Duck to fly supplies into the volcano during one trip, Whitey had a bit of a scare. Everything was going along fine until he realized that his J2F was slowing down as he climbed up the volcano's side. The thin air was having trouble supporting the old biplane, which was underpowered on its best day. Quickly, Whitey descended to pick up speed. He tried to pop over the rim of the crater, which was fairly large, perhaps three miles across, to drop the supplies to the group waiting below.

As he tried to climb back out over the rim, he realized he was not going to make it. He began circling around inside the crater trying to burn off fuel. He knew that O'Hare was watching him from his position on the crater floor. Whitey tried twice but just couldn't coax the old plane over the rim. He finally realized he was fighting the wind and decided to try coming out the opposite side, and sure enough he picked up an updraft that lifted him above the side and out into the clear air once more.

Feightner recalled that his CO was very safety conscious, which was not always the case at the time. Today's safety awareness programs grew out of this period where many young aviators paid with their lives for a lack of attention to operating safely during the war.

Heading Out for Combat

Eventually, the training and time for relaxation had to end as deployment neared. O'Hare and his men were ready, but the needs of the Navy threw them something of a curve. Lt. Cdr. Jimmy Flatley, late of VF-42 in the *Yorktown,* had plenty of pre-war experience and had seen a good deal of early Pacific combat, participating in the Battle of the Coral Sea in early May. He was then ordered back to San Diego to form a new fighter squadron, VF-10. During that time he watched the news anxiously as his friends fought the Battle of Midway in June, escaping with their lives as the *Yorktown* met its fate on June 4. The ship was badly damaged by enemy dive bombers and abandoned in the late afternoon. After drifting for two more days, several U.S. destroyers closed in to administer a coup de grace. Almost as in an act of heroic suicide, however, she settled, took on more water, capsized, and sank on June 7.

There were friends and a ship to be avenged, and Flatley brought his new squadron together with training and morale-building activities, including a name and insignia. He finally came up with "The Grim Reapers," and a diving skeleton with a scythe. For added measure, he devised a motto, "Mow 'em down." Eventually, the skeleton took on the sobriquet of "Ol' Moe." Soon, Fighting Ten was ready for deployment. It just needed a few more aviators to round out the roster. Wartime squadrons took a large number of pilots into combat.

Heading out with the *Enterprise*, Air Group 10 passed through Hawaii. During their normal workup exercises, VF-10 lost a couple of pilots and Jimmy Flatley needed replacements as he headed into combat. Looking over the list of availables, Flatley selected Whitey Feightner and his roommate Gordon Barnes of Butch O'Hare's VF-3. The time was critical. The ranks of the Navy's carriers in the Pacific had been drastically cut. With the loss of the *Yorktown* at Midway in June, that left only four flattops, the *Saratoga, Wasp, Hornet,* and *Enterprise.* The next big battle was coming in the Solomon Islands, namely with the invasion of Tulagi and Guadalcanal on August 7. The *Enterprise* had fought in the opening rounds of the invasion and had retired to Hawaii for repairs and to pick up a new air group.

On August 31, however, the *Saratoga* was hit for the second time in six months by a Japanese torpedo and she had to retire for repairs. Two weeks later, on September 15, the *Wasp* took three torpedoes from a lurking Japanese submarine and also left in clouds of flame and smoke. After the crew abandoned her, an accompanying destroyer sunk her. That left the *Hornet* and *Enterprise.*

The *Hornet* was the only U.S. carrier on station, against five Japanese carriers, including two large fleet carriers, veterans of the attack on Pearl Harbor. The *Enterprise* was desperately needed, and on October 16, 1942, she sailed from Pearl Harbor with Air Group 10, including the untried fighter squadron VF-10 and her two new additions from Butch O'Hare's VF-3.

CHAPTER 4
FIGHTING IN THE SOLOMONS

Whitey and his friends soon found that their new CO was much different than their previous leader. But it wasn't a bad thing. Where Butch O'Hare had been fairly reserved in his pronouncements, choosing to address a subject once and let his people digest it and work it out for themselves, Jimmy Flatley was talkative and had a streak of religious drive that he added to his instructions for a mission. After being brought up in a fairly religious household, it was OK with Whitey if his new skipper wanted to include verses from the Bible.

Actually, at first Whitey worked with Lt. (jg) John Leppla, the maintenance officer who by a happy coincidence came from Whitey's hometown of Lima, Ohio. Leppla had come from VS-2, an SBD scout squadron, and had seen action at Coral Sea, shooting down several enemy aircraft. He was aggressive and was not afraid to tempt fate when he wanted something. Leppla had been credited with as many as four kills at the time, but postwar scrutiny gradually reduced the count to one confirmed kill, probably a Zero.

As he got to know Flatley, Ensign Feightner came to the conclusion that he was "a true leader," epitomizing "what you think of as a squadron commander . . . typical of what we'd like to think everybody in the world is out there defending their country for." Flatley could be one of the boys, playing a hot game of volleyball against younger men who towered over his five foot six inch frame. In one such game, Butch Voris, a big young man who would become an ace and after the war founded the demonstration team known as the Blue Angels, came down hard on Flatley's right foot, breaking it.

In typical fashion, Flatley refused to be hospitalized and had his men rig a strap on the rudder pedal so he could keep flying. The rudder is important in all coordinated flight; a pilot doesn't turn the aircraft using only the stick to move the wing-mounted ailerons. But Flatley knew that once in the air, the pressure on his feet to move the rudder would not be anywhere as heavy as that required on the ground or flight deck to halt his aircraft with toe brakes, which required a definite flexing or pivoting of the pilot's foot on the top of each rudder pedal.

Whitey knew that Flatley was also concerned about safety in flight. One concern was the lack of a restraint in the cockpit, a harness to hold back the pilot in the event of a crash. Accordingly, Flatley came up with a chest harness and had it fitted to all the squadron's Wildcats. The CO's invention quickly saved various pilots from serious injury after a combat engagement that ended in a rough landing either on board ship or, later, ashore.

The *Hornet* hastened to the Southwest Pacific, where the invasion of the Solomon Islands had run into some trouble, both on the ground and on the sea. The Japanese were counterattacking and the small U.S. fleet was fighting for its life, with only the *Hornet* on station to help the hard-pressed Cactus Air Force, composed of U.S. Army and Marine Corps and a few Allied aircraft spread out against the enemy aerial armada coming from the northwest bases of Lae on New Guinea and Rabaul on New Britain.

The *Enterprise* finally arrived on October 24. It was now two U.S. carriers against four Japanese carriers. The American flattops could launch squadrons equipped with SBD Dauntless dive bombers, augmented by a few new Grumman TBF Avenger torpedo bombers that could also carry a sizeable bomb load for a shipboard aircraft, and the Grumman F4F-4 Wildcat, which was proving its value as the only American fighter capable of confronting the Zero with any hope of success . . . or survival.

On the other side, the Japanese navy could field the redoubtable Mitsubishi A6M2 Zero as the world's best naval fighter. A Nakajima-built variant of the Zero—the A6M2-N (later tagged Rufe)—used floats to fly from a few coastal bases. Even though weighed down by three floats that sapped speed and range, the Rufe still retained the Zero's incredible maneuverability and was not to be taken lightly by any Wildcat pilot. Then there were the Aichi D3A2 dive bomber, later called "Val," and the Nakajima B5N2 (Kate) torpedo bomber, which could also function as a horizontal bomber. The Mitsubishi G4M1 (later called Betty), a twin-engine land-based bomber, had outstanding range to deliver its ordnance. The Japanese also had a stable of utilitarian observation aircraft, usually on floats, that could if pressed give a fairly good account of themselves against a Wildcat.

The Japanese had a potent collection of aircraft and highly skilled crews whose advantage was often lost in wartime propaganda in the United States but who posed a considerable threat to inexperienced U.S. aviators flying nearly obsolete aircraft at that specific time in the war. The advantage would eventually change hands by mid-1943, but during the summer and fall of 1942, aerial encounters could be a real tossup and were often decided by pure luck and individual pilot skill.

By late October, the fighting had greatly intensified, especially in the air. The Marines of the Cactus Air Force had gradually assembled a force of Wildcats and Dauntlesses, augmented by a few Avengers. Their flight crews put up with disease, fatigue, and poor food and living conditions as well as constant harassment by the Japanese. It was a struggle to merely survive from day to day, with the terrible

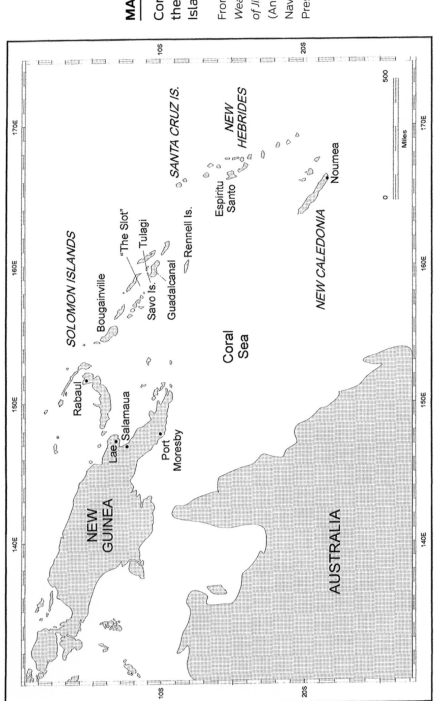

MAP 2

Coral Sea and the Solomon Islands

From Thach Weave: The Life of Jimmie Thach (Annapolis, Md.: Naval Institute Press, 2004), 51.

addition of having to rise every day from the muddy airfield they had wrested from the opponents to confront the aerial onslaught from the north. In some ways, one could liken the campaign to the Battle of Britain, where equally hard-pressed British pilots fought the streams of German bombers coming from captured fields on the French coast.

For his part, Ensign Feightner was learning fast and like many of his compatriots was eagerly awaiting his first action. Since December 1941, in addition to several hundred hours of civilian time, he had logged only a bare 324 hours of military flight time prior to October 1942. Yet by months end, he had added another 45, much of which was in heavy aerial combat. The only reservations he had were about his aircraft. Years later, he described his feelings about the little Wildcat. "It was such a poor performing airplane," he recalled. "But one thing, it had a lot of firepower and it was tough." The F4F-4 model VF-10 and other squadrons now flew had two more .50-caliber machine guns than the F4F-3 that Butch O'Hare and *his* friends had flown in earlier actions. The other advantage the young naval aviators took with them into their first action was the training their CO, Jimmy Flatley, had given them.

"One of the things he pounded into us—and Butch O'Hare had already told me this—was don't ever follow a Zero in a loop . . . with the difference in [our] performance, he'd be down, and before you ended up in level flight he's back on your tail again. They could turn such a much tighter loop than we could in the F4F, which was a very sluggish airplane. It was loaded down [with] armor plate, and we had self-sealing tanks . . . and all the things that you need."[1]

In one illustration of this strict warning, Ensigns Feightner and Maurice "Wick" Wickendoll had encountered two Zeros after coming around a cloud while on CAP over the task force. The Japanese pilots quickly began a loop, no doubt figuring the American fighters would follow them. Wickendoll peeled off after one Zero while Feightner, remembering his two COs' admonishments, made a tight turn to the right, refusing to follow the second Zero.

"The guy did a loop and came right down in front of me, and that was the last loop he ever made. It worked out like a charm. Fortunately, he wasn't too bright; he didn't look around much or he'd have seen me out there coming in on him."[2]

At 12:50 p.m. on October 25, a PBY Catalina found two Japanese carriers 360 miles to the south steaming rapidly at twenty-five knots. Although the flight would be a long one, TF 61 launched a strike with SBDs, TBFs, and a VF-10 escort. Flying at 17,000 feet on oxygen for three and a half hours, the *Enterprise* pilots found nothing and had to return in the dark. They couldn't know that the Japanese task force commander, Vice Admiral Chuichi Nagumo, who had led the attacks on Pearl Harbor and Midway, had turned his fleet around when the PBYs appeared.

Thus, CVG-10's (carrier air group) first combat mission was stillborn. Seven aircraft—three SBDs, three TBFs, and one F4F—had to ditch when their fuel ran out. The F4F pulled out of formation and dropped back behind Whitey, who was tail-end Charlie, the last Wildcat in the group. The VF-10 pilot, Lt. Don Miller from

Kansas, bailed out at forty miles from the task force after finding out he couldn't transfer fuel from his forty-two-gallon belly tank because of improper installation by the ground crew. Apparently, the mechanics did not tighten the connection sufficiently for the wobble pump to provide proper suction.

Miller bailed out successfully and was last seen floating down through ten thousand feet. Sadly, he and nearly a dozen other pilots and crewmen were killed when the PBY that had rescued them was set upon by Zeros and shot down the following day.

The rest of the squadron made its way back to the ship in the rapidly disappearing light. They had little night-flying experience, to say nothing of night landing. The situation was rapidly deteriorating. The group descended below a cloud deck only 800 to 1,200 feet above the water. They thought they were at the rendezvous point where the *Enterprise* was to be waiting for them. But all they saw was a black, featureless sea. The group commander, Cdr. Richard Gaines, flying a TBF, began circling. There was no moon and the sky was black.

The SBD pilots began jettisoning their bombs, several of which exploded when they hit the water, damaging the Dauntlesses that had released them. Whitey Feightner was flying Swede Vejtasa's wing when he became aware of Vejtasa's wing light reflecting off the water. Feightner immediately assumed a stepped-up position above Swede, putting some distance between himself and the water.

Now, Swede was slowly zigzagging back and forth until he steadied up on a westerly heading, the air group slowly falling into line behind him. He had discovered the remnants of the oil wake left by the task force and, like a trail of crumbs in the forest, he followed it. In a few moments, the task force appeared out of the murk, and the planes quickly lined up for the carrier's deck. Whitey declared, "Just amazing. We wouldn't be here today if it wasn't for [Swede]."

The next day, October 26, was a red-letter day for VF-10 and its new combat aviators. Much has been written about the general conduct of the crucial Battle of Santa Cruz, "a confused, complex battle characterized by multiple strikes airborne from both forces."[3]

As the two fleets drew closer, Adm. William F. Halsey sent an electrifying message: "Attack. Repeat, Attack!" At 0600, sixteen SBDs launched from the *Enterprise* to search for the enemy. More aircraft set off on submarine patrols. Except for the clouds at two thousand feet, the sky was clear and the sea calm. VB-10 Dauntlesses made the first contact, discovering three large combatants but no carriers. Twenty minutes later, VS-10 radioed it had two carriers in sight, and the battle was on. The SBDs ran through a gauntlet of Zeros and anti-aircraft fire. But although hits were scored, the two enemy carriers—*Shokaku* and *Zuiho*—remained afloat though heavily damaged.

The *Hornet* sent in the next strike as all sixteen *Enterprise* SBDs returned safely. Soon, another Air Group 10 strike followed. This was the second "Big E" (*Enterprise*) group, including eight VF-10 Wildcats with skipper Flatley leading a four-plane division. Lieutenant (jg) Leppla led the other division. The night before, he had written a letter home, to be sent if he did not return the next day. Climbing almost leisurely at 115 knots, the VF-10 Wildcats and their VT-10 charges were bounced by nine Zeros from *Zuiho*. Three Avengers were quickly shot down, and Leppla turned his fighters toward the Japanese, thereby depriving himself, his division, and the remaining torpedo bombers of Flatley's aid. Perhaps Leppla's natural sympathy for the bomber pilots—he had been one himself only six months before—clouded his judgment. But the Zeros took out Leppla and Ens. Al Mead and Ens. Raleigh "Dusty" Rhodes, leaving Ens. Willis "Chip" Reding with a damaged fighter.

Reding dove away with several Zeros in hot pursuit. Leppla was seen to parachute from his stricken Wildcat, but his chute streamed and did not deploy fully. His letter the previous night had been sadly prophetic. Leppla was posthumously awarded another Navy Cross, based primarily on Ensign Reding's report. Reding was obviously the only man from his division to return to the *Enterprise*. Rhodes and Mead were retrieved by the Japanese. Reding, Rhodes, and Mead were each awarded the Silver Star.

Leppla's roommate in the *Enterprise,* Ens. Jim Billo, was having his own troubles. Launching with the 0900 strike, Billo led the second section of Lt. Bobby Edwards' division. Climbing to 10,000 feet, Edwards' aircraft developed prop trouble—a common occurrence with the F4F-4—and he began to lose altitude. He told Billo and his wingman, Ens. Jim Caldwell, to continue with the mission while he, Edwards, dropped behind. Climbing to 20,000 feet, heading southwest, Billo saw a formation of Zeros about 8,000 feet below attacking a single Wildcat. He headed for the fight, watching as the F4F shot down two of the attacking Japanese.

Diving into the melee, Billo dispatched another Zero but ran into a hail of bullets from the remaining Mitsubishis. Billo spotted a white chute that might have been Caldwell's, but he could not be sure. He joined three *Hornet* fighters at 20,000 feet and after just circling for an hour, burning up precious fuel, Billo called the *Enterprise* but got no response. Finally the F4Fs arrived over the *Enterprise* and prepared to land.

Much to his surprise, Billo found himself the focus of attention from the gun crews of the battleship *South Dakota* (BB 57). He was in the clear and easily observed as a friendly fighter, but the jittery crews continued firing at him. Seeing an unidentified dive bomber head for a cloud above the Big E, Billo chased him in company with a *Hornet* fighter, but to no avail. They spotted another Japanese and the *Hornet* pilot, Lt. (jg) Henry A. Fairbanks, shot the bomber down. By this time, Billo was extremely low on fuel—an estimated nine gallons remaining in his F4F's tanks. He made two passes at the *Enterprise,* only to wave off twice for a fouled deck.

As he passed the carrier's island after the second attempt, desperately cranking up his aircraft's gear, he ran out of fuel and crashed off the port side of the carrier. His little Grumman sank almost immediately, but Billo was able to get out and climb into his raft. He was picked up by the destroyer USS *Preston* (DD 379). He did not rejoin VF-10 until two weeks later, on November 7, at Tontouta Airfield, New Caledonia, since the *Enterprise* had been heavily damaged. The XO, Lt. Cdr. William R. "Killer" Kane, was also forced to ditch and did not rejoin the squadron for two weeks.

Turning his flight toward VT-10's Avengers, Jimmy Flatley dispatched a Zero, but the enemy had done their work and disengaged, leaving the Wildcats and the remaining bombers. Three VF-10 fighters and three VT-10 torpedo bombers had been destroyed.

Meanwhile, the *Hornet's* strike group headed for the Japanese carriers, meeting the same stiff resistance from enemy interceptors and flak as their *Enterprise* cohorts had. Two VF-72 Grummans went down and skipper Mike Sanchez and the rest of the squadron did their best to keep the Zeros off the SBDs of VB-8 and VS-8 as they dove for the *Shokaku*. The attack was enough to put the carrier out of action.

The *Shokaku*'s strike group was now approaching the U.S. fleet, but the *Enterprise*'s radar did not find them until only fifty miles out. The Americans had several problems, not the least of which was the tubby little Wildcat's lack of climbing ability. Additionally, confusion on the radio was caused by the two carriers' fighter direction officers (FDOs), who gave conflicting directions to the F4Fs as they struggled to climb toward the incoming threat.

The first Wildcats to make contact were from VF-72. The F4Fs roared in against the Vals and Kates, while the escorting Zeros milled about for a few moments. Under heavy attack, the Japanese bombers pressed on, beginning a run on the *Hornet*. By this time, four planes of VF-10's Red Two Division, under Lt. A. D. "Dave" Pollock, reached the fight. Pollock attacked a Val and flamed it. Ens. Steve Kona finally shed a troublesome drop tank and dove on another Val. Kona caught up to his prey but spotted three more Vals astern of the *Hornet* and headed for them. He was forced to give up his attack when a Zero intervened, and Kona could only claim two probables. He and his wingman, Ens. F. J. Fulton, evaded the Zeros and headed back to the *Enterprise*.

Ensigns Wick Wickendoll and Whitey Feightner intercepted a Val beginning an attack on the *Hornet*. As they closed to firing range, Wickendoll's guns jammed because of frozen grease. The aircraft he was flying had just been taken out of storage prior to the flight. Feightner managed to flame the Val before the Wildcats were attacked by Zeros. It was his first kill *and* his first combat. Successfully evading the escort, Wickendoll and Feightner left the area.

The *Hornet* had been hit and was smoking heavily. To the returning crews from the *Enterprise*, it looked at first as though it was *their* ship that was in distress. They had watched the tracks of Japanese torpedoes as they headed for the Big E, which was zig-zigging "like mad" according to Feightner. Yet even under concentrated attack, their carrier was trying to recover them.

Whitey came aboard and managed to avoid the cluster of previously recovered CVG-10 aircraft now bunched up at the bow by trapping behind Swede, who was still in the wires. Whitey had no choice. He had run out of fuel and would never have made a go-round. "It was either that or ditch," he said later. But Whitey managed to grab one of the first cables and had room before running into his flight leader.

> I'll never forget the shock. They taxied me forward, and I got out of my airplane. There was no number 1 elevator. It was completely gone. I got down to the hangar deck. I was wading around in water and fuel and dead bodies. Something had burned on the ship; you could smell it all over the place. They had taken a bomb back on the starboard quarter. It knocked out the first three wires on the ship. In the meantime, not only are there torpedoes going by up there, but there's a dive-bombing attack going on at the same time.[4]

The star action of the day unfolded as Lieutenant Vejtasa had a field day. Leading Red Seven Division, Swede caught up with a group of Vals preparing to dive on the *Hornet*. He shot down the last Val in the lineup as it dove in front of him. He claimed a second Val as it materialized out of the mist.

A second Japanese strike was on its way with aircraft from the *Shokaku* and *Zuikaku*. The *Hornet*'s fighters met them first, claiming several. Vejtasa was ready for more action. His number four, Ens. Hank Leder, spotted eleven Kate torpedo bombers at seven thousand feet headed for the *Enterprise*. He got one of the Nakajimas just before Swede followed four of the bombers into a cloud bank, eventually shooting down all four.

Orbiting the scene, Vejtasa waited until the intense American flak subsided. His patience was rewarded as two more Kates emerged from the smoke. Together with another Wildcat, Swede engaged the enemy aircraft, shooting down yet another Kate. That made seven kills for the Montanan. He hit a fifth Kate with his remaining ammunition. The enemy bomber was heavily damaged and on fire, but the pilot retained enough control to steer his doomed plane into the forward turret of the destroyer *Smith* (DD 378), causing many casualties. Swede's last Kate was designated a probable, but it could have been considered his eighth kill of the day.

The destroyer skipper conned his stricken ship into the huge wake of the USS *South Dakota* (BB 57), which miraculously extinguished the fire, allowing the intrepid little DD to resume its station and continue the fight.

With the three kills credited to him flying his SBD at Coral Sea, Vejtasa was now the leading U.S. ace of the war with ten victories. At the time, it was thought that Flatley had recommended Swede for the Medal of Honor, but that cannot be confirmed. According to a junior pilot, Flatley "did not believe in awards for men or insignia on aircraft." Therefore, he must have felt Vejtasa's accomplishment all the more deserving of special recognition.[5] Vejtasa eventually received the Navy Cross. At the time of writing, a concerted attempt—seventy years later with Swede now age ninety-eight!—to upgrade Swede's Navy Cross to the Medal of Honor was denied. Swede Vejtasa passed away in January 2013.

The *Hornet* had absorbed the worst of the Japanese attacks, and by 1:20 p.m. she had been taken in tow by the cruiser *Northampton* (CA 26). A second Japanese raid, however, caused the cruiser to cast off the tow lines to protect herself, leaving the *Hornet* nearly helpless and drifting. A Kate put another torpedo into her and that, coupled with yet another strike, sealed the *Hornet*'s fate. By 5 p.m. she had been abandoned and two destroyers moved in to sink her, with no success. The *Hornet* refused to die, but continued to burn until Japanese destroyers came upon her long after the U.S. fleet had left the scene. The Japanese dispatched their drifting foe with four torpedoes. Soon after midnight on October 27, the *Hornet* finally sank.

With the *Hornet* gone, the aircraft returning from strikes and CAP duties had only the *Enterprise,* which herself had taken two bombs during the second raid at 10:15. The carrier was damaged but still operational. Through adroit ship handling, Capt. Osborne B. Hardison, who had relieved Capt. Arthur C. Davis on October 21, was able to avoid nine torpedoes from the Kates that swarmed over the two carriers. Many sources credit Vejtasa's one-man stand as being directly responsible for helping save the *Enterprise.* His actions could thus be compared to those of Butch O'Hare the preceding February.

Whitey also admired Swede, saying, "Talk about a really competent aviator. . . . [He] was about as cool and laid back as any guy you'd ever want to meet. Swede was single-minded. He was an airplane driver and nothing else. He was an absolute jewel as a squadron commander. And his men would have followed him any place."

The situation was desperate for the aircraft, and there was no choice but to take them all aboard the *Enterprise.* The carrier had two well-qualified LSOs (landing signal officers), Lt. Jim Daniels, the air group LSO, and Lt. Robin Lindsey, the ship's LSO. In a sequence that became a milestone in carrier history, these two men began recovering aircraft at 12:15, carefully signaling the planes down the groove to touch down as far aft as possible. The ship's number one elevator had been damaged and stuck in the down position, leaving a great hole in the middle of the flight deck.

Only six minutes later, the *Enterprise* came under attack from the third wave of enemy bombers, with twenty Vals dropping from the clouds through a hail of flak. One bomb bounced off the ship's starboard side and exploded, the concussion hitting the *Enterprise* below her vulnerable waterline and causing flooding as well as jamming the number two elevator in the up position. Now, there was only the number three lift available to move landing aircraft below to make room for more.

During the attack, Lindsey had jumped into the rear cockpit of an SBD and blazed away at the Japanese with the dive bomber's twin machine guns. As the carrier twisted and groaned through the attack, desperately dodging bombs, more damage resulted, especially to the all-important radar, without which the Big E was blind to incoming aircraft. Lt. Brad Williams, the electronics officer, and his men made a valiant and ultimately successful effort to repair the radar.

Finally, after a half-hour of concentrated attacks, the *Enterprise* found herself in the clear and began landing planes again. Not all the planes made it. This last strike had sent the fuel-hungry aircraft scurrying off to orbit helplessly. In the next three hours, Lindsey and Daniels brought planes aboard, jamming them quickly up to the bow, until the number two elevator was repaired. In conjunction with the number three lift, some of the planes could be stowed below. Still, the last plane came to a stop only twenty feet from the aircraft that preceded it.

All credit went to Robin Lindsey, who together with Daniels had done a magnificent job of helping to keep the Navy's only operational carrier in the Pacific on station. He was awarded the Silver Star for his day's work. Retired Captain Lindsey died in 1984. His passing elicited these words from CVG-10 alumnus, retired Rear Adm. James D. Ramage: "Lieutenant Lindsey had saved the Navy precious aircraft in precisely conducting an operation that permitted the last operational carrier in the Pacific to remain on station. The loss of *Enterprise* . . . would have been a major strategic loss to the Pacific fleet."[6]

Whitey remembered the heroic LSO's actions.

> Here was a guy that everyone respected as much as a pilot as an LSO . . . he was a very practical individual [who] instilled a lot of faith in everybody because when he said something, he did it. He was the czar . . . a senior lieutenant and, of course, most of the people up there were—we didn't have many lieutenants in those days—and what he said, people listened. Whatever he said, they did. He had the faith of people like Jimmy Flatley and Jimmie Thach. A phenomenal guy. This was entirely with paddles, too, no mike. Long before the days of microphones.[7]

Lt. Russ Reiserer was also grateful to Lindsey, who gave him the "cut" as the next-to-last aircraft, even though the LSO had been ordered to stop landing aircraft. Reiserer had been off directing a destroyer to a downed pilot and arrived late over the *Enterprise*. At one point, Reiserer recalls, Lindsey was going to be court-martialed for failing to obey orders. The charges were, of course, dropped.

The one-day engagement known as the Battle of Santa Cruz was one of a series of naval and air combats which made up the other half of the Guadalcanal campaign. VF-10 and VF-72 lost twenty-six Wildcats against forty-eight confirmed Japanese aircraft downed, nearly a two-to-one ratio. Several Navy Crosses and Silver Stars were awarded, with a scattering of Distinguished Flying Crosses and Air Medals.

Lt. Dave Pollock and Ens. Jim Dowden of VF-10 were cited for their daring strafing run against supposedly enemy torpedoes, amidst intense anti-aircraft fire from American gunners who couldn't distinguish them from the attacking Japanese. The torpedo struck the USS *Porter* (DD 356). In tragic reality, the torpedo had actually come from an American TBF of VT-10 whose pilot, Lt. (jg) Richard K. Batten, under fierce attack by intercepting Zeros, ended up ditching, unable to jettison his torpedo because his Avenger's bay doors were jammed. The force of the ditching impact apparently broke the torpedo free, however, and it broke surface enough to be spotted by Pollock and Dowden, who then attacked the wayward "fish" unsuccessfully before it slammed into the side of the hapless American destroyer. The *Porter* lingered for two hours before being sunk by another U.S. DD.[8]

The American flight crews, including the young fighter pilots of VF-10, had acquitted themselves well against a numerically—and technically—superior enemy whose nucleus crews could boast of up to five years of combat experience, beginning in China. Yet with all the heroic statistics, the fighters were furious, with both their equipment and their tactics.

Foremost was the disappointment with the F4F-4. Fighting 72's Lt. Cdr. Mike Sanchez railed at the increased weight and the reduced ammunition of the F4F-4. Flatley agreed, adding disgust over the fuel transfer system and the troublesome Curtiss Electric propeller. These variable-pitch props sometimes stuck in high or low pitch at the most inopportune times.

Whitey, too, even though a junior aviator, was disappointed with the Wildcat. "The F4F wasn't that good of an airplane," he claimed. "The landing gear didn't take much punishment. In fact, we got away with murder on the ship, but if we'd go over and land on the beach, we'd often put a guy over in the palm trees because they'd ground loop over there. And the brakes weren't needed that much aboard ship and the people didn't maintain them. They were hard to maintain, anyhow."

As far as tactics were concerned, both squadron commanders took the disappointing performance of the FDOs to task, citing improper positioning of the fighters too low and too close to the ships to allow forward interception. Dave Pollock, whose division had made one of the first contacts with the Japanese, wrote that the FDOs had sent the fighters too far north, where they wasted precious fuel and thus were too far away to be of assistance.

Pollock also noted the poor performance of the Wildcat, stating that it was "a heavily loaded airplane" that "cannot climb and flip around from place to place and up and down. Its rate of climb makes it a very clumsy weapon." Like his senior squadron mates, Pollock wished for more fuel, more ammunition, and only four machine guns. Commenting on their opponents, Pollock said, "In general, the Japs are no smarter than we are, except that they use some trickery that is clever, such as sending Zeros to 7,000 feet to draw our combat patrol down, if we had had some planes up to be drawn down."[9]

The Reapers lost eleven aircraft on October 26; four of the pilots were rescued and two were captured by the Japanese. Counting Lieutenant Miller's loss the previous day, the squadron had lost twelve fighters and six pilots killed (Leppla, Caldwell, Davis, Fulton, Barnes, and Miller); Kane, Billo, John C. Eckhardt Jr., and M. Philip Long were rescued after they had ditched. Rhodes and Mead ditched and were captured by the Japanese. It had been a rough initiation for VF-10. But there was more to come, and soon.

CHAPTER 5
WITH THE CACTUS MARINES

While the *Enterprise* was laid up for repairs, Whitey and his squadron were temporarily transferred ashore at Guadalcanal. Heavy fighting was still going on and the Japanese air raids were always a threat, so VF-10 was always on alert. The daily battles over the sea in August and September had given way to occasional sorties that tested the will and the available assets of the Cactus Air Force, which was still largely composed of Marine Wildcats and Dauntlesses. These aircraft and crews were augmented by Navy and Marine Corps Avengers and Army P-39s of the 67th Fighter Squadron, which arrived in August a few weeks after the Marine Wildcats and SBDs. These units were followed by assorted Royal Australian/New Zealand Air Force P-40s by mid-1943. P-38s of the USAAF's Thirteenth Air Force also arrived in November 1942. These aircraft were all flown by courageous aviators and often gave a good account of themselves, but the Japanese Zeros and Bettys were just too far ahead of their Allied opposition.

As relative peace returned to the task force, it was obvious that the *Hornet*'s aircraft could not remain. Thus, the SBDs and TBFs of both air groups took turns staying airborne for hours at a time. Because of the fear of another enemy attack, the normal CAP fighters orbited the carrier as well. For the better part of two days, the *Enterprise* kept this shuttle routine going until Espiritu Santo in the New Hebrides was close enough for all aircraft to safely depart.

Word soon came, however, that the Japanese were regrouping for what promised to be a final thrust against U.S. forces on Guadalcanal. Admiral Halsey ordered the partially repaired *Enterprise* out; she was all there was, after all. The Big E left her haven in Noumea, New Caledonia, where she had been undergoing refit, on November 10, in company with battleships *Washington* and *South Dakota* and cruisers *Northampton* and *San Diego*.

Meanwhile, the Japanese initiated a furious night battle off Guadalcanal on November 12–13. The U.S. ships came off much worse; all but one destroyer sustained heavy damage or was sunk. By dawn on the 13th, the carrier task force had arrived in the area and the *Enterprise* flew off a search party of SBDs. A second launch followed of TBFs and Wildcats. This second group found the damaged

Japanese battleship *Hiei,* a veteran of most of the previous battles as well as the attack on Pearl Harbor. She lay semi-immobile near Savo Island.

The Avengers tore into the *Hiei* while their escorts landed at Henderson Field to refuel and rearm. They were joined by Marine aircraft—Dauntlesses and a few Wildcats—as they flew back out to the *Hiei.* Soon, Army B-17s put in an appearance, though with disappointing, almost embarrassing results. Finally, after an incredible pounding, the old battleship stopped dead in the water and began to settle. She eventually sank that evening, the first enemy battleship to go down.

Throughout the rest of November 13 and 14, Navy and Marine planes hammered the Japanese, especially the transports assembled off the coast. The U.S. crews shuttled between the *Enterprise* and Henderson Field, depending on their direction. To the harried Marines, the activity and constant flow of airplanes was a mixed blessing. The previous month they had pleaded for more planes and crews; now they needed more mechanics, more fuel and ammunition, and extra sets of hands!

By November 15, the Japanese had consolidated all the survivors in the remaining transports. They had brought seven thousand troops to invade the island, but were left with only two thousand.

The Reapers had been kept busy through this period. On November 13, a Mavis had been shot down by a combat patrol led by Swede Vejtasa. The next day, another Kawanishi flying boat was destroyed by Lt. McGregor Kilpatrick and Lt. (jg) W. K. Blair. Later, on November 14, Lt. Red Carmody in an SBD had located a convoy of Japanese transports heading for Guadalcanal. Ten Reaper Wildcats led by Jimmy Flatley, escorting fifteen SBDs, chased off two Zero floatplanes.

The SBDs attacked the thirteen transports, and Flatley took his fighters down to strafe the ships and their destroyer escorts as well. Ens. Ed Coalson, in Lt. Dave Pollock's flight, shot down a Zero that attacked him as the tail-end Charlie. Following the furious action—only three transports survived to be beached the following day—the Dauntlesses and Wildcats landed at Henderson and spent the night.

Whitey landed on the fighter strip, which had portions of Marston matting—metal surfaces that could be linked together—installed along the sides where crews parked aircraft. As he landed, he saw a big geyser of dirt spring up to his left. The Japanese had a 6-inch gun on the side of a hill. Quickly looking around, he saw a Marine frantically beckoning him to head for the trees in which to bring his airplane.

As Whitey taxied over to the Marine, other crewmen grabbed the Wildcat's tail and swung the little fighter around. Thinking that the Japanese were bombing the airfield, Whitey jumped out of his Wildcat only to discover an eighteen-inch-diameter hole in the ground. He nearly fell into the huge opening, which had been dug by enemy ships' shells. The Japanese were, indeed, shelling the strip.

The Marines collected all the Navy pilots in a jeep and took them to the tent area back under the trees as the Japanese continued shelling the field. Once there, Whitey had a chance to meet Capt. Joe Foss, XO of VMF-121 and then the ranking U.S. ace in the Pacific with twenty kills.

Right in the middle of this, Whitey remembered, "this guy with a campaign hat on and smoking a big cigar comes strolling across the middle of the strip. . . . I'd heard about him before, but this was him. And he's strolling along across to the area, saying hello to all these people and he welcomed us. And we became part of the 1st Marine Division, Reinforced."[1]

By the time he left the Solomons, Foss had shot down twenty-six Japanese aircraft, tying Capt. Eddie Rickenbacker's record in World War I, a goal much sought after by most American aces during the war. Indeed, the push to reach that hallowed number placed undue burden on many capable combat aviators who certainly had enough to contend with without having to deal with daily inquiries from upper echelons and the press.

At the time, the Marines had only three fighters that were mission-capable. During the night, the Japanese gunners put another two Wildcats, the newly arrived Navy aircraft, out of commission. Feightner estimated there were only twenty fighters left when the morning came.

When the new day did dawn, and as the new "associates" of the Cactus Air Force began to come out of their tents, a Marine told them to stay inside their quarters. He was followed by a lot of automatic weapons fire coming from the treetops. During the night, the enemy had infiltrated the compound and installed themselves in the trees, prime positions for sniping. The Marines got a few of the snipers, enabling the American pilots to run toward their aircraft.

With quick instructions to man up and take off, Whitey and his friends launched to join up with a strike force of TBFs that was going to try to torpedo a Japanese battleship that had been lobbing shells at the Marines. The target was barely thirty miles from the field, and the Wildcats strafed the big ship ahead of the oncoming torpedo planes. The Avengers pushed through the flak, with two of them being shot down. The rest dropped their torpedoes, but they ran up against the battleship and failed to detonate.

Army B-26s had been ferrying more torpedoes to Henderson. More Navy and Marine TBFs attacked the enemy force, along with a Wildcat escort, including Whitey, flying wing on Dave Pollock, who was one of the more senior lieutenants in VF-10. Just as the attack started, two Zeros made a pass at the fighters. One Japanese pilot hit Pollock's propeller, which went into flat pitch, decidedly hazardous during a fight; he couldn't maintain airspeed and turned back toward the field on Guadalcanal. Whitey dutifully followed his leader. But Pollock's prop quickly froze, leaving the frustrated aviator with no choice except to prepare for a ditching.

Pollock was soaked, but except for lacerations of the scalp from his landing, he was OK. He had smacked right into the gunsight, a common hazard for Wildcat aviators at the time. Skipper Flatley had designed a restraining strap but not everyone used it all the time. As Whitey circled above watching for his friend, Pollock struck out for some safe haven, but Whitey was concerned because Pollock was swimming straight for the three enemy ships that had been struck and were on fire near the beach. He was swimming on his back and couldn't see his direction.

A Zero appeared and made a pass at the American in the water. Whitey drove him off without firing a shot. He kept making runs on the enemy fighter while Pollock kept swimming below him. A few rubber boats were coming out for Pollock, and Feightner was afraid they were the Japanese. He started another run when he realized they were Marines in the boats, themselves coming under Japanese fire. Feightner then went after the Japanese positions, allowing the Marines in the boats to finally scoop up Pollock, who was evacuated to Espiritu Santo the next day.

Following Pollock's rescue, Feightner was told that the field was in such bad shape from all the enemy shelling that he should land on the adjacent beach, which was fairly wide. He landed his Wildcat on the broad, hard beach and went to see his flight leader in the makeshift hospital. Aircraft were routinely dispersed along the beaches, although an Army P-39 overturned and burned, its pilot scrambling to safety as flames consumed his long-nosed fighter. It took a while to repair the landing fields, but the Navy Seabees and their bulldozers eventually filled in the holes sufficiently to permit "normal" operations to resume.

Taking off the next day at 1230, VF-10 mounted a patrol over Henderson and the surrounding area. Two and a half hours later, a second patrol was launched when bogies were called approaching the field. Flatley took his flight to 20,000 feet, holding over the water between Henderson and Savo Island. Twenty minutes later, Stan Ruehlow and his section spotted eleven Zeros and attacked, with Flatley quickly bringing his planes into the action. Ruehlow went after a Zero he had spotted and was just ready to open fire when Butch Voris' Wildcat cut him off. Ruehlow growled at his wingman to get out of the way.

"Voris, that's my Zero. Leave him alone!"[2] But moments later, Ruehlow was screaming for help as the Japanese got on his tail. Voris was slightly wounded in the scrap. Six Zeros were shot down, and the Vals, which the Zeros had been escorting, turned and fled. Voris eventually scored seven kills during the war and after the war organized the famous flight demonstration team the Blue Angels.

November 16 and 17 saw action taper off as the Japanese withdrew. The Americans sent a few raids against the three beached transports, which were left burning on the Japanese-held beachhead, but little aerial action occurred. On the 17th, Jimmy Flatley led five planes back to Noumea, while the rest of the squadron made the trip back in transport aircraft. Fifteen Wildcats were transferred to VMF-121 on Guadalcanal to augment the dwindling Marine fighter forces. During their time on Guadalcanal, the Reapers had accounted for eight Zeros confirmed, as well as contributing to the overall mayhem during raids on enemy ships. The Reapers suffered no pilot losses, and the only Wildcat lost was Dave Pollock's.

In his report detailing the action from November 10–17, Flatley commented on the effectiveness of strafing, a new area which his men had not been involved in before their tour on Guadalcanal.

It is felt that great damage can be inflicted on enemy surface ships by our own [fighters]. It is further suggested that every effort be made to strafe enemy carriers . . . during morning twilight . . . such an attack would result in destroying enemy air groups on the decks of their carriers.[3]

The *Enterprise* returned to Noumea on November 16 to continue the repair work interrupted by the previous days' action. Her air group straggled back from Henderson as schedules permitted, though the Marines inherited several Wildcats and SBDs from CVG-10 and were grateful for the hand-me-downs. At times, the Marines actually flew the Navy aircraft before the planes had been assigned to them. In reality, the Guadalcanal campaign had been decided in favor of the Americans, as the Japanese retired and never mounted an invasion of the island again. By December, the *Saratoga* had joined the *Enterprise,* fully repaired and ready for action. There remained only one final battle for the Big E, in January 1943.

Swede Vejtasa and Chip Reding made an interesting side trip on November 15 while en route to Noumea. During one of the periods when VF-10 was operating from Henderson, Swede and Chip were recalled to the *Enterprise* and directed to get into two prepared Wildcats. The mission was to hand-deliver correspondence to Admiral Halsey on a ship in Noumea Harbor. Provided a sandwich and a canteen of water each, the two pilots anticipated an easy, though lengthy, over-water flight. Vejtasa felt confident in his dead-reckoning capabilities because of his experience as an SBD pilot with Scouting Five, his VS-5 squadron on board the *Lexington* at the Battle of the Coral Sea.

The weather was overcast and rainy, so the two Wildcat pilots flew below a thousand feet, the better to see the water and check the winds. After three hours, Swede was becoming concerned as they had apparently missed a checkpoint, some reefs north of Noumea. There was nothing but water below. Continuing on course a while longer, they eventually turned west 90 degrees, straining to catch a glimpse of land on their new heading.

Fuel was approaching the critical point, and Vejtasa was considering his alternatives when he spotted a reef and breaking waves almost directly below. They had come across a small island, and after a couple of passes to inspect possible landing sites, Swede and Chip landed on what appeared to be a grassy but firm stretch of land.

Climbing out of their fighters, the Navy pilots encountered a large native chief in shorts, who directed a few of his people to cut down coconuts. Vejtasa indicated he was thirsty, and the natives were obviously relieved to find that the visitors were Americans, not Japanese. The islanders were anxious to help, and the chief ceremoniously ushered the pilots to his village.

A white man, who turned out to be the only French resident and a quasi-official receptionist, came out of his hut to welcome the pilots. A woman joined them, and since she seemed to be the "head lady of the island," she exercised some authority, even over the chief. He hustled off at her direction to fetch a young radio operator, who contacted Noumea.

Meanwhile, the native woman told the Americans they were on the island of Uvea, east of New Caledonia. In response to the radio message, Noumea asked for verification of Vejtasa's identity. He shot back, "Anyone with the name of Vejtasa needs no further identification!"

While they waited for rescue, Swede and Chip inspected the projected "runway" they would use for takeoff once they got fuel for their dry Wildcats. With the help of the chief and his natives, a path was cleared, trees cut down, and palm fronds put down to create a firmer surface. By this time, a Grumman Duck had appeared offshore and Swede clambered on board to deliver his letter to Admiral Halsey. The admiral's staff quickly aided Swede in lining up a PBY Catalina with drums of gasoline on the underwing bomb racks. The Catalina flew back to Uvea, where Swede and Chip refueled their fighters.

After thanking the natives for their hospitality, as well as the Frenchman who hosted them for dinner that evening, they took off the next morning and headed for Noumea, seventy miles away.

VF-10 had also arrived at Noumea and the reunion was a happy one. Upon inspection, it was revealed that the compasses in *all* the F4Fs were at least 12 degrees off, which would account for the navigational error that nearly put Vejtasa and Reding in the water.[4]

The *Chicago* and the Reapers

Smarting from their first land defeat, the Japanese continued to harass the Americans while evacuating their own troops with a massive sealift. So, even though U.S. carrier aviation was taking a breather at Noumea, the Marines and various Navy surface units were kept busy in December and early January 1943 fending off Japanese thrusts and bombardments.

By January 23, the *Saratoga* had come north from Noumea to conduct an attack on Japanese positions on the island of Kolombangara. With "Sara" in the area, Admiral Halsey now had two carriers, three battleships, twelve cruisers and twenty-five destroyers at his disposal to harass the Japanese withdrawal. Accordingly, he sent a group of these ships, Task Force 18, up "the Slot," a long channel between the main islands of the Solomons—roughly Guadalcanal, Santa Isabel, New Georgia, Choiseul, and Bougainville. This area had been the scene of some of the bloodiest naval battles in history, all within the previous seven months.

Task Force 18 entered the Slot in the early evening of January 29. Suddenly, a group of torpedo-armed Betty land-based bombers attacked in the dark, managing to put two torpedoes into the heavy cruiser USS *Chicago* (CA 29). The big ship came to a halt and was dead in the water, the entire bow blown off back to the number one turret. By morning, the cruiser USS *Louisville* (CA 28) was trying to tow her toward Noumea. The *Louisville* was relieved by the tug USS *Navajo* (AT 64), and as the slow-moving group neared Noumea, the larger force left the tug with *Chicago* and six covering destroyers.

At 3:45 p.m., though, radar picked up a group of aircraft approaching from the west. The *Enterprise* had left Espiritu Santo on January 28 with TF-16. It could only be another Japanese attack. At 4:10 p.m., Killer Kane launched with a division of Reapers to intercept the intruders. Sure enough, more Bettys appeared, twelve in all, making straight for the *Enterprise*. The raiders inadvertently stumbled on the wounded *Chicago*. Between the flak and VF-10 CAP, eight of the bombers were destroyed on their first run. They regrouped for a second approach. The remaining four Bettys dove for the water heading west. They outdistanced the pursuing fighters for a short but crucial time, time enough to drop their torpedoes.

By this time, both the Reaper CO and XO were up, leading divisions. Whitey Feightner, now a seasoned veteran, had dropped behind his section led by McGregor Kilpatrick, with a balky engine. Now, as the Bettys came in, he was able to intercept them, shooting down two of the fat green bombers. Forming up with Flatley's group, Feightner chased the remaining bombers right into the wall of flak hurled skyward by the desperate *Chicago*. Two bombers were left, one so badly shot up it was obvious it would never get back to its base. The Bettys dropped their fish, roaring over the cruiser with the Wildcats in hot pursuit.

As the sole surviving Betty disappeared, the Reapers turned back in time to see the *Chicago* begin a slow roll and start to sink. In his effort to protect the *Chicago,* the Ohio native shot down three Bettys; he had one previous kill at Santa Cruz. After Whitey had recovered on board the *Enterprise*, Flatley reportedly walked over to his junior ensign and said, "You're a fighting fool, aren't you?" Although originally put in for an Air Medal, Whitey's initial award was upgraded to his first Distinguished Flying Cross.[5]

The young Ohioan became a Buckeye celebrity as the subject of several hometown newspapers. The *Lima News* for June 11, 1943, headlined its story "D.F.C. [*sic*] Won By Elida Pilot For Combats In Pacific. Never Underestimate The Japs, Warns Lieut. Feightner." Whitey's exploits in the Solomons filled two columns. "He has to his credit one Jap dive bomber and three torpedo bombers, and probably another enemy torpedo plane."

A noncombat-related loss occurred on January 30th when Lieutenant Edwards had a ramp strike during landing, and the veteran flight leader was killed.

Reaper One Departs

The action involving the loss of the *Chicago* was formally known as the Battle of Rennell Island, as the ship was cruising off Rennell when first attacked on January 29. It also proved to be VF-10's last major combat for a year. By early February, the last Japanese had left Guadalcanal, effectively ending that historic and bloody campaign.

On February 13, Jimmy Flatley was detached from his beloved Reapers and headed east. He left Killer Kane in charge, as well as some mighty big shoes to fill. Reaper One was headed back to form a new air group and would eventually return to combat as commander of CVG-5 in the new *Yorktown* (CV 10), as she and the USS *Essex* (CV 9) introduced the F6F Hellcat to combat on August 31, 1943.

Flatley seldom addressed his troops in person for a pep talk and over the past few months had developed the custom of writing notes accompanied by appropriate prayers for all to read. Taking his leave, he continued this tradition. His parting letter read

> I can't find it in me to make a farewell speech. I'm afraid I'd get all choked up. I want you to know that I take my leave of you with deep regret. . . . I'm so darn proud and fond of everyone of you that my heart's about to bust. . . . Take care of yourselves . . . One parting word of advice.
>
> There is a definite tendency on the part of everyone of you to throw caution to the winds every time you meet the enemy. We've been lucky so far. But it's dumb. We've spent hours and hours on tactics, designed not only to destroy, but also to protect ourselves. Keep that thought foremost in your minds. Rip 'em up and down, but do it smartly.
>
> I trust our paths will cross in the near future. Meanwhile, keep your chins up and don't forget that little guy who called himself "Reaper Leader."[6]

CHAPTER 6
A NEW SQUADRON AND A NEW FIGHTER

ollowing Flatley's departure, VF-10 and her new skipper kept the Reaper aviators in shape while the *Enterprise* remained in Noumea. The carrier also sortied occasionally to maintain a presence in the area, even sending her aircraft back to Henderson Field in February and April to beef up the Cactus Air Force while the Marines continued to fight the departing Japanese.

While at Guadalcanal, Whitey had had a chance to meet several of the Marine aviators, many of whom would go on to become high-scoring aces and leaders during the war and long afterward. Naturally, as a junior ensign, his contact with these more senior personalities was limited, but he still formed lasting professional opinions of them. He did get a chance to see them in the air and appreciated the opportunity to learn from their expertise. Indeed, throughout his long, productive career, Whitey would have similar opportunities, and his admiration was always returned in kind.

He flew with Lt. Col. Harold W. "Joe" Bauer, a leading light and then the CO of VMF-212, which had actually been stationed at the rear-area base on Efate. He was usually called "Indian Joe" or just "Joe" because of his dark complexion. His pilots also called him "Coach" because they felt he treated them like a team and at thirty-four was quite a bit older than his lieutenants.[1] Without his aircraft actually at Henderson, Bauer had to rely on the good will of other COs like John Smith of VMF-223 and Bob Galer of VMF-224 to "lend" him one of their Wildcats. Even with this occasional arrangement, Bauer had established himself as a combat aviator of great value. Bauer was shot down on November 14 after making his last kill, his eleventh official victory. He never returned, although his friends searched desperately for him. He received a posthumous Medal of Honor for his work at Cactus.[2]

Of John Smith, Whitey remembered, "He was kind of quiet, but, boy, he was all business." This assessment rings true for the VMF-223 skipper, who kept himself aloof as he led his squadron of young aviators, even though sending them up to fight the highly experienced Japanese crews and often not coming back was eating him up inside.

Speaking of Marion Carl, Whitey said, "He just kept reminding me of Lindbergh. He looked like him." Several aviators Whitey met reminded him of Charles A. Lindbergh. Mike Murphy was the first, although it was probably more because of Murphy's flight suit and reputation when he met the intrepid interwar personality. Marion Carl was at least taller and lankier in keeping with Lindbergh's actual appearance. Carl was another of the shining lights of Marine aviation who went on to have a stellar postwar career, retiring as a major general. He and Whitey become close friends and often worked together. Whitey recalled, "He was unbelievable as an aviator."

During their off hours, VF-10 aviators had little to do on Guadalcanal, and their two main activities became relaxing with a favorite "beverage" and swimming. The waters around the island harbored incredible opportunities for sightseeing, and the men took full advantage, improvising swim goggles from bamboo, Plexiglas, and rubber bands. Russ Reiserer was an avid swimmer and was frequently accompanied by Tommy Harman and Whitey Feightner.

But Whitey was put off after an afternoon encounter with a giant Moray eel. Leisurely swimming just below the surface, Whitey poked around in an underwater ledge, his feet above him as he held onto an outcropping of coral with a gloved hand. Imagine his surprise when he spotted two eyes looking back at him from the dark depths of the cavern he was exploring. Feightner quickly found another pastime.

In April, a group of Reapers launched on a predawn mission. As it got lighter, other pilots could see a trail of smoke and fire coming from Jim Billo's Wildcat. After he landed and the cowling was pulled, Marine mechanics discovered a crack in an engine cylinder. The oil had pushed through and had created the smoke. After a mechanic supposedly fixed the cylinder, Billo flew a CAP mission the next day, only to have the entire cylinder blow. He made it back to Henderson and traded his F4F for that of Bill Blair, who was sick with malaria. Billo and the rest of the Cactus Reapers flew back to Espiritu.

VF-10 alumnus Swede Vejtasa, who had left after Santa Cruz, made a surprise visit in a brand-new F4U Corsair. The big gull-winged fighter was having trouble winning acceptance on board Navy carriers and was relegated to flying from shore bases. It would be a year before it went to U.S. carrier-based squadrons. Eventually, VF-10 would come to know the Corsair very well.

From May through mid-July, the *Enterprise* and her air group conducted training, but there were a number of personnel changes. Whitey, now a lieutenant junior grade, transferred to VF-8, originally scheduled to join the USS *Intrepid*'s (CV 11) air group. But the *Intrepid* had had trouble going through the Panama Canal and was laid up for repairs, and her air group was transferred to the USS *Bunker Hill* (CV 17). Jim Billo had already made it over to the new carrier as a member of VF-18 and had already seen combat with his new squadron over Rabaul in November 1943.

After the action off Rennell Island, where the *Chicago* was lost, and the last weeks of working from Guadalcanal, VF-10 and the group received orders to head back to Pearl Harbor to replenish and rest before their next deployment. For many it was going to be a time for reassignment and to become acquainted with a new fighter, the Grumman F6F Hellcat. The Navy hoped that the big new cat from the Iron Works would offer a much-needed advantage over the tight-turning Zero that had often overwhelmed the young aviators in the Wildcat and Dauntless squadrons. Killing time at Espiritu Santo, the tired squadrons were glad for the chance to head east for a measure of home.

Swede Vejtasa was then the maintenance officer for a time. Since Vejtasa was the premier fighter ace in the Pacific, Vought wanted his opinion of their new fighter, the F4U Corsair, and sent an example out expressly for Vejtasa to sample. Vejtasa was less than impressed. He didn't care for the gull-winged, long-nosed brute with its 2,000-hp engine and its massive prop, and he wrote up a list of eighteen concerns, some of which were addressed, albeit with some reluctance by Vought, after being pushed by the Navy. The Corsair's tail wheel was too low and gave the aircraft an unhealthy stance on the ground or flight deck, resulting in the propwash "blanking out" the rudder and greatly diminishing the Corsair's controllability on the ground. Several young new aviators ground-looped their big blue fighters. The wings were too wide, and in the early models, about three feet of each wing tip was hinged to fold upward. This modification was soon dispensed with in the main production run.

Whitey was Swede's assistant. When they got back to Pearl, Swede wangled them both a hop in the Hellcat, which was a single-seater; no two-seat trainers were ever made, which was typical for the period, no matter the country of origin. Few single-seat types were ever modified as two-seaters for instructional purposes. A flight manual accompanied by a cockpit briefing from a current pilot leaning into the cockpit, and a new transitioning pilot was sent off with a pat on the back or shoulder and a quick warning to be careful.

From the first, Whitey was impressed with the new Grumman fighter's size. It certainly was larger than the little Wildcat, with wide-tracked landing gear that kept the Hellcat from ground-looping, which had often plagued F4F pilots ashore. The landing gear was electrically powered too. No more having to *wind up* or *down* the main gear as in the Wildcat, producing a porpoising motion right after launch from a carrier or takeoff from a landing field. Most Wildcat pilots developed a big right bicep from this cranking activity.

The Hellcat's powerful engine had nearly twice the horsepower of the Wildcat, and its battery of six .50-caliber wing-mounted machine guns were much better suited to the larger wing than was the same number of guns in the smaller Wildcat. In other words, there was power to lift the increased weight and push the F6F along at a hefty speed that was much faster than the Zero. Overall performance was twice that of the little F4F. The Hellcat had the speed, range, and ability to carry a reasonable bomb load, as well as rockets later in the war. Everyone was eager to get back to the United States to complete the transition to the Hellcat.

After the return to San Diego, new squadron assignments were handed out. As mentioned earlier, several VF-10 veterans were to go to VF-8, which was forming on the East Coast to be part of the *Intrepid*'s air group. What was to become the naval air station at Oceana in Virginia Beach in the Virginia Tidewater had not yet opened, and the squadron was stationed at nearby Pungo, known for its annual strawberry festival. Other satellite fields eventually hosted the bomber squadrons. It was a remote area, well-suited for training, although farmers were occasionally concerned about the noise that disturbed their livestock.

By this time in the war, the training schemes of the U.S. military were in high gear, producing hundreds of new aviators every month as well as fine-tuning the more senior men who would head out to the Pacific or other fleet assignments. When Whitey arrived as a lieutenant junior grade, there were five lieutenants already involved in the training syllabus. The situation in the training mix was that several of the more junior officers like Whitey had already seen a lot of combat—remember, he already had tallied four kills—and were thus seasoned veterans.

Nonetheless, everyone got together to devise tactics for their new Hellcat fighter, and they were glad to see they could do things with it that they could never have done with the old Wildcat. For instance, someone had devised a delayed-action fuse for 250-pound and 500-pound bombs, four of which could be carried by the Hellcat, and Whitey and his friends spent a lot of time perfecting the delivery technique for these weapons.

All was not smooth within VF-8, however. At the top, the CO, Cdr. William M. Collins Jr., was not exactly a people person. The Wisconsin native and member of Naval Academy class of 1934 was ambitious, preferring to spend more time with senior officers outside the squadron than with his junior officers. His autocratic way of running the squadron also rubbed many of his men the wrong way, and they grumbled about it.[3] But there was no denying that he was a skilled aviator and gunner—he would eventually gain nine kills—and there was little anyone could do about how he managed the squadron. Thus, at the end of the training cycle, VF-8 was a well-trained if not exactly happy squadron. After his highly successful nugget tour with VF-10 and its beloved skipper Jimmy Flatley, Whitey knew he had a much different tour ahead of him.

Actually, the time in the Reapers had had its ups and downs as well, but at least the CO was a decent sort. The main problem was the limited amount of flight time many members had before the hurried deployment, coupled with the fact that most of the pilots with any operational experience had come from SBD squadrons. Another problem was the air group commander, whom Whitey remembered as "absolutely one of the worst air group commanders at that time . . . even as an ensign I realized the man was completely out of his element."

Remember, too, that Whitey had not been with VF-10 when it was formed in San Diego; he had been originally assigned to Butch O'Hare's VF-3 and had done much of his predeployment training with that squadron and CO. Such a drastic change could be disastrous for a neophyte aviator ensign, especially one going directly into combat for the first time, even for one as affable and easygoing as Whitey. But the disadvantages had been smoothed over by Jimmy Flatley's skilled and personal management style. Whitey did feel that his new squadron was gaining the cohesiveness so important in a combat unit. Although they had not had a lot of time together for training at the little base in Virginia, many of the pilots had gotten railroad tickets for the same train car and rode up to New York for a little predeployment party.

After that "soiree" they had gone down to the Caribbean for a shakedown cruise in the *Intrepid*, which they found in Trinidad. It was then that VF-8 discovered that their new carrier might be jinxed! There had been a fire while she was still in the yard, then a rumor of some five hundred deserters permeated the air group. It was obvious that the ship's crew was not doing well, either. To have 20 percent of a wartime carrier's complement go over the hill was incredible.

The *Intrepid* was one of the first carriers to be built on the East Coast, which presented the problem of getting her over to the Pacific. The normal route west was through the Panama Canal, but it had been built before the advent of the aircraft carrier, which was much bigger than the largest Navy ships of 1914. The first American carriers could just barely squeeze through the canal, but as they grew in size and girth, it became increasingly more difficult to pass them through. But the captain, Thomas L. Sprague, decided to try it.

When the ship got down to Panama, it anchored and waited for a ship's pilot. No less than *five* finally arrived, but none had ever taken such a large ship through the canal, which was not surprising. The *Intrepid* was pulled alongside the pier, but she had too much way on, meaning the ship was moving too fast to control at such close quarters. The pilot held the carrier off from the pier.

From the beginning there was trouble. The carrier's big 5-inch gun mounts stuck out at the same level as the lights that lined the waterway. For a moment, it appeared to all who were watching that they just might make it into the lock. But the *Intrepid* kept moving and soon there was a crunch as she hit a retaining wall that ran along a highway. The bow was over the road as people scrambled to reduce the damage as much as possible. Needless to say, the pilot was relieved immediately.

The first thing that had to be done was to take down all the light poles that lined the lock. But after only two poles, the ship was again pulled through, which resulted in more light poles being destroyed. All Whitey could think at the time was, "Gosh! What a waste!" The options were to either remove the lights or the gun mounts. Messages flashed between Washington and the ship, and finally the decision was made to keep going even if more lights were destroyed, and about a hundred were.

Somehow, the *Intrepid* and her crew got through the first series of locks and entered Gatun Lake, which was a welcome stopping point before continuing on. By this time, another pilot had arrived, and he quickly got two other pilots to stand, one on each side of the bridge, to monitor the progress through the next challenge of Culebra Cut, which had been blasted out of solid rock. The carrier eased into the narrow lock, but even at eight knots, the physics of the operation took over, with a Venturi effect sucking the stern in, which made the bow turn to starboard instead of port. Captain Sprague called to drop the port anchor, but as the ship was already in full reverse, it was the starboard "hook" that came down!

As the crew, both ship's company and those from the air group, struggled to secure things around them, the carrier finally stabilized as her anchor restrained her forward movement. The bow hung over the lock and the adjacent road and was cut off where it had folded over. After the repairs had been made, the carrier went through the remainder of the canal and headed to San Francisco for major repair work. On the way, the air group did manage to conduct operations, so the time was not a total loss.

The group was now equipped with the SBD's replacement, the Curtiss SB2C Helldiver. The SB2C had had a long gestation period and was not an easy aircraft to fly or maintain. Whitey called it "an absolute hydraulic nightmare." He had even ferried a couple of the new planes from Columbus, Ohio, back to the east coast and he had learned just how much of a problem the Helldiver could be. "The problems we had with hydraulic leaks were just enormous."

The *Intrepid* finally arrived at Hunter's Point and, happily, repairs were accomplished fairly quickly, mainly because the shipyard already had a replacement bow ready. The new bow was supposed to go to another ship under construction. Still, although the grafting of the new bow went easily, the need for a new air group in the Pacific was acute, and Whitey and Air Group 8 were reassigned to the *Bunker Hill*, which was heading out for its deployment. CVG-8 now had VF-8 as its designated fighter squadron, with its F6F-3s. The rest of the group included VB-8 (SB2C-1Cs), VT-8 (TBF-1Cs), and a specialized night-fighter squadron, VFN-76 with modified F6F-3Ns.

CVG-8 was glad to leave the luckless *Intrepid*, which was holed up in dry dock, and join a ship headed for combat. The *Bunker Hill* would not be like the *Enterprise*, which as so many have written was a special ship with a special esprit. There was also the system of rotating air groups in and out of ships after only one tour, not like today where most air wings remain with a specific carrier for several years, if not for most of the ship's career.

Before he made the switch, however, Whitey was ordered to Norfolk to make a series of tests on a new development for the Hellcat. Ordinarily, the job would have been the concern of the people at the new naval aviation test group at Patuxent River in southern Maryland, but "Pax" was not that well organized in those early days and the Navy wanted a fleet pilot to make the tests. Whitey never could find out exactly how or why he was selected for the job.

The test involved a new supercharger that was being installed in the F6F, and the Navy wanted to determine what the absolute operational ceiling was with the new device. In June 1943, Whitey was briefed on the new supercharger in Norfolk and given a Hellcat with the advanced "blower." The Hellcat had a dedicated radio frequency installed so that the people on the ground could listen in to the test as Whitey climbed out. Every 5,000 feet he had to call in to report how things were going. Arriving at 35,000 feet—a very high altitude—everyone was amazed to see he still had something like an 800-feet-per-minute climb rate. He broke 41,000 feet and was still climbing.

Finally, he could feel the fighter shudder as it approached a stall, indicating it had run out of "breath" and had reached its ceiling. He started to descend, and when he got to what the altimeter read was 15,000 feet, he took off his oxygen mask. He was, after all, supposedly at a safe altitude. He quickly realized that he didn't feel right, but he didn't put the mask back on. Imagine his surprise—at least—when after landing the mechanics realized that the special test altimeter had been set at 10,000 feet *below* sea level! Everyone was dumbfounded. He had never gotten to 40,000 feet! He had taken his mask off at 25,000 feet and had gotten hypoxic. He was really at 35,000 feet. No wonder things didn't look right without it! The altimeter's design was faulty and it was not delivered to the Navy.

After that little escapade, Whitey was tasked with yet another test, this time to "exercise" the arresting gear during an acceptance trial for the *Intrepid*, which had by now come out of dry dock. The plan, however, was for the captain of the ship to have the honor of making the first landing, so while he headed out in an SNJ trainer, Whitey circled, waiting for his turn.

After several traps—arrested landings—Whitey was finally moved up to the ship's starboard catapult. The situation was changing as the carrier was running out of "sea room," room to maneuver and turn away from land or other obstructions such as decreasing depth. Undeterred, the crew ran the *Intrepid* up to thirty-two knots and, while they were at it, figured they would see how the ship felt while making a full rudder turn. First to starboard, which made the carrier heel hard over to port. During this maneuver, the bridge realized they were, indeed, running out of water below the keel and that it would be prudent to launch the Hellcat strapped to the catapult. In the meantime, Whitey had been holding on, strapped into his seat as the deck wallowed and swung beneath him. He watched as the catwalk at the edge of the flight almost went under the water during the tight turn. The extreme movement was certainly not conducive to his stomach's well-being.

Nevertheless, a third of the way through the corrective turn, he had his head down adjusting trim tabs for his landing approach. It was then that the deck crew fired the catapult, with no warning to the Hellcat's pilot! Whitey, of course, had not been prepared, and his engine was actually at idle. Somehow, the engine went to full power and the fighter went straight up in the air, quickly stalling.

The young aviator fought to regain control, all the time thinking he was going in the water. But somehow something happened—he could never determine what—and he regained control and was flying. But by this time, because the ship had continued to move forward after his launch, it was now in front of him and he was headed straight for the stern! Thinking he might have actually done a loop off the cat, Whitey found himself below the flight deck rounddown. He had to make a hard turn to miss the ship. It was incidents like these two—the hypoxia episode and the unexpected cat shot—that would fill Whitey Feightner's life and career, even out of combat.

After returning, Whitey was called up to the bridge, usually not a good sign. But when he had made the climb, he was surprised to see the catapult officer *with a rope around his neck*. The captain handed Whitey the rope, saying, "He's all yours." Although there was no really good explanation, the story was that the cat crew was getting things set for Whitey's shot, and someone simply fired the cat. In today's Navy, such an incident would have set off a full-blown investigation and probably would have got the poor cat officer fired, although not off his own catapult.

Since no one was hurt, however, not even the Hellcat, everyone simply had a good laugh. It was still something to contemplate. If Whitey had not shoved the throttle forward—although he never remembered doing it—he might have gone over the side and through the onrushing carrier's screws (propellers). His reflexes and luck were to follow him throughout his storied career.

Before finally heading out with the *Bunker Hill*, Whitey had one more test assignment. He had become so experienced as a test pilot that his services were in demand for even the most menial tasks. "Why I suddenly became an F6F expert I don't know," he mused, "but I was a typical fleet pilot, I guess." In this case, his job was to find the minimum wind over the deck needed to bring in an F6F safely.

His carrier in this case would be the USS *Charger* (CVE 30), one of the first escort carriers that was originally built for the British but which was reclaimed by the United States. Its tiny flight deck measured 440 feet by 81 feet versus the new *Essex*-class, which featured flight decks measuring 862 feet by 108 feet. (For modern comparison, the recently completed eleven-ship *Nimitz*-class of nuclear carriers averages a flight deck of nearly 1,100 feet by 250 feet.) Whitey went out to do field carrier landing practice (FCLP) at Virginia Beach. Whitey approached the field in his Hellcat, and the LSO, whom he knew slightly, signaled for him to come in and land. Heavy with fuel, Whitey decided to circle for a time before landing. The LSO became impatient and strongly indicated that Whitey should come in.

"Back in those days," Whitey admitted, "I did a lot of foolish things, and I came by and rolled on my back at about tree level." He flew by the LSO inverted, then rolled upright, dropped his landing gear, and landed. The LSO had been beating his paddles on the ground, a strong signal to land, now! Whitey obeyed and was immediately confronted by the training group commander, who stood the lieutenant at attention while he railed at him for his antics, threatening him with all sorts of disciplinary action. But, after venting his frustration, the commander left.

Whitey finished his FCLPs and went out to the *Charger*. After several approaches, he found that with barely four knots of wind, he could recover safely. They had actually been working with an F4U Corsair as well, but unfortunately the one they were using broke in two, cracking right under the fuselage aft of the wing. That left only the Hellcat. With continued tests, landings were achieved with zero wind over the deck, with the ship actually *stopped* on what was a really calm day. Another rarity was that Whitey didn't need a catapult for launching. At that time, lengthy deck runs were enough, with a good pilot at the controls, to take off from a carrier.

One other unusual variation was landing while the *Charger* was actually backing down, moving *backward* at four knots. Whitey caught the No. 1 wire, actually running the cable out to its full extension, where it hit the stops. Whitey was to do more unusual shipboard ops throughout his career after the war. He always considered times like the testing assignments he had between wartime deployments as giving him great experience that would help him when he reported to Patuxent for a full tour as a bona fide test pilot.

But now it was time to find his new ship and head out for his second combat tour. Just twenty-three, he had seen a lot and had developed a typically youthful acceptance of his personal situation, mainly that he didn't expect to survive these forays. But he and his friends were at the tip of the current spear and were fighting for their country at a dangerous time in its history. Pep talks from various combat leaders helped reinforce these feelings, and he felt good about it all. He recalled, "I had no trepidation about doing anything. We knew when we took off that if anything happened at all you weren't coming back. We knew we had a job to do. There wasn't any question of why we were there. . . . It's easy to accept when there are no alternatives."[4]

It was around this time that word came that Butch O'Hare had been killed in action. Promoted to lieutenant commander and given command of VF-6 in July, Butch's squadron was developing the U.S. Navy's night-fighting capabilities using Hellcats with radar and assisted by Avengers. VF-6 sent detachments to several carriers, and Butch's detachment was on board the light carrier *Independence* (CVL 22). Although history has questioned whether he actually shot down five Japanese bombers during his February 1942 Medal of Honor mission, he did get two kills during this deployment, shooting down a Zero and a Betty on October 5, 1943.

Now named to command CVG-6, he moved to the *Enterprise*, flying with VF-2. Butch launched on the night of November 26, 1943, along with his wingman and an Avenger from VT-6. Their mission was to confront a force of Bettys headed for the fleet. While the TBF circled, Butch and his wingman, Ens. Andy Skon, maneuvered to meet the oncoming enemy bombers. The story becomes confused, but the result was that as the Bettys approached, Butch's Hellcat was between the Avenger and the bombers and was caught in the crossfire. Then Ensign Skon saw his CAG slumped over in the cockpit as his Hellcat began to spiral down toward the sea. The twenty-nine-year-old ace was dead.[5]

The situation was much different from one year earlier on board the *Enterprise* in the Solomons. Although the Japanese were still a threat to be considered, they no longer had superiority in numbers or quality of equipment, especially with the appearance of the Hellcat, which was faster and at least as maneuverable as the Zero. Also, the Japanese had lost many of their most experienced flight crews during the Battles of the Coral Sea and Midway. Time was no longer on their side to replace those highly experienced aviators with the new trainees going through the Imperial pipelines. It takes at least two years to produce a properly trained aviator ready for combat, and while the United States had taken full advantage of the intervening years to produce squadrons of such aviators, the Japanese found themselves having to nearly start from scratch in the face of an oncoming juggernaut of American aircraft and men and carriers.

CVG-8 got into the action fairly quickly. The ship and its task force were was deep into the Pacific combat theater, all the way to the Palau Islands. The air group carried out three days of strikes against the enemy airfield on Woleai, about three-quarters of the way to Palau. The purpose of these strikes was never quite clear but Whitey later thought they had propaganda value, much like the Doolittle raid of April 1942, driving home the point to the Japanese that the Americans could get in there with their carrier and hit whatever and whenever they wanted. CVG-8's strikes destroyed a lot of aircraft on the ground that although staged fairly well forward were still—or so the Japanese must have thought—safe from such direct attacks.

Whitey and his squadron made a lot of fighter sweeps, establishing what came to be called the "Big Blue Blanket" of American naval aviation coverage. At times the strikes were composed of some 250 aircraft, with the fighters orbiting over the airfields to polish off any Japanese that might be foolish enough to come up to contest their presence. It was a great training exercise for the group, for every flight crew from every carrier. It was like getting your feet wet, much like the concept some twenty years later in Southeast Asia, off Vietnam, where the southerly Dixie Station allowed newly arrived carrier air wings to fly relatively uncontested missions on targets in South Vietnam before heading north to Yankee Station and the more dangerous combat over Hanoi and Haiphong.

Actually, there were at times so many aircraft in their air—sometimes as many as four carriers operating in the same general area—Whitey and his friends had to be careful about the crowded air space and overlapping landing patterns. Shipboard radar came of age here and controllers gained a lot of experience with large numbers of aircraft in the same space.

The size of the carrier groups had also expanded. In the earlier F4F days, there was little anti-aircraft artillery support from the various ships. They shot at everyone, friend or foe, but now, battleships and cruisers were outfitted with incredible arrays of guns of all calibers and radars. The Hellcats could fly four-hour combat air patrols with 150-gallon fuel tanks on the fuselage centerlines. If the duration of the patrol permitted, the tanks could be filled with powder and jellied gasoline— napalm—and the Hellcat pilots could drop these terrifying weapons on likely targets with devastating effect. Later, the fighters could also carry air-to-ground rockets under the wings.

Added to this lineup were the SB2C Helldiver replacements for the SBD Dauntless. The SB2Cs could carry 500-pound or 1,000-pound bombs. The strikes delivered by the air groups suffocated the Japanese bases because on the other end of the line, U.S. submarines and other air groups were making it impossible for the Japanese to resupply their far-flung bases. Now a lieutenant, Whitey Feightner was seeing fantastic changes in the squadrons and also how the war was being fought, and he had been a part of it.

And yet there was room for individual attention. On one mission, Whitey's wingman had gone down on the return home. Whitey circled over the young aviator in the water until he was recovered. When Whitey returned to the *Bunker Hill*—late and responsible for holding up the schedule operation at the time—he faced an angry two-star task force commander. The admiral told the lieutenant that finding the downed wingman was his problem, not Whitey's.

This admiral had the reputation of being an alcoholic and made several gaffes during his tour. In one case, Whitey recalled, he had been to the *Bunker Hill* to hand out awards. With the men lined up in formation, he started out with, "Men and officers of the USS *Wasp*, I am proud . . ." His chief of staff led the inebriated admiral away. Something like this was bound to have a demoralizing effect on people, and this particular incident was not a single occurrence. In contrast, the men of the *Bunker Hill* had a great captain as well as air group commander, in other words great men where it really counted.

CHAPTER 7
BUNKER HILL ACTION AND FINAL KILLS

Whitey was now a mature combat aviator, and he started showing his leadership skills and also became an ace. On one mission over Saipan, he was leading the fighter sweep over the island and saw two Nicks, twin-engine Nakajima Ki 45s, trying to take off. Whitey pushed over and tried to slow down to get behind the two enemy fighters. Just as he was about to start shooting, all the U.S. fighters behind him began firing, catching him in their crossfire. Whitey quickly broke off to avoid being shot down.

On April 29, 1944, he was flying with the CO, leading the second section. Lieutenant Commander Collins was leading the strike against the Japanese bastion at Truk, assigned to high cover at nearly 20,000 feet. Everyone else was at various altitudes. The flights went in and there were about a dozen Japanese planes taking off, as well as many floatplanes on the water. Although the enemy had known the Americans were coming for several days and had tried to move their aircraft out of harm's way, there were still enough to constitute a good interceptor force. The Americans, however, had something like three hundred aircraft in the air, which would certainly overwhelm the much smaller number of Japanese defenders.

Whitey saw a Hamp—a "square-cut Zero," as he called it—that had managed to get above his division. The Hamp was actually an A6M3, Model 32, a Zero with chopped wing tips, supposedly to give it more speed. The plane was originally code named "Hap," but Gen. Henry H. "Hap" Arnold of the Army Air Force took offense at the name, and the department responsible for the names quickly changed it. The Hamp was carrying bombs that had magnesium streamers that at a preset altitude would burst into flame that would settle onto the wings of the target American aircraft. The terrible fire would be fed by the oxygen of the surrounding air and would not go out until it had burned through the wing, severing it from the rest of the unfortunate plane.

Whitey went after the Hamp as it started dropping its horrible weapon onto the other fighters. Nose to nose, the Hellcat and Zero raced toward each other. Then, with what Whitey estimated as less than a thousand feet of separation, the Japanese pilot rolled to his left, then leveled out, leaving Whitey flying thirty feet off his right wing.

Whitey was slightly below the Hamp and climbing when the Zero pilot looked behind him and spotted the blue-gray Hellcat closing in. After waiting a moment, Whitey kicked left rudder and began firing his six .50-caliber machine guns, hitting the Zero behind the cockpit and in the engine. At 26,000 feet, the little fighter quickly caught fire and began spiraling toward the ocean. The pilot bailed out, pulling the ripcord on his parachute. Whitey timed it, and it took him thirty-seven minutes to hit the water, as long as the Navy strike force was over the target. Later, back in the *Bunker Hill*, a visiting newspaperman recorded the story of Whitey's high-altitude kill for a Chicago newspaper. It was Whitey's sixth kill. He figured the pilot had frozen to death, jumping out at that altitude without sufficient oxygen to make it all the way down. He received the Air Medal for this mission.

He had made ace a month earlier, on March 30, during a strike on Palau after leaving Hawaii as part of Vice Adm. Marc A. Mitscher's Task Force 58. The strikes were big, large-scale affairs involving three carrier groups, including five fleet carriers and seven light carriers. The Navy was finally organized and eventually headed for Japan.

On March 30, the first wave attacked at dawn, with seventy-two Hellcats attacking the assembled Japanese lineup, followed by more, including Army and Navy forces the next day. On the 30th, Whitey, flying an F6F-3, got a Zero as well as another probable kill over a Zero. He was now officially an ace.[1] He received the Air Medal—his third—for this mission. His CO, Lieutenant Commander Collins, also got his *first* kill on this mission, although he nearly missed his chance.

While Whitey watched, the skipper, who had little combat experience even though he was a good aviator, rolled over to attack a formation of twelve enemy aircraft at about three thousand feet, well below the Americans. Whitey had always placed great store in situational awareness, knowing who and what was around you, and at that point Lieutenant Commander Collins did not seem to know *all* those Zeros were there. Collins flew right in front of the Japanese fighters and Whitey wheeled over to lend a hand. He pulled up alongside Collins and frantically pointed back toward the Zeros. Collins finally understood and patted his head and pointed, giving Whitey the lead. The two Hellcats swung back toward the Zeros. Collins picked out the lead Japanese and blew him out of the sky with his six machine guns. The rest scattered "like a bunch of chickens," as Whitey said later.

The question of confirmed and probable kills affected most combat pilots around the world and even today remains a sure-fire trigger for discussion. Whitey is one of those highly experienced aces who believes his official total of confirmed kills is incorrect. But at this late stage of life and career, it is difficult to revisit the circumstances. Several people have made themselves specialists—some call them "aceologists"—in determining the final disposition of victory claims. It remains a hard task, one often without the reward of realizing the truth to everyone's satisfaction.

Whitey said during a 1990 interview, "In my own heart I know I have shot down twenty-two airplanes. I have credit for nine, but I didn't waste any time watching to see what happened to them. And no one could verify it. . . . I have been credited with six probables . . . everyone agrees they probably went down but nobody saw them hit. . . . I was interested in staying alive, and I was looking somewhere else by the time. . . . I have gun camera film of pieces flying off a Zero. Believe me, I've flown the Zero and pieces don't fly off a Zero and it keeps going. They come apart . . . at speed, that airplane just disintegrated."[2] Besides his nine official kills, Whitey claims six probables, with two being officially credited, plus one damaged.

The operation against Truk had been cause for apprehension. The Navy thought the big base was a heavily fortified bastion that would deal harshly with any American task force that dared to attack it. Truk was a group of small islands in the larger Caroline Islands group, which in turn was included in the Japanese Mandated Islands (along with the Marshalls and the Gilberts, all of which saw some action and eventually became bases for the Navy as the war pushed steadily westward). They had been originally the property of Germany, which had invested a lot of money and men in the development of an Asian empire for the kaiser, but were given to the Japanese following World War I after they had joined the Allies against the Central Powers.

The secretive Japanese did not permit outsiders—namely Westerners—to visit the islands as they built a huge base in preparation for war to foster their own expansive empire in the Pacific. Originally, the Allies planned to pound Truk into submission before attempting any landings, but they finally decided to simply bypass the enemy base and its anchorage, allowing it to wither from lack of resupply from Tokyo. Actually, U.S. forces destroyed some two hundred Japanese aircraft and thirty-six ships of various classes in the initial stages of the operation.

Whitey recalled:

> What a shock! We got in there and there was practically nothing there. There was a lot of triple-A, and we did get a lot of people shot down. [But] the morning strike on April 29, 1944, with that many airplanes over there and many of our airplanes on the fighter sweep and so few enemy airplanes airborne, and there's no place they could resupply it. Once we had them out of there, why they obviously mostly pulled out. We shot up everything . . . then came back the rest of the day with bombs. There were a lot of ships in the harbor, civilian-type ships, and we proceeded to take those out one by one . . . we had all the skip-bombing training [and] our squadron was allowed to go into the main harbor [with] delayed-action fuses . . . each plane with two bombs. I led a division and we saw a big transport sitting there. I made my run, coming in at a shallow 30-degree dive, while my wingman

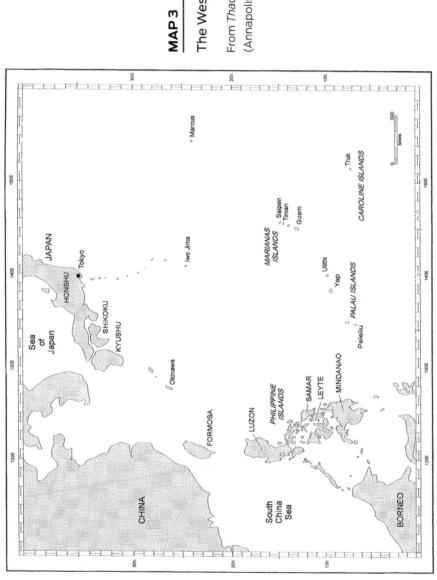

MAP 3

The Western Pacific

From *Thach Weave: The Life of Jimmie Thach* (Annapolis, Md.: Naval Institute Press, 2004), 110.

strafed to keep their heads down. I waited until we were about at ship's level, then put another 10 degrees nose down so that the bomb would hit the water just short of the ship and would ricochet into the ship and explode. On this particular delivery, I got a little too low and my delivery was flat. I dropped the bomb and immediately pulled up over the ship and rolled up on my right wing to watch the thing go off. When I looked down, my bomb was flying wing on me! It was flying formation with me! I could see the fuse prop spinning and it was winding up. I made a *square* turn, pulling back on the stick so that the bomb went one way and I went another! The bomb actually skipped over the ship and went a mile up the beach before blowing up![3]

Whitey also found himself flying several combat reconnaissance missions in specially equipped Hellcats. These fighters, either F6F-3Ps or F6F-5Ps, carried large 150-pound F56 cameras that took huge twelve-inch negatives. The cameras were nearly four and a half feet long and were mounted behind the cockpit and looked out of a hole on the right side. All the pilot had to do was to put his starboard wing tip on the target and the results were, hopefully, large, high-definition photos. Each load usually carried enough film for sixty pictures. The favorite targets of these photo flights were beachheads.

One day, in the second week of early June 1944—perhaps the 11th (his sparsely written logbook is unclear on the activities during this period)—Whitey launched to take pictures of the beaches on the northern coast of the island of Tinian and the southern coast of the island of Saipan in the Marianas. The photographs were needed before the huge operation scheduled to begin on June 15 with amphibious landings by Marines followed later by Army troops on Saipan to reclaim the important strongholds as future B-29 bases. He was actually part of a twenty-six-plane group, with the remaining twenty-five assigned to escort him and then attack the Japanese barracks that housed the troops that would contest the American landings. There were also gun emplacements that were targets of interest. The cloud base was 2,500 feet, which suited Whitey because he wanted to make a straight run over the guns to take pictures. The fighter lead told him they would come down with him and shoot up the emplacements, but Whitey said he would make the photo run alone to take advantage of whatever surprise he might have. Lead agreed, and the lone VF-8 Hellcat pilot started his descent.

Whitey flew at fifty feet above the water, the better to get a more realistic view of the approaches to the beach as might be seen by men on the ships and in the landing craft. As he flew along the coast, the Japanese defenses opened up on both islands, bracketing the Hellcat as he flew straight and level to take the photos. With all that lead in the air, he flew two passes and returned without a single hole in his fighter. His friends followed later and destroyed the barracks and guns.

Then he flew another mission more inland to take photos of more gun emplacements at the airfields. The day was bright and the strong Pacific sun made for a postcard picture, complete with puffy, fair-weather clouds. Whitey went in low, the better to prevent his being seen. Then, as he flew over palm trees that ringed the area, he climbed to eight thousand feet off one end of the runway and made his run, heading toward mountains at the opposite end, now followed by increasing amounts of flak.

What no one in the carrier knew was that this base had radar-directed guns, and now he found himself the target of these heavy weapons, maybe of 75-mm caliber. He was hit and lost his entire port horizontal stabilizer on the tail, as well as cutting the cable to his trim tab, an important flight control that helped ease the pilot's task of maintaining easy flight. The shell had actually struck just behind the cockpit near the camera and had flipped the Hellcat over.

Now flying at 400 mph, *upside down*, the young pilot struggled to maintain control as he exited the area. "All I could see was ground," he remembered later. "I was headed right toward the ground." Somehow, he was able to roll right side up again at what he estimated to be barely five feet to ten feet over the runway, actually *below* the palm trees. As he swept by he realized he still had his finger on the camera button, taking pictures. His photos would show the ground as a blurred streak, as well as the enemy gun crews staring bug-eyed at the crazy American pilot invading their space.

As he finished his runs, he was hit once more, and this time his aircraft was engulfed in smoke and flames. As he pulled back his canopy, he thought he might have to bail out over a very hostile area. He actually had his right leg over the cockpit sill and waited for the Hellcat to slow down so that he could exit more "safely."

Now the fighter was nosing up and he pushed the stick forward. Time seemed to slow down as he thought about pushing the stick further forward. He considered his options: stay with the airplane and probably blow up with it, or come down among the Japanese he had just been terrorizing and who were not known for treating aviators with any compassion. He decided to take his chances with the burning airplane and pulled his leg back inside.

The ocean was about five miles away and Whitey made a gentle turn as he crossed a line of hills. If he could get to the water, he figured he could bail out and wait for rescue. The hills were actually about six thousand feet high. The smoke was blowing into the cockpit, so Whitey closed his canopy, but the cockpit was heating up with the fire.

He had just cleared the tops of the hills when there was a big explosion. Dazed, he sat for a minute before realizing that the fire was out and the engine was still running. He pushed forward then looked out at his port wing. Most of it was missing! A section remained that went from the fuselage to the wingtip and perhaps two feet back, chordwise. (The chord measures the surface from the leading edge to the trailing edge. In this case, the remaining section was more like a single spar.) What was left looked like an inverted "L." And yet the rugged Hellcat still flew.

The fire had probably struck the hydraulic lines to the brake, resulting in the oil and the main wheel tire going up as well as the fuel tank and the ammunition cans for the three machine guns on that side. So now the young lieutenant was flying a Hellcat without much of a port stabilizer or port wing. But he still had a vertical tail and starboard wing and elevator, which continued giving him some control. He kept flying out to the ocean.

As he stood up, preparing to bail out, Whitey looked ahead, and his incredible eyesight spotted the task force some thirty miles away. Without a radio, he couldn't call in, but he kept heading for the ships. As he neared his goal, however, he discovered that one of the connectors was loose on the radio. He simply tightened the wire and suddenly he had communications.

As he approached the task force, he explained his situation and soon he had another Hellcat from the CAP on his wing checking him out. Unfortunately, there was another recovery going on and naturally, no one wanted to take him aboard with his badly damaged plane for fear of blocking other landing traffic. Instead, Whitey was told to bail out near a ship where he would be rescued. He lowered what remained of his landing gear anyway, including his tailhook, right main gear, and his tailwheel. There was only the stub of his left main gear remaining. But the Hellcat seemed to be flying OK. He kept coming.

Of course, he had no flaps, which would have provided him with a much lower, safer landing speed. Right now, the best he could get was ninety knots instead of the normal sixty to sixty-five. Gingerly, he reduced power as the controller finally told him to bail out.

Instead, he called, "Permission to come aboard." The amazed controller said, "You have no left wheel!" Then, "It's your option. The skipper says if you think you can bring it aboard, fine." Obviously, the CO had a lot of confidence in his young pilot, and Whitey was also bringing back important film now taken at some cost. The ship offered to rig the barricade webbing. Whitey kept coming around until he was in the groove, on final approach now at a steady ninety knots. Close in to the flight deck, the LSO gave him the cut, signaling him to chop his power, and he caught an arresting wire.

The deck crew counted more than 170 shrapnel holes in the battered Hellcat. Yet, the fighter flew again ten days later, a tribute to the Grumman's rugged construction. Apparently, he did not receive even an Air Medal for this very dangerous mission. On another mission, Whitey returned with one lower cylinder of his engine completely shot away, resulting in oil streaming from the cowling as he flew back seventy miles *and* recovered without incident. The man from Ohio certainly had his share of luck but he also had his share of flying skill.

The Turkey Shoot

Whitey found himself in the middle of what came to be known as the Marianas Turkey Shoot in June 1944. Many historians have written about this aerial engagement that saw hundreds of Japanese aircraft shot down and the fabled nighttime recovery of many U.S. Navy aircraft and crews, as well as the loss of many more men and machines when they ran out of gas before they could reach the fleet and a flight deck. There were many individual goals met during those missions, one of which was to get Skipper Collins his fifth kill to qualify him as an ace. He had scored a kill over a Zero on March 30 near Peleliu, the same day Whitey got his fifth kill, a Zero.

Early on June 19, Whitey and the CO launched for a CAP, and as they orbited their station, a vector came for an enemy intruder, which turned out to be a Pete, one of those Mitsubishi float biplanes that could give a good account of itself against more heavily armed and more powerful fighters. The contact was at about 1,500 feet and he obviously saw the U.S. fighters coming. Whitey and his wingman split to go up on either side of the little floatplane, sitting off on his right and left side so he couldn't turn away to escape. The enemy pilot must have panicked because the plane's nose pulled up abruptly and it turned over into a spin. There was nothing any of the American pilots could do but watch as the Pete hit the water. No credit for anyone.

Later, two of the night fighters attached to the ship were out on a day patrol and they found the wreckage of the Pete, with two of the three-man crew forlornly sitting on a wing. The two American pilots decided to have some target practice and made several strafing runs on the wreckage, something that most U.S. veterans would deny seeing or doing. But in a darkly humorous turn, the two Japanese would dive off the wing as the Hellcats approached firing their guns, eventually using up their entire load of ammunition without any results.

The *Bunker Hill* was one of a huge force of fourteen carriers—six fast attack carriers (CVs) and eight light carriers (CVLs)—carrying a total of nine hundred aircraft. All told some five hundred U.S. ships were part of the massive operation called Forager, all headed toward major enemy bases including Saipan and Guam, which had been wrested from American control shortly after Pearl Harbor two and a half years earlier. In turn, the Japanese fleet included nine carriers, three CVs and six CVLs, as well as the two largest battleships in the world, the *Yamato* and the *Musahi*, each armed with 18.1-inch guns, the world's largest. The Imperial carriers also carried 450 aircraft, and there were 200 land-based bombers and fighters that could strike the American force when it came in range. All in all, the operation was shaping up to be one of the last great sea-air engagements of the Pacific War.

In reality, the best the Japanese could hope for was to contain the huge opposing force heading straight for them. The fear that had ridden with the huge Japanese strike force that hit Pearl Harbor in December 1941 had finally reared its head, and there was little they could do about it. The Japanese made their first appearance over the U.S. fleet early in the morning of June 11. Flying boats and bombers came out from the shore bases only to be destroyed by the alert CAP launched from the carriers. The first U.S. strikes launched just before noon and continued for three days, hitting Guam, Saipan, and Tinian, all important islands that would eventually become bases for the Air Force B-29s headed for Japan's home islands and industrial heart.

All the U.S. Navy carrier planes and crews were busy, especially the fighters protecting the fleet. At mid-afternoon on June 11, Whitey was up and quickly found action, namely a beehive of Zeros that surrounded him as he returned from another photo mission over the beaches on Saipan before the Marines landed. Fortunately, Ens. Lester E. Gray of VF-10 was available and he spotted Whitey beset by two Zeros. The Reaper aviator hammered one of the Zeros, which quickly fell away in flames. A few days later, Whitey was only too glad to confirm Gray's kill and to note that his old squadron was very much alive. Missouri native Lee Gray would eventually become an ace with five and a quarter kills, earning two Distinguished Flying Crosses along the way, flying a second tour with VF-10, equipped this time with F4U Corsairs.

Whitey also has credit for sinking a Japanese ship. On October 10, 1944, he was originally to be part of a strike in the Philippines, to the north. But planners were more interested in whether the airfields in the Nansei Shoto islands of the Ryukyu chain some seven hundred miles southwest of Kyushu had any aircraft on them. The retasking resulted in using straight fighters. His regular plane was having generator problems and was dropped from the mission. He took another F6F, but one that was still carrying a bomb with a delayed-action five-second fuse for the earlier strike. The armorers said they would take a few minutes to unload the bomb, but Whitey was impatient to launch and told the ordnancemen to forget it; he would take the bomb with him!

Whitey joined his group of twenty Hellcats; he was the only one with a bomb. When they got to the island, they discovered a small, maybe 15,000-ton ship steaming out of the harbor. Whitey called the flight leader to tell him he had a bomb and to request permission to skip-bomb the enemy ship. Lead agreed and said he would send a few other Hellcats down to strafe ahead of Whitey, to keep the freighter's crew's heads down for him as he made his approach.

But Whitey was concerned with the amount of potential defense guns on the ship and asked to go in alone. "They won't even see me," he said. "They'll be too busy looking at these other planes up here." Again, lead agreed and Whitey made a steep dive above five miles short of the ship. His bomb hit the ship, perhaps in the engine room, and created a huge explosion. The ship's entire stern fell off, and the rest sank quickly, right in front of the surprised American formation. "I had the most confirmed ship sinking of World War II," he declared. All the pilots, including his leader, circled taking pictures. Whitey eventually received an individual Air Medal for the mission (as opposed to the Air Medals awarded for a cumulative amount of points for each strike mission). He would eventually gain another Air Medal, his sixth, this time "for a series of meritorious acts . . . from March 30 to April 21 [involving] flight in a combat area where enemy anti-aircraft fire was expected to be effective or where enemy aircraft patrols usually occurred."[4]

Whitey flew on the June 19 mission against the Japanese carriers later called the Battle of the Philippine Sea, where 380 Japanese aircraft were claimed to be destroyed (perhaps 55 to 60 percent of those claims were confirmed). Twenty-two U.S. Navy pilots made ace that day. This part of the battle was nicknamed the "Marianas Turkey Shoot."[5] The enemy fleet had been at the extreme range of most of the American aircraft, and the U.S. crews were launched with the possibility that they would not have enough fuel to return to their carriers. In many ways, it looked like a one-way mission.

But Whitey's war consisted of flying a CAP, and there was little action to be seen. Whitey and his division did flush out another Pete and proceeded to take their turns harassing the chunky little green biplane, which finally stalled and spun into the water. Since none of the four VF-8 pilots could claim any real part of the kill, now Commander Collins (he had been promoted on June 11) denied credit to anyone. It was a disappointing end to a day when many of his friends were coming back with claims for at least one kill. Commander Collins eventually finished the deployment as the high scorer for VF-8's second combat cruise with nine kills.

To the PI

Eventually the task force made its way to the Philippines, making a detour to satisfy General Douglas MacArthur of the Army, who had promised in 1942 to return and retake his adopted country from the Japanese, who now held the island nation under a harsh boot. The Navy side of the fight took place largely during the Battle of Leyte Gulf in October 1944 when Admiral Halsey took his fast carrier task force to hunt for the remnants of the once imposing Imperial fleet.

After flying through stormy weather, Whitey and his air group struck Palawan, on the west side of Leyte. The Curtiss Helldivers hit the target without any aerial opposition, but a Hellcat pilot had to bail out after being hit by flak, and he was now in the water. Whitey escorted an OS2U Kingfisher floatplane from a cruiser to pick up the lonely fighter pilot, Lt. (jg) Zeke Holland.

They spotted him, and the OS2U pilot landed close to Holland, who clambered aboard the blue-gray Kingfisher stark naked after discarding everything but his life jacket as he was being strafed by Zeros. As the Kingfisher took off and joined up on his escort, the OS2U pilot radioed that he was getting low on fuel and that he wasn't sure he could make the trip back to the cruiser.

Whitey gave him the lead, which relieved the other pilot of maintaining formation with the Hellcat, and told him to make a straight line for open water. But they soon found themselves directly over the enemy airstrip, tangled up with a few

Zeros. Whitey drove the enemy fighters off and he and his charge got out over the water once more just as the OS2U pilot called that his gauge was showing empty tanks and that he would have to set down somewhere. They were about thirty miles from the task force.

Whitey called them and the fleet dispatched a destroyer, which was on the outskirts of the force, fifteen or twenty miles from the inbound aircraft. The Kingfisher pilot landed by the DD, which gave him enough fuel to make it back to his cruiser by water taxiing. Although most destroyers didn't carry aviation gas, with a higher octane rating, a few did, and more DDs were converted to seaplane tenders as AVDs (tenders converted from older flush deck, four-stack DDs). The cruiser by now had come over the horizon to pick up its wayward floatplane and its passenger. But the story wasn't finished.

After the cruiser's recovery apparatus had been hooked onto the OS2U, the ship's crew began hoisting the floatplane up toward the stern deck. But one wing float dug into the water, flipping the aircraft and ejecting the crew and Hellcat pilot into the water. This was the third dump for Holland in one mission, and it was enough for him. When he was finally retrieved on board, the ship's doctor gave him a thorough examination and decided the young aviator had used up most of his luck. Holland had had enough, too, and he decided he was through flying and returned to the United States.

The task force hit Formosa—later renamed Taiwan—the large island off the Chinese mainland where the Japanese had built a large and well-stocked airfield at Tainan. Earlier in the war, it had been the base for one of the best-known fighter groups in the Japanese navy. On October 12, 1944, the Navy encountered forty to sixty enemy aircraft arrayed against a mere fifteen on the American side. Undeterred, the Hellcats tied into the Japanese. Whitey shot down three Zeros, his final kills, bringing his overall score to nine. The Zeros had actually been above the Americans and had dived down through the U.S. formation, taking a quick shot and continuing their dive toward the water to escape. It was a tactic similar to what American fighter pilots had used earlier in the war.

Kwajalein, Eniwetok: strange South Pacific names to be added to the list that Americans came to know as the Allied juggernaut made its slow way toward Japan. Task Force 58 plowed its way through the ocean's deep waters.

Finally, the deployment ended, and CVG-8 and its carrier turned back to the east to begin the long voyage home. Eventually arriving at Pearl Harbor, the weary crews had a surprise waiting for them. Instead of another transport ship or a fleet of transport aircraft, the Navy was going to put them aboard luxury passenger liners. Whitey embarked in the *Polk* and settled in for a week-long trip to San Francisco, the war now seemingly behind them.

But three days out, while they were about to have lunch, the general quarters alarm sounded. The ship made an extreme turn, an evasive maneuver, sending plates and pots flying. Each man raced to his state room to get his life jacket and then headed up to the deck to see what was going on. Their two destroyer escorts were firing Hedgehog antisubmarine mortar shells. Their aim must have been very accurate because, to the amazement of all, a Japanese submarine came blasting up to the surface, its huge red "meatball" showing bright and wet, only to stand on its end, roll halfway, and hit the water like a broaching whale before disappearing beneath the sea. The *Polk* changed its course immediately; its new destination was Seattle, Washington.

Arriving in Seattle, however, the task force crews were held on board for two days while higher-ups discussed sending the ship back down to San Francisco. But the crews were finally taken off the liner with the admonishment not to say anything about the engagement with the Japanese submarine. The Navy then flew the tired crews down to San Francisco.

After two weeks' leave, Whitey received orders to report to VF-98 as a fighter instructor. With two heavy combat tours and nine kills, he certainly was well qualified for that job! The squadron was then under the leadership of one of naval aviation's icons, Cdr. John Crommelin.

Crommelin came from a family of Navy men, including several naval aviators, and he was a fighter pilot to the end. Whitey often went out with the skipper in Wildcats, and the two would spend their time practicing fighter maneuvers. On one flight, though, Crommelin announced he wanted to do "fighter formation acrobatics." Their first maneuver was a loop, and as they neared the top Whitey could tell the CO was putting on more power, then reducing it. In fact, he was flying formation with his junior pilot. Then there followed barrel rolls.

On a later flight, Crommelin was ready to teach Whitey something.

> "Here's an exciting thing for you in an F4F," he said in the brief. "When I drop my hand, I want you to kick right rudder and throw that stick as far over to the left as you can." In effect, this was a cross-control maneuver, resulting in a snap roll. Whitey did as he was told and the two Wildcats made "a very nice over the top and right formation." Perfect for showing off over their ship, followed by a zoom pass along the flight deck. Modern aviators—70 years later—can appreciate this little bit of aerial showmanship for the troops. Nothing changes in seven decades. But it definitely won't be the same with unmanned aerial vehicles (UAVs)!

In this training unit, Whitey flew all the current types operating in the fleet, from the FM (the General Motors–built version of the F4F), to the F6F and the F4U. On one hop, Whitey took a flight of newly minted Marine aviators out for a run to shoot rockets. At the time, the Marines were experiencing a terrible safety record, which wasn't helped by their flying Corsairs, which were still having trouble finding a home in the carrier fleet. The CO of the ship they would be using was not favorably disposed to having leatherneck aviators try out his ship for landing practice. He briefed them on how he wanted things to go. At first, the weather didn't cooperate, resulting in the flight schedule being canceled.

The next day things improved a little, but conditions were still not that good. Nevertheless, the ship called flight quarters. A Corsair was coming in, but the ceiling was barely eight hundred feet. As everyone watched, the big, blue fighter dropped from the overcast and zoomed down the flight deck. And who was the pilot? Why, John Crommelin! He quickly set up his approach and trapped. He told Whitey to get all his pupils into the wardroom for a little "talk."

When they were all assembled, Crommelin said they could all do what he had just done. "There isn't anything wrong with anyone in this room," he declared. "You're all capable of doing this. It's just a matter of confidence. And just to show you what I am talking about, I want you all up on the flight deck, and I am going to demonstrate what I want to see you do."

Afterward, Crommelin went up to the flight deck, which was pitching badly. He climbed into his Corsair and launched. He had no more cleared the deck when he had wrapped the big fighter into a climbing turn up to pattern altitude. He made a big, circling pattern, although quite low. The LSO signaled he was low but the determined aviator kept coming, aiming for the heaving deck.

The LSO gave him the "cut" signal and the Corsair's wheels were barely on the deck, the tail still over the rounddown. He *taxied* up to the No. 1 wire. He no sooner had stopped than he gunned the engine and took off again. The LSO gave him another cut signal and this time, Crommelin raised his altitude perhaps another ten feet from the first landing. He made four of these recoveries, all the time watched by as many people as Vulture's Row could hold. On the fifth launch, he disappeared into the clouds, headed for home, leaving behind him a crowd of extremely motivated young aviators.

They didn't fly that day, but the next day everyone went out and qualified without any mishaps. It was quite a show put on by one of the Navy's best, something that stayed with all who saw it, including Whitey Feightner.

The war ended when Whitey was still instructing. Now not yet twenty-six, he had shot down nine Japanese aircraft during several important campaigns and had been awarded four Distinguished Flying Crosses and twelve Air Medals. But there were more exciting times ahead, including flying the Navy's first jet aircraft.

CHAPTER 8
TESTING JETS

Flying with Major Bong

While in VF-98, Whitey received a unique set of temporary orders for a young fighter ace at the time. He was given the opportunity to fly the latest thing in aviation development, one of the first jet-powered aircraft. His instructor for this terrific new experience was none other than Maj. Richard I. Bong, who with forty kills flying P-38 Lightnings in the Pacific was America's ace of aces for all time.

Much has been written about the boyish-looking Bong, a native of Wisconsin. Suffice it to say that he was a good combination of flying skill and exceptional marksmanship. He had received the Medal of Honor for his work and was an easy-going though occasionally intense operator who exuded confidence and ease in the cockpit. Just the type of person Lieutenant Feightner could warm up to.

Whitey got a temporary assignment, along with Lt. Reuben James, who was assigned to a staff as an admiral's flag lieutenant, to go up to March Air Base south of Riverside, where the Army was conducting the initial flight testing of the P-80 Shooting Star. To be among the first Navy pilots to fly the latest fighters was indeed a real plum. Whitey came to regard the jet course as being well-designed, and he felt comfortable when he soon strapped in for his first jet flight.

Jet aviation was, of course, in its infancy; there was a lot to be learned, especially in operating the new engine technology with its greatly reduced endurance compared to the reciprocating engine still at the heart of all aviation, civilian and military. Whitey found the P-80, with its straight, tapered wings and its simple design, "an honest airplane." It was easy to fly with a "straightforward stall" that didn't snap off on one wing.

Flying jets versus props involved using much less rudder because of the greatly reduced amount of torque normally associated with props. A new jet pilot used to props soon learned to be much lighter on his feet when applying the rudder. A jet didn't slow down as rapidly, however, because of its momentum, and a jet was a much cleaner aircraft with less drag. Jet fuel consumption rates were also something to be considered. The short-legged P-80 kept its pilots always thinking about fuel.

The new arrangement of having the jet exhaust at the rear without prop airflow blowing past the wings and tail-mounted elevators required more speed, but as he later recalled, the P-80's clean design, without large engine nacelles or paddle-bladed propellers offering resistance, made the Shooting Star a "beautiful little airplane."

So now, with the almost perfect mount, Whitey was assigned to the nearly perfect instructor. In Major Bong, he found an unassuming but highly confident personality to match his own. Someone who had seen a lot of heavy combat but had a mild demeanor that allowed the business of training to proceed, unhindered by ego, something some people might have found unusual in a fighter pilot.

Bong was proud of being an instructor and went the distance to make a student at ease as they explored the new thrill of flying jets. "He was meticulous in everything including his dress. You know he wasn't one of these laid back, sloppy individuals. Without being overbearing, you know he was just a great guy. . . . He was an instructor in the truest sense."[1]

The jet course lasted only seventeen days, and although Whitey was satisfied with the course, given his own level of flight experience, he left with a strong impression of the contrast between Army air force and Navy aviators. He felt that the Army pilots did not get the training that helped them understand *how* an aircraft flew, whereas the Navy put a lot of time into the subject. In the early days of the war, the Army desperately needed pilots and pushed them through training without the same amount of attention to basics given to Navy pilots.

During his stay on Guadalcanal, he had encountered a P-38 pilot with only *nineteen* hours in his fighter. Yet he was being sent into combat. It seemed almost like the same situation the Royal Air Force was managing during the Battle of Britain in 1940 when it was sending newly winged aviators with often no more than ten or fifteen hours (sometimes less) in their Spitfire or Hurricane into the intense fighting over England. Of course, the young P-38 pilot did have perhaps two hundred hours acquired during his so-called undergraduate training before getting his wings. But there was little subsequent training in his log book on the plane he was to fight with, perhaps for his life.

Unfortunately, Dick Bong did not survive the war. He was killed on August 6, 1945—the day the A-bomb was dropped on Hiroshima—while flying a P-80. He had not accumulated much time in the jet, only four hours all told in eleven flights, barely 1 percent of his total time, including combat. He wanted to add more, of course. He took off and climbed to two hundred feet. Witnesses saw the Shooting Star dip its right wing as black puffs of smoke popped out of the exhaust. Only a few seconds later, the plane hit the ground even as Bong had almost managed to extricate himself from the cockpit. It was too late. The crash destroyed the little gray fighter and killed America's ace of aces.

The field where the P-80 crashed indicated that even in his last moments Bong had aimed for an unpopulated site to keep from hitting civilians. The investigation focused on fuel pressure and the probability that the undependable fuel pump had stopped feeding fuel, causing a flameout. In all probability, many people believed, the young ace had simply not turned on the auxiliary fuel pump, which was a checklist item. Thus even with his considerable flight experience, but with only four hours in the P-80, he had made a simple mistake that cost him his life after accumulating all that combat time. Bong would have been too low to try a relight and all he could think of just before he tried to bail out—the early jets did not have ejection seats—was to keep his doomed plane away from people and buildings around the field. It's sad to think that an ejection seat might have saved his life, catapulting him up and away from his aircraft.

Bong's death was only one of two losses Whitey experienced involving great instructors. Two years before, on November 26, 1943, Butch O'Hare, now a lieutenant commander and commander of Air Group 6 on board the *Enterprise*, had become a proponent of night fighting. On that date he had led two other Hellcats, accompanied by a TBF radar plane, on an interception of Japanese intruders near Tarawa. What happened on that fateful night has been open to long discussion by several authorities, but it would seem that after his flight had destroyed several of a large force of Mitsubishi G4M Betty bombers, O'Hare was caught by an alert nose gunner of another Betty. The Navy's first ace of the war went down. He received a posthumous Navy Cross, the citation of which highlighted Butch's "brilliant leadership and courageous initiative."

As one recent account pointed out, O'Hare had met his old enemy. The Betty was the same type he had triumphed over on his Medal of Honor flight on February 20, 1942. This time, however, the result was much different and America lost one of its most important heroes.[2]

Admiral's Aide

Shortly after finishing jet training, Whitey found he would become the aide to newly selected Rear Adm. Samual P. Ginder, who was on the staff of Carrier Division 3. Taken aback by the prospect of leaving flight status, especially after the thrill of flying jets with Dick Bong, he tried to convince the chief of staff, Capt. "Nappy" Kinnette, that he wasn't the best choice for the job. The captain listened to the young fighter pilot plead his case, but in the end he told Whitey that the admiral had asked for him personally and it was a done deal. There was nothing to do but give the age-old salute and "Aye, aye, sir!" and start packing.

Whitey did try once more. He found his former group CO, now Rear Adm. Ralph Shiffley, and asked him to help. At first Shiffley, who was involved in helping to form a Navy flight demonstration team that was eventually called the Blue Angels, was thrilled at the prospect of having one of his best and brightest young aviators on the team. But when he found that Whitey had actually already been selected as Admiral Ginder's aide, he backed off, saying, "Go back and do your job."

There was nothing for Whitey to do but accept the circumstances. He would find his way to the Blue Angels soon, though.

So Whitey joined the new admiral and quickly found himself headed back to the Pacific in 1947 to make a series of goodwill port calls, beginning in Australia. Unfortunately, the protocols for the ceremonies had been lost. No one knew what to do!

Then there were other things, such as obtaining an Australian flag. With instructions by radio, the parachute riggers made one. There was also the matter of a band: they didn't have one! Admiral Ginder called for a band and it was flown out by seaplane, which landed by the carrier USS *Shangri-la* (CV 38) and was hoisted on board.

Finally, the carrier group left Hawaii and headed for Australia, arriving in Sydney Harbour with its two gigantic sandstone cliffs, called the Heads. The visitors were greeted by nearly half a million enthusiastic Aussies standing on the cliffs. The Australians had a warm spot in the national heart for Americans, whom they considered a major reason why Australia was able to repel a Japanese invasion in 1942. Then, too, the American psyche and history are close to those of the Australians. So the arrival of a large American naval force for a visit was especially welcome.

The harbor itself was filled with boats of every shape and size. The enthusiastic Australians were thrilled that their American friends, who had helped them defend their island continent from the Japanese, were coming to visit for the first time since the war. Whitey remembered the carrier's communications officer, a short, bald man with a strong Boston accent, strolling down the dock with a voluptuous young Aussie woman on each arm.

As soon as they were secured, the visitors began their rounds, which were enthusiastically returned by their hosts, who were hard drinkers. The pace lasted for ten days. In the middle of the visit, a message came telling the Americans that the next day was a special holiday and that they were to "dress ship," deck each ship out with colorful flags. Although the message proved to be a hoax, the American fleet did look good.

Two days before their departure, Admiral Ginder decided to hold a dance to reciprocate their hosts' enthusiastic hospitality. As his aide, Whitey had his hands full completing all the arrangements.

Finally, the Americans left, but it wasn't until the ships were under way that several Australian women were discovered still in many ships, including the carrier, various destroyers, and a cruiser, willing stowaways with the genial help of American sailors. With the women finally back on shore, the fleet headed out to the Coral Sea, scene of the furious battle in May 1942 that helped turn back the oncoming Japanese. Then, on to Guadalcanal, where only five years earlier, Whitey and many of his friends were holding the island against a determined Japanese effort to retake their airfield. Whitey inspected several rusting hulks, taking special note of many holes from .50-caliber machine guns, perhaps from his own Wildcat.

After Guadalcanal, the carrier division headed toward Truk, scene of many aerial battles that would certainly have memories for everyone. After anchoring outside the atoll's lagoon, littered with the rusting, half-submerged hulks of Japanese ships, the Americans paid a call on the island commander and went touring. Escorted by their native hosts, the sailors took lots of pictures, some of which were of groups showing the islanders in native dress, which for the women meant going topless and the men only loincloths.

When the fleet returned home, Whitey's wife produced a cruise book for the admiral. As the producer and editor, Vi Feightner had exercised her rights and pasted small cloth brassieres on the women in the Truk photos. The admiral was amused at Mrs. Feightner's unabashed censorship. The carrier division continued its tour, making Palau, Saipan, and Tinian, all scenes of terrific landings and battles. Although there was little diplomatic business to accomplish, these detours were important to show the flag for the people of these islands now under direct American control.

Guam became the most colorful port because Adm. Charles A. Pownall, who had been the second CO of the *Enterprise* from 1938 to 1941, challenged Admiral Ginder's command to a boat race. He enjoyed sports, especially intramural competition within his units and different ships. Ginder was delighted to accept. He had an ace up his sleeve, and he was a man who also loved a good time. Before leaving Hawaii for Australia, Ginder had obtained an aluminum skimmer, which he officially designated as his barge. He also had the traditional wooden barge, but the aluminum boat could be broken down and easily brought on board the carrier. The admiral's coxswain was apparently also something of a frustrated racing pilot. With a good coat of polish, the little skimmer was thought capable of fifty to sixty knots.

On the day of the race in Agana Harbor, there were quite a few offside bets going. The saluting battery's cannon fired its starting shot, but it was no contest. The CarDiv 3 barge went screaming down the course, way ahead of its competition. To add genial insult to injury, the CD-3 coxswain, now halfway down the track, circled the Guam boat *twice*, then took off and crossed the finish line. There was little for Admiral Pownall to do but accept the outcome with good grace.

Whitey commented, "[Pownall] was a real gentleman. Absolutely just great, and he wanted to organize this race because it was a morale raiser for all the people. . . . I can't think of a better man to be put in charge of a place like Guam. They loved him out there." After the race, the admiral organized a beach party to be remembered. A real South Sea island type of affair.

Along with others in his group, Whitey toured various sites of interest, including the bomb-loading area on Tinian where the atomic bombs had been loaded into the B-29s that struck Hiroshima and Nagasaki on August 6 and August 9, effectively ending the war. Salvaging all the wreckage was big business throughout the Marianas. There were sites where many aircraft had been discarded. Whitey even went into caves the Japanese had used as staging areas and found brand-new rifles, some in wooden racks, others in crates, never unpacked. Many were brought back to the ship where they were auctioned off.

Immediately after the war, there was great concern in the War Department about returning salvaged material, even brass screws, to the United States because it was thought that to have so much construction items come back would ruin the postwar industry that made them in the first place.

As CarDiv 3 made ready to return to the United States, orders came to instead sail up toward China and the U.S. Seventh Fleet. The Red Chinese were making their move to claim all of China. Although they had fought together against the Japanese, Mao Tse-tung's huge army was now moving to oust the army of Generalissimo Chaing Kai-chek and claim the huge country as their own. It was a vast and frightening undertaking, and China's one-time allies now found themselves preparing to try to stop the takeover by a communist enemy.

Several towns were still outside communist domain, such as Tsingtao on the southeastern coast, a one-time stronghold of the German kaiser. CarDiv 3 launched reconnaissance flights over the center of the town. One of the AD Skyraider pilots apparently wandered over enemy-held territory and was shot at for his trouble. The AD crashed on a beach, and a rescue mission was launched to successfully retrieve the crew. Meanwhile, time was running out to get everyone who wanted to leave out of the city. There was less than a week left before the communists came. Whitey was sent ashore to look things over, and he found a ghost town. Dead bodies littered the streets.

"People were just dying everywhere," Whitey remembered. "People were starving to death . . . we contacted the local officials . . . we actually had some U.S. representation there at the time."

The Americans soon sent several LSTs toward the beach and lifted people out and took them to safe havens farther down the coast. Later, Whitey and the admiral visited Shanghai, a bustling metropolis that was the center of Chinese trade, and then conducted several maritime exercises with Australian forces in the Yellow Sea. It was a good chance for the two allies to try out new communication technologies as well as hone their war-fighting skills.

As the flag aide, Whitey was also the assistant force Combat Information Center (CIC) officer, standing staff watches under way, and getting familiar with airborne radar, a new addition to the array of implements developed during the war. TBMs with radar were the first examples of airborne early warning radar and as such were obviously of great use to defenders.

"We assigned sectors to each one of the ships for air defense and tried to coordinate the targets coming in," Whitey recalled. "We didn't have a good method of matching, though, and we'd often end up with two tracks of the same airplane because it was from two different radars. We didn't have a way to grid those things so that we'd identify positively."[3]

The next stop was Japan, as the Americans made a port call at Yokosuka. They found another busy trade in American salvage; this time the material was a healthy mix of American and Japanese stuff. Liberty ships were sailing in and out of the port, their holds crammed with material. For their part, the former enemies seemed to be very much involved, and happily so, with this new industry. There was money to be made and the Japanese were always known for their industrious attitudes. If the Americans had been planning to invade the home islands, then decided not to, it was polite of them to leave all these war machines and implements to be turned around into surplus and junk.

Immediate postwar liberty in Japan, however, was not that good a deal. There were a lot of restrictions, too many places where American sailors or GIs couldn't go, and probably with good reason. Even so, Whitey found that he came to enjoy the time he spent in Japan. He had also enjoyed his time with Admiral Ginder. In fact, the admiral had given Vi away at the wedding just before they sailed (Vi's father had died several years before). Her mother was there, however, and the admiral was pleased to stand up for one of his officers and his new bride. Whitey had met his future wife while he had been an instructor with VF-98 at Long Beach. Vi had been working at the *Long Beach Press-Telegram* newspaper and living with her sister and brother-in-law, a commander in the Navy station at Los Alamitos. He introduced Whitey to Vi. Like so many military marriages, the wedding was soon followed by a long separation.

"He felt very protective of us in those days," Whitey remembered of Admiral Ginder. "He was looking after our career at that point. . . . He was very gregarious and always liked to have people around. As a result, he was forever inviting visitors." Admiral Ginder was not always one to involve himself in operational matters, rare for a flag officer, especially one who probably wanted to continue moving up the chain with another promotion. He had briefs during the day to keep him advised of matters that might concern him, and as the senior officer present (SOP) in San Francisco (when he was there), he was well served by his fellow admirals in the area and in California in general. Most of them seemed to get along with each other, and the flag officers melded into a comfortable ol' boys club. There were exceptions, however.

Rear Adm. (later Admiral) John H. Hoover (1887–1970) was Commander Air Fleet West Coast at the time. His nickname was "Genial John," an ironic reference to his normally strict, even sour demeanor. The ever energetic John Crommelin wanted to set a cross-country speed record, which was held by the Air Force's P-51 (later F-51 when the designation system changed).

One of Crommelin's mechanics got hold of a Corsair with extra fuel tanks. After modifying the fighter's engine with water injection, Crommelin began planning his flight, figuring it would take about four and a half hours, using water injection the entire flight, a daring and slightly dangerous plan. Water injection uses water from an internal tank that is sprayed into the engine with the throttle wide open. The water keeps the engine from detonating while delivering more horse-power. This method was normally intended for only short periods of time. All was in place, but the Army decided to break its own record, this time using a jet. One of the Army's F-80s accordingly broke the record by an hour and a half. Undaunted, Crommelin now wanted to continue the plans and break the prop speed record. But Admiral Hoover said no and forbade Crommelin from working on the attempt, and he ordered him to stop modifying the F4U. It was not a happy camp.

The Corsair was reassigned to the Marines, who decided to take the pumped-up F4U onto a carrier off Jacksonville, Florida. The major who flew the Corsair ran into problems and quickly returned to El Toro, the Marine air base near Los Angeles. He had lots of fuel, and as he landed the plane caught fire and the major was terribly burned.

By this time, naval aviation was beginning a major transition from props to jets. Yet there was still the last generation of high-performance prop types trying to find work on the flight decks. Among these was Grumman's barrel-chested little F8F Bearcat, perhaps the ultimate expression of the piston-engine fighter-interceptor. The F6F Hellcat did not remain in front-line service very long after the war. The Avenger and its stablemate, the SB2C Helldiver, were also serving out their last deployments. The Avenger at least found work as a radar-carrying aircraft, and the Helldiver went to work for other countries fighting other battles, such as with the Greeks and the French. The only World War II type that maintained its place in the fleet, at least until after the Korean War, was Chance Vought's redoubtable big blue F4U Corsair. The long-nosed, gull-winged "hose-nose," "angel of Okinawa," or "whistling death" still had a lot of life in it. It could drop bombs with the best of them and when required could take care of itself in a dogfight.

The Marines, especially, retained their Corsairs, flying them from carriers as well as from shore bases throughout the Korean War and even longer. But there was no doubt that the jet was coming up fast, and the prop-driven fighter and light bomber's days were numbered.

On March 10, 1948, Whitey was on board the USS *Boxer* (CV 21) off San Diego as it conducted carrier qualifications (CQs) with the Navy's first jet fighter, the North American FJ-1 Fury, a singularly rotund design that did not seem to offer anything except that it was powered by a jet engine. The Fury, with its 4,000-pound thrust Allison J35 engine, could attain a top speed of 547 mph at 9,000 feet and had a range with wingtip fuel tanks of 1,500 miles. VF-5A—that August the squadron was redesignated VF-51—under Cdr. Pete Aurand came out to make the first traps, followed by his XO, Lt. Cdr. Bob Elder, who many thought was the Navy's best officer and aviator, on a par with John Crommelin. For the first day and a half, the CQ went well enough. Then one pilot crashed three times before being sent home.

The *Boxer* had received modifications to handle jets, including to the cata-pults and arresting gear. The jet's speed was much higher than the prop-driven types, which made the landing cycle much shorter and required a jet to be brought on board more quickly. The ship's LSO was not qualified to "wave" jets, so the squadron brought their own LSO. Waving jets required an understanding of the new technology that would come with experience. A jet's wave-off characteristics were also different from those of a prop. Three Furys ended up in the water in five months. Fuel was important. After making several passes, a pilot might not be able to divert to a field ashore. Of course, this was well before air-to-air refueling was instituted.

At this time, all carriers had so-called axial decks, or straight decks. A landing aircraft had nowhere to go but forward up the deck, up toward other aircraft that might be parked at the bow. Crashing into this cluster of various aircraft usually proved costly and often fatal. Today's familiar angled deck that allows aircraft to land and if need be take off again away from other planes at the bow was several years in the future.

The years immediately following World War II were periods of intense development, some unsuccessful, but some pointing the way to greatly improved operations and aircraft. Nowhere was this success as dynamic as in naval aviation, especially tactical aviation, that is, carrier aviation with its brash, noisy, and growing cadre of jets. The sleek, dark blue types like the F9F and F2H, and soon the F4D and A3D, heralded a new era of military aviation. Even the heavier, clunkier designs like the F3D were examples of American expertise in designing world-beating aircraft.

Occasionally, there were disasters, like the Vought F7U, a radical, nearly tailless design that struggled to find its place right from its first flight in September 1948. Underpowered and hard to fly, the early Cutlass really never had a chance, even when a highly redesigned F7U-3, the only Cutlass to see production and fleet service, albeit for only four years, entered squadron service. Whitey Feightner accumulated more than his share of time in the F7U, but we're getting ahead of our story.

Back to Pax . . . and Loving It

After two years serving as flag lieutenant, Whitey received dream orders to the growing group of test pilots in southern Maryland's Patuxent River naval air station, universally called simply "Pax." But in November 1948, he and Vi were about to head east when a hiccup developed. His replacement had arrived with a previously unseen alcohol problem and was fired after only one week on the job. Whitey was recalled just as he was about to get on the road. He had been detached, meaning he had been released from his previous command and was in a travel status to his new assignment. But he now had to return to the admiral's staff for a while until a more suitable replacement was selected.

The incident put a dent in the Feightners' travel plans but there was little that could be done. Another aide was finally selected and Whitey and Vi were on their way. He had been slated to join the first class of the newly established Test Pilot

School (TPS) but his place would now be with the second class because of the delay at his previous command.

TPS had been collecting aircraft for its students to fly. Nine had reached Pax, including an F6F-5, F7F-3, and an F8F-1. Class 2 added an F4U and another F8F, as well as several other types to bring the small "fleet" to fourteen, including the first jets: one F9F-3 and one Vought XF6U-1 Pirate. The Pirate was the first U.S. jet to have an afterburner, which raised the output of its single Westinghouse engine from 2,300 pounds to 4,000 pounds, enabling the aircraft to reach a speed of 540 mph. Of the twenty-eight students, eleven would only take the academic course. They were actually test pilots already stationed at Patuxent. The academic course would give them a better grounding in writing reports as well as a better understanding of the mechanics of flight and of their aircraft.

During three field trips, Class 2 visited the National Advisory Committee on Aviation (NACA) organization at Langley Air Force Base near Norfolk, Virginia, the David Taylor Model Basin, which developed hull designs outside Washington, D.C., and the Grumman Aircraft Corporation Headquarters at Bethpage, Long Island. The class ran from January to July 1949.

When they checked in at Patuxent, Whitey and Vi ran into a little bit of housing trouble. There was none available. The air station had just been opened and several different groups including test division as well as fleet bomber squadrons had taken up all the small number of houses on the base. For a time, Whitey found himself commuting from Anacostia up in Washington, D.C., which meant driving at least three or more hours each day. They tried several little towns around the Patuxent area, including Port Tobacco, halfway between Anacostia and Pax. Then La Plata. Better, but still a long drive each way. A house finally opened up on the base.

Whitey found that the station was run by then Capt. (later Vice Adm.) Frederick M. Trapnell (1902–1975), one of the initial shining lights in the early development of postwar naval aviation. As a lieutenant, he had been a member of the Heavier Than Air (HTA) Unit flying the diminutive Curtiss F9C Sparrowhawk "trapeze fighter" from the airship USS *Akron* (ZRS 4) in 1932. He had been the first naval aviator to fly a jet, the XP-59A. The field at Patuxent was eventually named in his honor.

Trapnell ran his command like "an absolute czar," according to Whitey. "He knew he was way ahead of everybody else and he got to the point where he just made the rules. . . . There was no conversation about it at all. He just said, 'Do it,' and people did it, whether it was right or wrong."[4]

When Whitey was the project officer for the early performance of the Douglas AD Skyraider—the AD-3 was being used at that point—Captain Trapnell wanted some numbers, especially the force needed to move the control stick when there were two Gs, then three Gs, and so on, working on the aircraft. Whitey went up and got the readings the captain asked for. He found that some forty pounds of pressure were needed, which was quite a lot. Unfortunately, when Captain Trapnell saw the division report, he replied, "That's ridiculous!" He ordered then Lt. Col. Marion Carl, the well-known Marine Corps fighter ace and highly respected aviator and now head of that division, to go up himself. Carl came back with the same numbers, which didn't satisfy the boss at all.

The next thing anyone knew, Trapnell called for the AD. He would make the flight himself! The captain went up, flew the same flight as his two other pilots . . . and got the same readings. He landed, thanked everyone, and left, muttering, "Fix it!"

"That's the last we ever heard of it," Whitey chuckled. It was an example of how Trapnell worked. There were several circumstances surrounding this story. Captain Trapnell had actually flown this particular Skyraider brand-new from the factory back to Pax. It was the job of Whitey's division to check out a representative example of a production aircraft to ensure that it met the manufacturer's claims for performance and capability. Apparently, this particular AD felt heavy on the controls and Trapnell wanted to know why. He probably knew but wanted his men to confirm his suspicions.

The problem was traced to the improper installation of a simple weight connected to the control column that helped balance the stick's operation by the pilot. Somewhere in its assembly, an unknown workman had placed the weight in the wrong position, thereby requiring the pilot to impose a greater pull when flying any maneuver.

As noted, following classroom studies, Whitey went to work for Marion Carl, who had seen action at Midway and Guadalcanal and had been awarded two Navy Crosses among other awards. He would go on to do much good work after the war, eventually rising to the rank of major general, but not before he had flown in combat once again in Vietnam, flying everything from helicopters to fixed-wing jets, including Vought's ultimate thoroughbred, the F-8 Crusader.

Carl had been one of the Corps' earliest jet aviators, and he had also flown several so-called X-planes, setting several performance records along the way. As highly regarded as he was, Marion Carl could be aloof and something of a scary figure, especially to junior aviators. Many younger men would remember their encounters with the tall man from Oregon, whether flying as copilot in a transport or in a helicopter headed for action over the lush jungles of Vietnam. Even Whitey, who had seen combat in much the same areas in the Solomons as Carl and certainly didn't have to take a back seat to anyone, had a quizzical take on him. Comparing Carl to Dick Bong, Whitey recalled a few things.

> The two were probably equally adept at handling the airplane but Dick Bong thought things through. Carl was more or less the typical fighter pilot. He had absolute confidence in his own ability [he had soloed in only two and a half hours] and he did things in the air. I think he was just one of those natural-born pilots.

[He] was a very poor instructor. I don't know that he ever was an instructor. [Actually, Carl had served as an instructor in 1940 at Pensacola after a tour with VMF-1 at Quantico, Virginia.] But having worked for him for quite a while, I don't think he believed in passing things on. He just expected everybody to do his job, and he forgot that a lot of people weren't as talented as he was.

I remember one distinct time we were out with F9Fs carrying bombs and in those days we weren't very sophisticated. The engineers would estimate what the lowest wind was that an airplane would fly at a particular weight. We were in identical airplanes, and we're dropping these bombs one at a time. Each time we'd drop one, we'd lower the wind a little bit two knots to see what the lowest practical wind was to fly the airplane from a carrier. He went off the bow and just sank clear down to the water, and we figured, "Well, that's it." [The tests were to determine the lowest end speed for the Panther at which to launch carrying a specific bomb load.]

I was about to shut down when he called, "That was my fault. I mishandled it. Drop it another three knots." Well, believe me, he was almost to the end because when I went off, that *was* the end. But that's typical of Marion Carl. He did it by feel, whereas Dick Bong did things more thoughtfully, more well planned. He thought everything out.[5]

There were other notable aviators at Pax during Whitey's stay, such as John Hyland, who had been the CAG in the *Intrepid* in 1945 and who retired as a four-star admiral, and Gus Widhelm, who had fought the war from Santa Cruz where he was the CO of VS-8 and had shot down a Zero just before his SBD's engine had been heavily damaged by another Zero. He eventually had to ditch, and he and his radioman/gunner spent more than two days in their raft bobbing around watching the ongoing battle before being spotted and picked up by a PBY Catalina.

But now, Widhelm was head of Tactical Test, and Hyland was his XO. Both were highly respected aviators and worked well with all the other experienced pilots at Patuxent. It was a dream group and Whitey would have a great time flying with them.

There were new planes coming in all the time: the Martin AM Mauler, which could carry an incredible load of underwing ordnance, the futuristic Martin P6M jet-powered flying boat, and helicopters of various designs and capabilities, to name but a few. Many of the fixed-wing pilots, Whitey included, quickly grabbed the chance to qualify on helicopters. Carl was the first, although historically—and because he apparently did not submit the proper paperwork to qualify for the new rating—he is not listed as the first Marine helo pilot. Probably the second, however.

Other heavy types included the Convair R3Y Tradewind, a four turboprop-powered flying boat that could deliver tons of equipment right to the beachhead, and the Lockheed XR6O-1 Constitution, a huge four-engine (each offering 3,500 hp), double-deck transport that could carry 168 passengers as well as a huge payload. Handicapped by a short range, the XR6O never entered production, and the only two built were finally assigned to VR-44 at Naval Air Station (NAS) Alameda, California, and made their way until 1955 hauling midshipmen to various activities or making the California-Hawaii run.

In an aside, civilian George A. Spangenberg, later Whitey's highly respected associate, was working in the Bureau of Aeronautics (BuAer) in 1943. In a 1994 letter to the editor of *Naval Aviation News*, he commented on the Constitution's development:

> [T]he R6O program actually landed in our development program without any warning. [We] were not involved in large landplane transport studies. Such developments for the military were undoubtedly considered the responsibility of the Army Air Corps, which had at least one, the C-74 [the precursor of the R6O], under contract.[6]

Spangenberg elaborated on how the big transport was part of a development group that included Pan American Airlines and Lockheed, which made the R6O an obvious hopeful for postwar commercial use to, as Spangenberg wrote, "compete with our British cousins." After the war, though, there was little support for continued work on the Constitution, and with the coming of the jet age, the requirement for large, piston-engine airliners and military heavy haulers eventually passed.

Somewhere, someone got the idea to try jet-assisted takeoff (JATO) on the big Constitution. Cdr. Ira Brown, who was head of that particular section, went to see Marion Carl about it. Carl quickly said, "Take Whitey. He's our JATO man." Whitey had in fact been working with the assisted takeoff bottles with several seaplanes, so sending him to work with Commander Brown was a natural suggestion.

The fleet of aircraft, while including many fighters, also used a good number of heavy aircraft such as transports and flying boats. These were intended to give the fighter pilots who made up the majority of the classes a chance to compare their smaller, lighter types against the heavier machines that were part of other communities and that were an important part of the overall fleet. The "P-boat" section had the ponderous R6O for evaluation.

The R6O was fixed up with ten bottles and lightly loaded. With Commander Brown in the right seat of the huge transport, Whitey taxied to the runway and ran up the engines. As they started to move, Whitey prepared himself. At 90 mph, he rotated, lifting the nosewheel off the runway. "Fire the JATO!" he called, ready for the kick as the bottles ignited. Because there had been a strong wind from the west, Whitey had decided to use the shorter east-west runway—runway 26—to take advantage of the added lift as he headed west. But there was a large drill hall next to the other end of that runway.

The aircraft was now approaching 110 mph, and Whitey repeated his call to fire the JATO bottles. But nothing happened. Passing the airfield control tower, he pulled back on the control yoke, gently lifting the behemoth off the ground. However, the R6O refused to continue climbing, and that large, brick drill hall was coming up fast.

By now, they were in ground effect, which gave them some measure of lift, raising them over the drill hall and thankfully avoiding a catastrophic collision. Passing the building, the ground effect assistance disappeared, but Whitey was able to gain a measure of flight control. He raised the Constitution up and flew her some five miles away from the field. He now had good control and was able to bring the plane around and land. Investigation discovered a problem with the JATO's circuitry. Through human error, a safety switch had remained open and therefore the circuit could not fire the bottles in the air. The error could have cost the Navy a large building and an expensive airplane, not to mention the lives of the six crewmen.

The mortality rate at Pax was fairly high. In one eight-month period during Whitey's tour, nineteen pilots and crewmen were lost. It was hard for all the people assigned to the air station. Whitey's wife, Vi, in particular had a rough time. Not only did she worry about her husband every time he went up, she had developed some medical problems that severely handicapped her. She was diagnosed with acute compulsive neurosis, which stayed with her for the rest of her life, and she and Whitey searched for a cure or at least relief from the condition, without real success. They tried hypnosis as well as other forms of treatment, but nothing seemed to work. Whitey tended to his wife as best he could, accepting her condition as part of their lives together.

Whitey got qualified in helicopters, quite a challenge after flying chunky Grumman fighters with huge radial engines and six .50-caliber machine guns. He would occasionally check out more senior aviators, some of whom had been squadron COs and CAGs in the Pacific. It was an awkward juxtaposition for a newly promoted lieutenant commander.

During one cross-country to Bethpage in a Sikorsky HO3S, Whitey flew as check pilot for Gus Widhelm and Tom Connolly (later vice admiral). The weather was bad and Whitey had his "students" file an instrument flight plan. It was a complicated route because the New York City area through which they would be traveling was so busy with other traffic, mostly commercial airline flights going everywhere.

The ceiling rapidly went down to four hundred feet. It was not a good setup for a training flight even with two such experienced aviators. Whitey leaned over to Widhelm and said, "Commander, I'm sorry but I've got the airplane." Widhelm had to give up the right seat (because of the control arrangement, helicopter commanders normally fly in the right seat instead of the left seat common to fixed-wing types) to his junior instructor. Whitey refiled from VFR to their IFR plan and flew an instrument approach into Bethpage, on Long Island. He commented that while he never doubted the two commanders' ability to make the approach, they hadn't had the formal training in the helo and as instructor it was his responsibility to ensure a safe conclusion to the flight.

Actually, Whitey had taken his helicopter transition instruction from Marion Carl, his boss. One time the helicopter began swaying back and forth like on a pendulum. Whitey couldn't stop the disorienting motion and Carl said, "OK, I've got it," and steadied the helo up once more. Whitey had been flying a lot with the service test division, and he had only sporadically been in his TPS class. He rejoined his class, which was also trying to fly as much as possible. Captain Trapnell had kept a busy hand in running an informal test pilot curriculum, occasionally talking to individual pilots.

The classwork *was* demanding, with an emphasis on math and physics, all subjects Whitey had studied in college. Some students struggled because they didn't have a math background. But he was happy with the overall class, especially the amount of flying he was doing.

The division kept a Grumman F7F Tigercat mainly for Captain Trapnell to use as a high-speed transport. The sleek Tigercat had two large radials and was a treat to fly. As the F7F project officer, Whitey had the chance to check out Charles Lindbergh, who liked the aircraft very much. The F7F was meant to fly from carriers, but it had structural problems that were exacerbated by the two huge engines aside its slim, graceful fuselage. It eventually ran up a good record in Korea, flying with the Marines from shore bases on day and night missions.

As the class work stabilized, standardization became an important product, resulting in a growing crop of highly competent test pilots. Captain Trapnell's strong personality had a major effect early on, but by the fourth or fifth class, the TPS curriculum was running on its own. The process of screening TPS candidates was fairly demanding: two thousand hours of command pilot time, a math background, and a strong recommendation from your CO, all before a rigorous string of interviews up the chain, which often eliminated otherwise strong personalities.

CHAPTER 9
THE RADICAL, DANGEROUS CUTLASS

oon after the episode with the Constitution (at one point, there was some danger of Whitey's being sent out to VR-44 to fly R6Os, something he vehemently—and successfully—objected to), Whitey was assigned to the Vought F7U Cutlass, one of the most radical designs the Navy ever developed. Whitey thought the Cutlass was "a great airplane . . . way ahead of its time [with] a lot of innovations . . . and a lot of potential." Unfortunately, the fighter never realized that potential, perhaps because it was never combined with a satisfactory engine or weapon system.

Three XF7U-1s were built and tested, the first flight coming on September 29, 1948. The following F7U-1s all had difficulties with control and engine performance. The plane was decidedly underpowered with its two Westinghouse J34s, delivering barely 5,000 pounds of thrust each with afterburner, and less than 3,400 pounds each in basic engine setting without afterburner. The fourteen production F7U-1s were never assigned to squadron service but remained for testing. Two of the F7U-1s were lost, along with their civilian Vought test pilots in July and September 1950.

With the last fatal mishap, the Navy decided it wanted one of its own at the controls of any further tests, and its choice was Lt. Cdr. Edward L. Feightner, highly regarded fighter ace and highly respected ace test pilot, currently assigned to the service test division at Patuxent River. When he heard the "good" news, Whitey wasn't exactly thrilled at the prospects of flying the Navy's newest fighter, which had killed or injured several good fellow aviators. Accordingly, he paid a visit to his boss, Lieutenant Colonel Carl. But the choice had been made and Whitey had found a true test of his abilities.

The Navy was then also considering equipping its newly formed flight demonstration unit, the Blue Angels, with the Cutlass. After all, it certainly had racy, almost futuristic good looks and it would look great in the team's blue and gold colors. There was also consideration of giving command of the highly public group to Whitey. But his competition was Lt. Cdr. Roy M. "Butch" Voris, another Pacific ace who had also flown in a VF-10 with Whitey and an eminently qualified aviator in his own right. The choice was made in Voris's favor as he was senior in date of rank to Whitey, which Whitey certainly understood. Two F7U-1s were painted up in the blue and gold scheme. Whitey would fly one, and Lt. Harding C. "Mac" Macknight, now in the Training Command, would fly the other.

Whitey had to check out in the Cutlass first. He would try one of the F7U-1s at Pax. Since the Cutlass was a twin-engine aircraft, it offered several interesting flight characteristics. Since the engines were positioned side-by-side, there was not much concern about asymmetric control if one of them cut out or had to be shut down. During his checkout flight, fifteen minutes after takeoff, he made some rolls to the left. Suddenly, the port engine quit, which startled Whitey but didn't present any control problems.

Looking around, he found he couldn't restart the J34, and he made a single-engine landing. With the low thrust of each engine, he couldn't maintain level flight with the landing gear extended, so it was a "modified" emergency. He had to land on the first pass because getting airborne again would be difficult if not impossible. He landed, taxied into the hangar, and was quickly surrounded by the ground crew. The problem turned out to be something simple: his oxygen hose, which was lying on the left console, had hung up on the fuel-control handle and had shifted the handle in flight during his rolls. The hose had simply shut off the fuel to the left engine. Needless to say, the crew fixed that problem before any further flights.

The Cutlass had another feature that set it apart from most other conventionally tailed aircraft: an extremely high rate of roll. In fact, it was nearly impossible to use full aileron and stop the F7U upright. Whitey tried making a series of five rolls, which averaged 535 degrees per *second*, a high rate of spinning around the lateral axis of the plane's fuselage.

"Believe me," Whitey laughed, "that's enough to uncage your eyeballs! After a series of rolls like that, the horizon still oscillates even though you've finished."[1] The airplane would reverse instantaneously from a 90-degree right bank to a 90-degree left bank as fast as the pilot could move the stick, a feature that suggested many possible air show demonstrations for the Blue Angels.

The Cutlass also offered, for its time, one of the best sets of speed brakes. Two panels came down from under the fuselage, between the two engines. The operation was so smooth that there was no attitude change whatever. Again, this feature gave extra maneuverability in air-to-air maneuvering. Using a combination of speed brakes and full throttle, one could make a nearly *square* turn.

Whitey found the Cutlass easy to fly, with excellent low-speed handling characteristics. In a high-drag configuration, it was easy to accurately control it using just the throttles. The aircraft was stable with no tendency to drop off on either wing. In fact, he also found it hard to get into a spin and finally wrote in one of his test reports that the Cutlass was "unspinnable." More junior aviators, however, were not that comfortable with the F7U; its lack of power certainly didn't help.

Whitey's comment that the Cutlass was unspinnable was later proven wrong when another service test pilot took off and started climbing. For some reason, he pushed the stick forward at low speed, and the Cutlass started to tumble at only three hundred feet on takeoff and entered a true spin from which he couldn't recover, and the pilot ejected. Vought made a series of tests and found that the F7U did, indeed, "tumble" into an unrecoverable spin.

The Cutlass was one of the first aircraft to use a hydraulic control system, but because it was unreliable, pilots were uncomfortable with the new arrangement. The hydraulics were backed up by a traditional manual control system and many times pilots would end up using the mechanical backup when the hydraulics failed. But it took eleven long seconds for the aircraft to shift from hydraulic to mechanical, and for that time the pilot was merely a passenger with no control over his aircraft. The Cutlass was also short-legged, with little internal fuel capacity. It was, after all, originally intended as a point-defense fighter.

Whitey turned out to be the only man who took the F7U-1 aboard ship for its initial carrier qualifications. After field-arrested landings at Patuxent, a normal training cycle before actually going out to a carrier, the Cutlass was considered ready for its first real test as the next generation of carrier-borne fighters.

Among its many unique characteristics, the Cutlass used a long nose wheel strut that placed the cockpit some fourteen feet above the ground. Its control system consisted of elevons, which functioned as elevators and ailerons, and twin rudders. Other innovations were leading edge slats and a two-position main landing gear. There was one position for landing that put the gear in an aft position to ensure clearance for a carrier landing, followed by a position 36 inches forward for takeoff. Normally, the pilot shifted the gear while he taxied out for takeoff. With the gear in the forward position, the F7U could rotate earlier, requiring less elevator power with a shorter takeoff.

The pilot also enjoyed outstanding visibility, but, as Whitey was to find out, carrier landings generated an extremely nose-high position, which greatly restricted that visibility. The problem was later corrected in the F7U-3, but that was later, with a redesigned seat and a lower nose that gave a better view on approach.

There was one other problem concerning the holdback fitting, a small device that attached the catapult's tow bridle to the aircraft. On the test shot at Pax, the holdback fitting broke improperly and ricocheted off the runway, to be quickly sucked down the Cutlass's port air intake. The engine exploded and the aircraft caught fire. Whitey was airborne but at only fifty feet altitude, on one engine, the landing gear down, and insufficient hydraulic power to raise the gear without losing control of his aircraft. Plus, he was too low to eject. All he could do was make a 180-degree turn and hope to get the damaged plane back on the downwind runway. After he landed, the ground crew extinguished the fire.

Further landing tests went well, and finally the real tests were scheduled on board the USS *Midway* (CVB 41) in July 1951. As often happens, the carrier qualification (CQ) would combine the Cutlass with other types, including Panthers and Banshees. An available aircraft carrier is too precious a commodity for just one aircraft. Everyone was expected to take advantage of the rare chance to practice operating around a ship.

The *Midway* was off the Virginia Capes, a well-known area east of Norfolk and Virginia Beach. The weather was clear but gusty. Whitey found that his aircraft was flying well and he made a dozen landings before the other jets. He had only one problem during the first cat shot. As he left the carrier's deck and picked up the landing gear, the plane immediately started to spin to the left off the bow, a dangerous situation so close from the ship and the water, barely eighty feet below. Whitey instinctively knew that retracting the gear had caused the problem and he just as quickly threw it back down and recovered safely.

Later, he and the ground crew discovered an interconnection between the gear and the leading edge slats on the wings, which had not been thought to be a problem. At the speed at which the plane left the catapult, though, with the slats retracted the aircraft was not flying yet. When Whitey put the gear back down, the slats came back out, returning control to the pilot. He had flown off the deck at a 70-degree left bank instead of proceeding straight ahead and climbing. Fortunately, the situation was corrected.

The first recovery had also been "interesting" because the LSO and Whitey had decided that because of the high angle of the nose when approaching the flight deck, the pilot was actually *sitting* on the jet. Coming over the rounddown of the flight deck, Whitey had anticipated that the Cutlass would settle rapidly when he chopped the throttles. Thus the LSO and Whitey had decided that he would ensure he could make the deck before the LSO gave him the cut signal.

Coming around on the landing, Whitey was looking out the left side at the LSO. After getting the cut signal and returning his view to look ahead, he was shocked to find that he didn't see the carrier at all. He was forty-two feet above the deck! Whitey had schooled himself never to do what he did next, which was drop the nose because he thought he was way up the flight deck and about to go into the barricade. The moment he dropped the nose, the aircraft lost lift and he *taxied* up to the No. 1 wire. He had barely made the ship. The F7U had a lot of lessons to teach its pilots.

After he had notched up seventeen landings, it was the turn of the other aircraft. The Panther pilot, George Duncan, came around, setting himself up for a trap. But he was heavy and got into trouble, settling at the ramp. He hit the rounddown, a ramp strike, and the plane exploded. A piece of debris hit the LSO in the head, knocking him off the deck and into the safety net. Miraculously, the F9F pilot survived the spectacular crash, but the LSO was the only one familiar with F7U. He couldn't continue, and the CQs had to be held up until another LSO could be flown out from Patuxent. The replacement had actually only worked the Cutlass on one occasion during the field trials, but he was the best to be had at the moment.

The *Midway*'s deck was pitching quite a bit during the following session and the new LSO was, of course, justifiably concerned because he was not that familiar with the new fighter. He knew the plane dropped, and he kept bringing Whitey in at a higher and higher attitude. The last landing was photographed with the landing gear measured to be thirty-three feet above the flight deck when Whitey received the cut signal. It took so long for him to get down to the deck that it had actually bottomed out and was coming back up, resulting in an extremely hard landing.

The aircraft's fuselage was cracked vertically, just behind the cockpit.

"I'll never forget that sound," Whitey commented. "It sounded like someone had taken a board and slapped it down on the wing. The crack was wide enough that you could see daylight through it." That ended the CQ for the F7U-1. The aircraft was repaired and later flown back to the Vought plant in Dallas.

An Abbreviated Tour with the Blues

As noted earlier, Whitey had been originally asked to reform the Blue Angels on the Cutlass. But Butch Voris, an original member of the team, was senior to Whitey, and he was tapped instead for the lead slot. Also, after Whitey had made several trips to Washington, the Navy decided that because of its unreliable control system, the Cutlass was not a good choice for the team's close-formation maneuvers. The F9F-5 Panthers were considered much better, and the team was equipped with this aircraft. The Cutlass was still a good-looking airplane in blue and gold, however, and two F7U-1s and pilots were added to the Blues for solo maneuvers. Whitey agreed with these decisions, and the combination of two entirely different aircraft would make up the 1952 team.

Whitey checked out Mac Macknight on the Cutlass at NAS Corpus Christi, where two F7U-1s (bureau numbers 124426 and 124427) had been delivered. He tried to build a show around his unique fighters. Unfortunately, the Panthers were all grounded because of engine problems and with the show season fast approaching, the team decided to fly two-seat Lockheed TV-2s, the Navy designation for the T-33, which was a two-seat trainer version of the original P-80 (later F-80) Shooting Star. The advantage here was that the team could also take up VIPs. The Cutlasses would be used for special demonstrations.

"The Cutlass was a spectacular plane for air show work," Whitey remembered. "Not only because of its radical appearance, but because of its very tight turn radius. In one maneuver, Macknight and I would oppose each other at 450 knots, pass in front of the crowd, pop the [air]brakes, go to full power, and pull a hard left turn to exit the field going in the opposite direction. The crowd loved it."[2]

The first show with the Cutlass was at Pensacola when the Secretary of the Navy brought 150 guests to see the exhibition. The winds were gusty, and since Macknight only had ten hours in the F7U, Whitey decided to fly a solo show—after all the guests who wanted to take advantage of the opportunity were given rides in the TV-2s.

Immediately after takeoff, Whitey started a vertical climb. But at one hundred feet, he lost the hydraulic control system. All the hydraulic fluid poured into the port engine as he left a smoke trail that resembled a JATO takeoff, with one exception: he had no control! Whitey was fond of saying, "I have more 'passenger' time in single-seat aircraft than any other pilot. I've lost the control system 75 to 100 times. It was a regular occurrence."

With the Cutlass, the pilot had to bleed off pressure before an interlock would activate and springs snapped into place, which took those long eleven seconds. His Cutlass kept climbing to two thousand feet, then it stalled and turned nose down, heading for the ground. Whitey sat there watching the ground rushing up at him. Finally, the springs and pins all lined up again for manual control, and he made a square turn at the bottom. There was some question whether he'd actually touched the ground. He was still flying, except there was a row of trees in front of him that he couldn't climb over. He went through the trees, his port engine sucking up a branch, which required him to shut the engine down. Now he was on manual control and unable to climb. But he landed successfully and taxied up to the crowd. As he was getting out, the admiral came up and said, "I really hate to do this, but will the other Cutlass fly?"

The intrepid aviator replied it could, and, undaunted, Whitey took the second F7U up and completed the show without any problems. It was incidents like this that showed Whitey's truly unflappable character that served him well throughout his career in and out of the cockpit. After what he had gone through with the first Cutlass, no one—even the admiral—would have blamed him for saying no for another flight, especially right after the first hop that nearly put him into the trees.

Later, Whitey and Mac put on a show for schoolchildren near Corpus Christi. The ceiling was only about eight hundred feet—low for high-speed fighter jets in wheeling maneuvers—so Whitey decided to just do some high-speed flybys, tight turns, and whatever else he could come up with. He had developed a routine where he did three high-speed rolls to the left and then would reverse into three rolls to the right, which would help clear his vision from the previous rolls by the time he would roll upright.

In the middle of his left rolls, a light plane popped out of the clouds dead ahead of him. The blue and gold Cutlass thankfully missed the little airplane, but in doing so Whitey seriously overstressed his aircraft, tearing off the left wing slat, which went down the port intake. The port landing gear disintegrated and parts flew in every direction. Whitey came out of the overcast still flying and managed to land safely. The schoolchildren had certainly got their money's worth.

In June 1952, the two Cutlass pilots were asked to participate in the opening of the new airport at Pittsburgh, Pennsylvania. Flying their F7Us up from Pensacola meant several refueling stops. Crossing Columbus, Ohio, Lieutenant Macknight's aircraft developed hydraulic problems and he landed while Whitey continued on to Pittsburgh. Mac followed him later but as he came over the field at Pittsburgh, he lost his starboard engine. He was able to land but they decided not to fly him for the air show, letting the Cutlass become a static display instead.

After repairing the second Cutlass, the two aviators went farther north, up to NAS Glenview, near Chicago, Illinois. Pittsburgh's weather was bad with 800-foot ceiling and rain. After Whitey and Mac took off, at about 3,000 feet Whitey's starboard engine quit. But they pressed on to Glenview, which was clear. Whitey declared a modified emergency and asked to have a crash crew standing by. They came across the field in formation at 1,500 feet, headed for Lake Michigan. Right over the field, Mac called that he had had an explosion in *his* starboard engine with a fire warning light.

"There goes the port one," he added. "Now both engines are on fire."

Whitey looked to see his wingman *upside down* at 1,500 feet, doing a split S (rolling onto one's back and diving toward the ground) onto the runway.

"The Cutlass was the only jet I knew that could have done a split S from that low an altitude," he later declared. He followed Mac down and managed to be on his wing as he crossed the edge of the field. He reminded Mac to blow his gear down, which he did. Mac touched down at the edge of the runway, with his nose gear still coming down to the locked position. As soon as he was on the ground, Mac went over the side of his cockpit while his Cutlass did a 360-degree ground loop.

The ground crew quickly extinguished the fire, but chances of resuscitating the damaged fighter were out of the question. Mac would stay at Glenview. Since the crew couldn't clear the runway soon enough, Whitey continued on to Chicago's O'Hare Airport. The field had been originally called Orchard Airpark, but it had been enlarged and renamed after Whitey's old boss and Chicago native Butch O'Hare. Vought provided a dozen civilian technicians to repair Macknight's Cutlass.

The runway was still being worked on and was actually closed. Peach baskets littered the strip as a warning to approaching aircraft, but the tower told Whitey to ignore the obstructions and land. It was the first landing on what is now Chicago's O'Hare International Airport. Whitey left Macknight and flew back to Corpus Christi, where he took the team's R5C Commando, the Navy version of the C-46 transport. His copilot would be a chief NAP (naval aviation pilot), one of the enlisted aviators still flying with the Navy and Marines. The flight would be a check flight for the chief.

Taking off, Whitey encountered a strong wind. A Texas "Blue Norther" had decided to put in an appearance, and its strong winds quickly affected the flight. To make matters much worse, at nine thousand feet, north of the field, both of the plane's two engines cut out, leaving Whitey flying a 50,000-pound glider! The problem was later found to be fuel lines that had not been properly reconnected after maintenance, but that didn't matter now. There was no way to fix the problem in flight and Whitey had to either get down safely or have everyone bail out.

On leave in 1944, Whitey poses by the family Christmas tree with his father (left, standing) and his grandfather (sitting). *(Feightner family photo)*

Whitey and his three sisters, from left to right: Virginia, Marian, and Eleanor. Eleanor was the mother of Whitey's nephew, Jim McBride, whom Whitey helped raise. *(Feightner family photo)*

On the day he and his friend Red went up to enlist, Whitey and Red pose with Red's uncle by the uncle's Piper Cub. *(Feightner family photo)*

Newly winged and commissioned, Ensign Feightner and Second Lieutenant Hall pose in their whites. The two friends would soon become aces. *(Feightner family photo)*

Newly promoted Captain Hall leans on the propeller of his F4U Corsair shortly after getting his sixth and final kill, a Zero that followed him down to wave-top level and crashed into the water. *(Tailhook Association)*

Whitey's first flight instructor, Mike Murphy, stands by his red-and-white-checked Jungmeister in 1970. The large trophy on the right is the Freddy Lind Trophy for the National Aerobatic Championship, which Mike won three times to retire the trophy. The name and reason for the smaller trophy are unknown. The restored Jungmeister now resides in the Smithsonian Institution's Air and Space Museum near Dulles International Airport in Virginia. *(Mike Heuer)*

Whitey married Vi in Long Beach on August 15, 1948. Admiral Ginder, Vi's mother, and Whitey's mother and father admire the happy couple. *(Feightner family photo)*

"Uncle Ed," his cover characteristically tilted at a jaunty angle, poses with his young nephew Jim McBride, nattily dressed in a sailor suit. The year is 1948 and they stand by the house in Elida where they both grew up. *(Feightner family photo)*

Nearly twenty years later, still in Elida, Captain Feightner shares his nephew's pride as a newly commissioned ensign. *(Feightner family photo)*

Lt. Butch O'Hare sits in his VF-3 Wildcat, which is marked with the five kills he is credited with during his Medal of Honor mission in February 1942. Whitey still has fond memories of this early mentor in the field of aerial combat. (*Tailhook Association*)

During the Battle of Santa Cruz on October 26, 1942, the USS *Enterprise* is under attack by Japanese aircraft, two of which can just be seen wheeling above the carrier. The battleship *South Dakota* is in the distant background firing her anti-aircraft guns. *(National Archives and Records Administration via the U.S. Naval Institute)*

VF-10 ace Swede Vejtasa in the cockpit of his Wildcat. *(Barrett Tillman)*

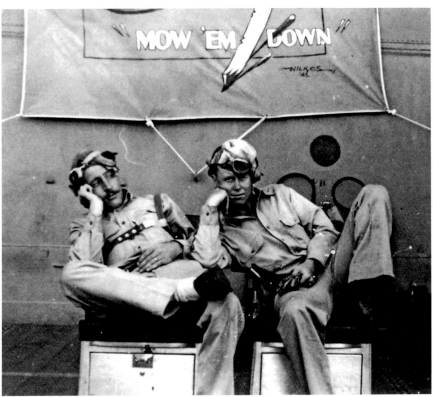

To illustrate their boredom, Dave Pollock and Swede Vejtasa pose on the *Enterprise* flight deck beneath the VF-10 banner. Three days later, these two would have all the action they wanted at Santa Cruz. *(Author's collection)*

After surviving action in the Solomons, Jim Billo, Whitey Feightner, and Chip Reding (left to right) pose in Hawaii in May 1943. They were no longer young men. *(Jim Billo)*

The inspirational leader of the Reapers of VF-10, Lt. Cdr. James "Jimmy" Flatley, gave his squadron a fighting tradition that remained throughout the war and three combat deployments. *(National Archives and Records Administration)*

A squadron photo in February 1943 shows the surviving pilots of VF-10, among them Whitey (front row, second from left), James "Jimmy" Flatley (front row, fifth from left), Swede Vejtasa (second row, second from right), and Butch Voris (second row, second from left). (National Archives and Records Administration)

A wonderful photo of the First Tour Reapers and their hostess in Hawaii, the gracious Countess Alexa Von Tempsky Zabriskie. John Leppla is on the extreme right in the last row. Jimmy Flatley sits to the countess's right, with Butch Voris in front of him in the front row. (Author's collection)

Fellow Buckeye John "Jack" Leppla had only a few chances to show his combat skills before being lost on October 26 at Santa Cruz. After downing one Zero, he had to bail out of his Wildcat, but his chute streamed and he was killed. *(National Archives and Records Administration)*

On October 24, 1942, deck crews move a VF-10 F4F-4 (Buno 5229, F-17) while others manually unfold its wings. Although the plane was assigned to Ens. James "Jim" Dowden, the pilot is Ens. Lyman Fulton. Dowden flew the plane two days later and was lost. *(National Archives and Records Administration)*

Deck crews move a VF-8 Hellcat down the deck on the *Bunker Hill*, on October 12, 1944, just before a raid on Formosa. *(National Archives and Records Administration via Dave Lucabaugh and Jim Sullivan)*

Feightner, at the time a lieutenant, sits in a VF-8 Hellcat marked with his nine kills. This may be the only photo of Whitey in an aircraft during the war. (*U.S. Navy Photo via Rear Adm. E. L. Feightner*)

A Douglas AD-4 Skyraider takes off from NAS Patuxent River with a load of bombs and rockets. The "NATC" on the tail indicates the Naval Air Test Center. (*U.S. Navy*)

Lt. Harding C. "Mac" Macknight and Lt. Cdr. E. L. "Whitey" Feightner, the two F7U-1 Cutlass pilots for the Blue Angels. One of the few photos of Whitey in a flight suit. *(Tailhook Association)*

The Lockheed XR6O-1 Constitution. Even in the air without any other references, the plane's massive size is apparent. *(Tailhook Association)*

The two Blue Angel Cutlasses with Lieutenant Commander Feightner in the foreground and Lieutenant Macknight on his wing. *(National Museum of Naval Aviation)*

Whitey and Mac talk things over by Whitey's F7U-1. The Cutlass gave these two men more than their share of problems and could not be depended on for a complete flight. *(National Museum of Naval Aviation)*

Lieutenant Commander Feightner, the only man to operate the F7U-1 Cutlass from a carrier, comes aboard *Midway*. *(Vought)*

Whitey taxis past the *Midway*'s island. The carrier qualification period was full of problems. *(Steve Ginter)*

Naval Air Test Center (NATC) aircraft fly over Detroit in August 1951. Left to right, FJ-2: Lt. N. G. "Bud" Sickel Jr.; F9F-6: Lt. G. G. Watkins; F9F-5: Lt. A. B. Shepard Jr.; F7U-3: Lt. Cdr. E. L. Feightner. The flight had a near catastrophic ending at the air show they were visiting. (NATC)

Two F2H-4 Banshees of VF-11 fly over Jacksonville, Florida, a few months before deploying on board the USS Coral Sea. (Tailhook Association)

The USS *Essex* in the mid-1950s. Many of the aircraft of CVW-10 are on the flight deck as a proper background for a presentation ceremony forward of the island. The new A-4s can be seen on the starboard half. (*Tailhook Association*)

An F4D from VF-13 in the groove as it approaches the *Essex* in January 1960. (*Tailhook Association*)

The USS *Chikaskia*, Whitey's first deep draft command. *(U.S. Navy)*

The USS *Okinawa*. Whitey was surprised at how much he enjoyed his LPH command tour after not getting the promised *Forrestal*. *(U.S. Navy photo by W. A. Hutchinson)*

Two famous aces still enjoying life. Brig. Gen. Robin Olds and Rear Adm. Whitey Feightner at the 1987 Fighter Fling at NAS Oceana, Virginia Beach. *(Author's collection)*

Rear Adm. E. L. Feightner in a BuPers portrait, complete with gray gloves but sans his Legion of Merit awards. *(Feightner family photo)*

He told the chief to go back to the cabin and tell the Vought people to strap on their parachutes and be ready to jump when he got to a lower altitude. But he decided to try to dead stick into another field, if he could find one. When the chief returned, he spotted something through the clouds. It was Corpus. The wind had been so strong that it prevented them from moving any great distance from their departure point. Whitey told the chief to tell the passengers to sit tight; he was going to bring the plane back to the field, which he did, thereby saving a valuable airplane, not to mention the Vought techs.

The fuel-line problem was quickly fixed, and Whitey and the chief were soon ready to take off again, this time minus the company people, who had decided to fly airlines up to Glenview, at Vought's expense. Whitey couldn't blame them. When the techs arrived they fixed Mac's Cutlass, and Whitey eventually flew it to Memphis for a show, along with the F9F-5s, which were now up and flying. It would be the first official show with all the team and all the aircraft. Mac thought he needed one more flight in the F7U that Whitey had brought in from Glenview, mainly because the repairs had also included an engine change.

So, off he went. Everything was fine until he put the gear down to land. For the first time since the two Cutlasses had arrived, one main gear locked in the forward position, while the other locked in the aft position. Frustrated, perhaps desperate, Whitey prevailed on a Navy Reservist pilot to lend Mac his F8F. He took off and formed on Mac over the field. Both men decided that Mac could land in that staggered configuration. He landed without further difficulties. Ground crews drop-checked the gear, meaning they propped the Cutlass on supports and extended the gear. Everything seemed all right.

The following day, Whitey and Mac flew the two planes on to Memphis to meet the team. Just as they landed, Mac had *another* hydraulic failure. His plane's hydraulic fluid poured out onto the runway, which the emergency crews foamed to prevent a fire. It was just too much. With all the problems the team had experienced with the Cutlass, it was decided to keep the two troublesome fighters for static display only. But even that arrangement was not satisfactory. The Cutlass was a maintenance nightmare, so the two aircraft were left at Memphis to be used by the Naval Air Technical Training Command in the field of hydraulic control systems.

The Blue Angels' experience with their racy but troublesome Cutlasses might have been brief, but Whitey's time with the F7U would continue for a while. After leaving the Blue Angels in September 1952, his next assignment was with VX-3, the test and development squadron at NAS Atlantic City, New Jersey. This new squadron was more involved with testing aircraft systems as opposed to the aircraft itself. Whitey found himself flying several different types of aircraft from the prop-driven AD Skyraider to the McDonnell F2H Banshee, and the latest development of the Cutlass, the F7U-3. As the man with the most Cutlass time, flying this new F7U would be a real challenge for him.

Vought revitalized the design with the F7U-3, completely redesigning the airplane with larger engines, increased armament, and various fixes or upgrades to other problem areas. As one of the most experienced Cutlass drivers—he had tallied 370 hours in the F7U-1—Lieutenant Commander Feightner was a natural choice to keep on to test the new variant.

While the F7U-3 generally looked like the F7U-1, it was much larger, a totally different aircraft. It featured a dual-hydraulic control system, a larger wing, new afterburning Westinghouse J-46 engines, and a completely redesigned cockpit with good night lighting. The F7U-3's landing gear was larger to support the increased weight, and the speed brakes under the fuselage had been eliminated. There were now split brakes between the engines.

The new Cutlass was the first Navy airplane to use the Mk 12 20-mm cannon; it carried four of them. There was also an efficient canoe-type pod containing thirty-two 2.75-inch rockets under the fuselage. There were bomb racks under each wing as well.

The F7U-3 was easier to fly than the F7U-1, with excellent slow-speed characteristics while retaining the F7U-1's outstanding roll rate. It was a great carrier aircraft in its earlier, more lightly loaded version, although in the heavier -3M and -3P versions it had marginal wave-off abilities. The nose wheel assembly also failed repeatedly in the fleet. So as good as the redesign was, it still had several problems.

The F7U-3 was still short-legged and didn't fit into a carrier's cycle time. As a result, many Cutlass squadrons—there were eventually twelve fleet squadrons, and four VX and one VC shore-based units—remained ashore because of these scheduling problems. The fighter could refuel in mid-air. Where the F7U-1 had a nose-mounted refueling probe, the F7U-3's probe was ten feet below the cockpit and was retractable. The Cutlass was also, in Whitey's words, "an outstanding dive bomber. You could put the brakes out and hang there."

Like the F7U-1, the F7U-3 had a maintenance arrangement where the entire underside of the plane was made up of two access doors. When they were opened, the entire engine bay was exposed. But if there were any stores on the plane, they interfered with opening those doors, and they had to be opened after almost every flight. There were also hydraulic and fuel leak problems, as well as electric system headaches. Whitey considered the rocket pod "beautifully designed," but something of a bother; it weighed around 1,500 pounds.

The F7U-3 had afterburners and a high climb rate, which was fairly spectacular. One British test pilot loved to split S from 30,000 feet, go through the sound barrier, open the speed brakes, slow down, then close the brakes and repeat the sequence twice more before landing. Needless to say, the squadron leader (equal to a lieutenant commander) caused great consternation in the local area around Atlantic City.

Eventually, the time came to test the new Cutlass at sea. A few engineers expressed concern about the nose wheel. The Navy had designated a design sink rate of 21 feet per second (fps), but when the aircraft was finally built, the rate was 18 fps. Pilots were told to get the maximum impact on the nose strut as they trapped. A Cutlass pilot sat directly over the nose gear, and any movement of the strut translated directly into his rear end.

Try as they might, no one could increase the sink rate to the required 21 fps. Whitey tried a number of fly-in engagements. He made an approach just above the ground, dragging the tailhook, and engaged the crossdeck pendant on the field. The minute the hook caught the cable, he pulled back on the stick and rammed the throttles forward. He climbed, of course, and was eventually snatched back to the ground, a violent maneuver to be sure. One of these engagements was so violent that he injured his spine, for which he paid for the rest of his life.

For all this effort, however, and even though nothing would change the sink rate, everyone agreed to be satisfied with the rate. As it turned out, though, the F7U-3 was no sooner in squadron service than pilots began shearing off their nosegears, not because of the impact loads but because of side loads in off-center engagements. There were enough of these mishaps that carrier COs began feeling uncomfortable with Cutlasses on board. There's nothing worse for a carrier skipper than a deployment with a brand-new aircraft in which he has little confidence. It doesn't do much for the air wing's collective confidence, either.

As noted, the Cutlass had afterburners, but most pilots didn't use them on shore. But carrier launches were another story, especially with the heavier F7U-3M missile carrier. The aircraft was fairly sensitive to high loads. With the guns and rockets, Whitey thought the Cutlass a "decent fighter, with good visibility." Then there was the matter of recovery, landing back on the ship.

"We knew the dash-3 was going to be a 'blind airplane' in the carrier approach, like the dash-1. To its credit, Vought redesigned the pilot's seat to that he could raise and lower it, as well as rotate it forward some 20 degrees until he felt comfortable. This arrangement helped resolve the problem coming aboard."[3] Whitey believed that one of the best of the F7U-3's innovations was its night-lighting system with a curved console. It was easy to monitor the instruments without moving around, and it was a good all-weather aircraft too.

The new Cutlass's hydraulic control system was much more reliable than the F7U-1, but there were few failures. Considering how much trouble the hydraulics had been in Blue Angels service, this was no doubt a major relief. The fuel-transfer system, though, did have its share of problems. To increase the range, the designers had stuffed fuel everywhere, and the transfer system was complex. There were *twenty-two* red warning lights in the cockpit, and the panel was often referred to as "the pinball machine."

The navigational system in the F7U-3 was way ahead of the earlier F7U-1, which had only a low-frequency range receiver and an automatic direction finder (ADF) that only worked sometimes. The F7U-3 used TACAN (tactical air navigation), an ultra-high frequency (UHF) system that included directional and distance information in one instrument and one-dial presentation in the cockpit. Some of the later Cutlasses even included a rudimentary inertial navigational system.

Another experienced Vought test pilot, Boone T. Guyton, who had also tested such aircraft as the F4U Corsair during the war, offered his opinions on the unusual Cutlass.

> There are some 1,700 pieces of tubing, totaling about 5,000 feet—a mile of plumbing—to handle the oil, fuel, hydraulic fluid and air flow. The Cutlass had some 40,000 feet—roughly eight miles—of electrical wiring threading fore and aft. . . .
>
> Fuel cells pack areas in both the wings and fuselage, wherever space was available. . . . The Cutlass has eight self-sealing tanks, spaced throughout the wings, center section and fuselage. They all have to be joined together, permitting unrestricted and completely reliable automatic fuel flow to the engines at all speeds and altitudes. . . .
>
> The cockpit of the F7U-1 is a mass of controls, instruments and dials, switches, knobs of various shapes and sizes, and lights and selectors. . . . Surprisingly, there is ample room for the pilot, the control stick and rudder pedals.
>
> The landing gear has to fold into the airplane somewhere, hundreds of rounds of ammunition, armor protection, and an oxygen supply for the pilot. . . . Gun heaters, oil tanks, emergency systems for the landing gear, canopy and controls have to be provided, too.[4]

The Cutlass did offer many advances over earlier aircraft already in service, but because of problems with such things as the engine bay doors, the low carrier cycle times, and a lack of internal fuel, it just wasn't what the Navy wanted. Even after its lengthy test-and-development time by men like Whitey Feightner, who certainly knew their business and wanted the new fighter to succeed, it only served the briefest of time in the fleet and was out of service by 1960, not even enjoying the customary time in the reserves allotted to aircraft that had left front-line service.

CHAPTER 10
MORE TESTING AT NEW COMMANDS

By this time, Whitey and his compatriots realized the F7U-1 was not that good an airplane, or at least it had too many problems to put it into production. When they went out to the USS *Midway* (CVB 41) in June 1951, though, they took it along to tabulate additional data for a proposed development, the F7U-3. Another reason was to create a decoy away from the major reason, which was to bring the F2H Banshee out to test its configuration carrying a nuclear "shape," a euphemism for a small nuclear store, usually carried under a wing on a centerline rack. A third aircraft that accompanied the group was the new F9F-5 Panther, just about to enter squadron service. The CQ for this aircraft was described in the previous chapter, but there are more details to include in this portion and how they affected Whitey's immediate assignment in the coming months.

A graduate of the Annapolis class of 1939, Cdr. George C. Duncan was the chief engineering officer, and he would make the first traps with the F9F-5. Duncan was an ace with thirteen and a half kills, having flown Hellcats with VF-15 on board the USS *Essex* (CV 9) with the Navy's leading ace, Cdr. David McCampell (thirty-four kills). After World War II, Duncan had spent time in various assignments, including Patuxent. He was therefore a highly experienced aviator in many types of aircraft.

With Whitey in the F7U-1, he and Commander Duncan launched simultaneously. Problems soon arose when Duncan realized he was flying with a full load of fuel, including the wingtip tanks. Before he could attempt to trap, he would have to burn down to landing weight; his Panther was much too heavy to try to trap. He also had to jettison the tip tanks.

As Duncan stood off from the landing pattern, Whitey brought his Cutlass in for the first traps. He had made five arrested landings when Commander Duncan called that he was ready to come aboard. Whitey made another trap and was taxiing forward to clear the landing area as the deck crew lowered the barricade normally in place during flight operations to protect the planes parked in the forward flight deck (this was before the advent of the angled deck).

A movement in his rear mirror caught Whitey's eye and he looked around to see the deck crewmen running. He looked in the mirror again just in time to catch a huge flash as George Duncan's Panther hit the ramp a half deck behind him. The F9F was still too heavy, and crash films would show the terrible sink rate as the Panther went below the ramp.

With the LSO calling frantically for power, Duncan tried to respond, but the F9F's J48 Pratt & Whitney engine couldn't give him enough to climb over the rounddown, and the Panther struck the deck with the forward part of the fuselage. The struggling fighter exploded in a terrible ball of flame and broke in two as it hurtled down the flight deck, leaving the rear fuselage and engine on the fantail. Commander Duncan was apparently not properly strapped into his ejection seat, and as the fuselage rolled over and over as it careened down the deck, he was tossed around, his head and helmet above the cockpit sill with little protection. He finally rolled out of the flames and into the barricade net. He suffered major injuries to his head, as well as burns to his arms and shoulders. The deck fire crew quickly extinguished the fire and the battered pilot was hustled down to sick bay.

When Whitey managed to get to sick bay, his friend was in a bad way. Duncan, however, survived and recuperated for a year with the aid of a superb plastic surgeon, and he was assigned as the commanding officer of VF-51 in Korea and then Air Group 5 after the Korean War. He had received the Navy Cross, Silver Star, and seven Distinguished Flying Crosses.

While he was mending, Duncan spent a lot of time as the duty officer. One day, he received a call from his two-star boss, who was stuck in New York and needed to get back to Washington the next day. The weather was foul and Duncan knew he needed a really top-notch aviator to retrieve the admiral. And after warming a chair, he was also anxious to log a few hours himself, even though he was not cleared to fly solo. His wounds still looked bad.

He called Whitey into the office. As the duty officer and senior to Whitey, a lieutenant commander, he told him to take a C-45 Twin Beech up to get their boss, Rear Adm. Malcom F. Schoeffel, who had recently relieved Captain Trapnell. As the senior instrument and check pilot, Whitey could handle it, although he wasn't really looking forward to taking the clunky but dependable Beech out in this terrible weather. But someone had to get the CO, and he was elected. The admiral had been up at the Bell Company's headquarters near Buffalo, New York, for three days so that Bell could show him some of their latest projects. The building was a huge, two-million-square-foot structure on the grounds of the Niagara Municipal Airport.

Imagine Whitey's surprise when after changing into his flight suit and filing a flight plan, he prepared to walk to the plane only to find his friend George Duncan also in a flight suit waiting for him. There wasn't much Whitey could do but take his unscheduled copilot along in the right seat. With his left arm still in a cast, Duncan couldn't have done much if he had had to fly the plane with the power controls between them, to Duncan's left! But, as Whitey recalled, as the duty officer,

Duncan felt it was his responsibility to bring the boss home. And since he could not do it alone, he called on his friend Whitey, who also had a "green card," which allowed him to make individual decisions regarding flying in bad weather.

As they plodded through the dismal clouds and rain, making the cumbersome position reports required at the time, George flew while Whitey made power adjustments and operated the radio. The two naval aviators suffered through it all and landed at Niagara Muni, as it was called then. Although he was glad to see the C–45 and his ride home, the admiral was furious when he saw Commander Duncan in the right seat. "Are you out of your minds?" he roared at his two senior aviators.

In Navy fitness reports there's an important column titled "Judgment," which forms a good part of how the subject officer looks to promotion boards considering him for positions such as squadron or air wing command. One wonders how the admiral graded his two energetic pilots after they came to pick him up. Actually, both Whitey and George enjoyed excellent future assignments, so perhaps his boss was not that harsh when making out their next fitness reports.

Whitey had come to believe that the F7U–3 was "a piece of cake on the ship," meaning it was easy to bring aboard. But as soon as the F7U–3 entered fleet service, problems arose involving the landing gear, which younger, less smooth pilots began breaking off the wheels with rough off-centerline landings. Lineup is everything in carrier flying. Often there is little room as the landing aircraft's wings approach the carrier's island—the E–2 with its large-span wings is especially noted for this requirement—and to touch down at an angle to the centerline produces a lot of stress on landing gear. The F7U–3's gear did not take kindly to such treatment.

Whitey thought the F7U–3 was a good bombing airplane, and he especially liked the under-fuselage rocket pod that carried forty-four 2.75-inch unguided rockets, a piece of ordnance that was to find favor in later generations of aviators in Vietnam. And with a dual hydraulic system, the F7U–3 seldom had any problems in this area.

Before leaving Patuxent, Whitey asked permission to get together a small air show group to take to the August 1951 Detroit National Air Races at Wayne Major Airport, something of a descendent of the iconic Cleveland Air Races and Bendix Air Races of the pre–World War II days where military entries dominated the lineup. He organized some of his test-pilot friends, including George C. Watkins, who became the first naval aviator to make one thousand traps in 1962. His younger brother James D. Watkins became Chief of Naval Operations in 1982 under Ronald Reagan, and then secretary of energy for George H. W. Bush in 1989. Another member of the select group was Bud Sickel, an excellent, highly capable test pilot. Perhaps the man to become the most famous in the group was future astronaut Alan Shepard, a spirited but also highly capable aviator. Whitey would lead the group in an F7U–3, while the others flew F9F Panthers.

The men took off from Patuxent and were scheduled to put on a show before landing at Detroit. An AJ tanker accompanied them with the idea they would put on a low-level demonstration of the new art of aerial refueling. One of the fighters would plug into the tanker in front of the crowd and follow it around in a great circle to show the people what the new operation looked like.

As the group from Pax approached its destination, the weather was obviously not the best. In fact, it was smoggy with reduced visibility. At 20,000 feet, conditions got better, but down at crowd level, the air was cloudy with less than half a mile visibility, definitely not air show conditions. Another group of fighters, sixteen Banshees from VF-22 under their skipper Lt. Cdr. Donald E. Runyon, a colorful former enlisted ace (eleven kills in Wildcats and Hellcats) of the early Pacific War, was also overhead, orbiting the show checking out the lousy conditions. At the time it was not unusual to have as many as twenty-two aircraft with twenty-eight pilots assigned to one squadron. Runyon had been one of the more senior test pilots and was certainly ready to help with the exhibition. He said he could come off one of the beacons to make a pass in front of the stands. Finally, the directors called for Whitey's flight to come down and fly past the crowd before going home to Pax. Whitey took his group down from 20,000 feet, stroking the burners as he passed 5,000 feet, going just under Mach 1, the speed of sound.

About a mile from the airport, he looked up and saw Runyon's Banshees right in front of him. Actually, Whitey was moving extremely fast, and the Banshees seemed to simply materialize like ghosts out of the mists. He called Runyon to pull up so he could fly under the Banshees. Runyon thought that was a good idea and started to comply. By this time, the Banshees had gotten low, and it was a close call as all the F2Hs did their best, leaving their tail-end Charlie ensign to pull so hard that he dropped a wing tank as the fighter went inverted right in front of Whitey's oncoming Cutlass.

"I had no place to go," Whitey remembered. "The tank came off and I could see it flipping up, and it went down the flight line in front of the crowd spewing fuel all over the world. Why it didn't blow I'll never know. The last thing I saw was the tank as I quickly did a turn to the right, intending to go behind the grandstand."[1] Just as he turned, however, Whitey spotted four Army helicopters lifting off. He had just enough time to roll back. Fortunately, the Cutlass was very maneuverable with its high roll rate, and he had just enough time to get straight and fly up in the face of the crowd, perhaps ten feet over their collective heads with both afterburners aflame, going just below Mach 1.

Needless to say, the combined effect was something the people probably never forgot. Some had clothes ripped right off by the Cutlass's shock wave (hats at least), and the ensign's tip tank barely missed a young boy as it spiraled away only seventy-five feet from him. The ensign regained control and simply flew out of the area to find his squadron. With two radio stations, one on either end of the field, the Navy crews could position themselves properly right in front of the stands below. But the weather was getting worse and consideration was given to canceling the show. Finally, all the Navy aircraft landed at nearby Selfridge Air Force Base (AFB).

The next day the weather had cleared and the second air show went on as scheduled but with a bunch of restrictions. The Navy aircraft flew their passes without incident, but the Air Force's contribution, an F-89 Scorpion, a huge two-seat radar-equipped interceptor, made a simulated dive-bombing attack—the big plane was definitely not a dive bomber! During the pullout, the tail came off and crashed right in front of the stands, sending wreckage all over the area, including the parking lot. The crash ended the air show and also any planned future races for quite a while. It wasn't until 1964 that a National Air Race was scheduled, this time in Reno, Nevada. These new versions of the race enjoyed large crowds, but there were incidents, crashes, and dangerous near-misses, including a fatal crash of a P-51 Mustang that came down in the crowded viewing area in 2011. Unfortunately, large air shows also have an accepted risk of dangerous mishaps.

In June 1972, a huge aerospace exhibition called Transpo 72 featured many different aerial exhibitions, including a rare appearance by both Air Force and Navy flight demonstration teams, the Thunderbirds and the Blue Angels. Both teams flew the Phantom II, with the Thunderbirds using the F-4E and the Blue Angels the F-4J. On June 4, the last day of the exhibition, the Thunderbirds had their first fatal mishap at an air show. The F-4s were normally only flown with one man in the front seat of the normally two-man heavy fighter. As the crowd watched, the team started a vertical maneuver. But one Phantom exited the area with mechanical problems. Its pilot soon ejected and seemed to be all right, but he was blown back into the fireball of his F-4's crash and killed. It was one of three fatal crashes during the week-long exhibition. As Whitey recalled, the terrible crashes closed down any further national displays for a while, at least at Dulles.[2]

During his testing time, Whitey met several Navy and Marine aviators whose names would soon become household names, including Alan Shepard and John Glenn. Although the two men were highly competent, extremely intelligent aviators, their personalities were at opposite ends of the spectrum. Whereas Shepard was always ready for a good time—"a typical fighter pilot . . . sort of a rebel in a lot of things" as Whitey put it—the studious Glenn was always focused on the job at hand, thinking things out thoroughly, always planning his missions and jobs down to the last letter.

Even with all his experience and expertise, Whitey was too old for the astronaut program, if in fact he had ever thought about applying. His predilection was more like that of Charles Yeager, who pursued his flying in the traditional cockpit and not from an orbiting space capsule. It suited Whitey best. He never lost his love of flying hands-on and probably would not have been happy with the constant checks and communications from a distant band of mission coordinators.

By now, the main specialty was all-weather weapons delivery, especially nuclear delivery. VX-3 developed the loft maneuver, and VX-5 in California continued that research. Whitey worked closely with another Pacific ace and future four-star admiral, Noel Gayler, whose personality was more like that of Marion Carl, an excellent, gifted aviator, but one given to periods of aloofness that often frustrated other people, junior and senior.

Whitey and Gayler concentrated on low-level, all-weather nuclear delivery, certainly a demanding, occasionally frustrating arena. Gayler eventually developed an antagonism toward anything having to do with nuclear weapons, but at the time, he was working with Whitey Feightner, and he gave all his effort to developing the proper delivery method, which was not easy. In Whitey's estimation, Gayler was a good aviator, "good enough to become an ace in World War II," but he often over-extended himself, getting into situations, such as poor weather, that probably would have been better left alone.

Another highly respected personality Whitey dealt with was Donald D. Engen, who at one time was the youngest naval aviator and who had earned the Navy Cross as the pilot of an SB2C Helldiver attacking a Japanese ship. Engen was another one of those Pacific aviators destined for great achievement. He eventually rose to three-star rank, was head of the Federal Aviation Administration, and was the director of the National Air and Space Museum when he died in the crash of his glider over the Sierras in Nevada in 1999.

Engen had been the CO of the USS *America* (CV 66) in 1967 and had launched a force of A-4s and F-4s to rush to the aid of the USS *Liberty* (AGTR 5), which was then under attack by Israeli aircraft during the June Arab-Israel Six Day War. Eventually, he was ordered to recall his planes, but it had been a brave move by a highly motivated senior combat leader in the face of an unknown danger and force.

Engen had been a test pilot on several interesting projects, including the way-ward XF8U-3 Crusader III that competed with the F-4 to be the next Navy carrier fighter. Even today many people believe it was the best fighter ever developed by the Navy, but it lost out to the Phantom. Few aviators logged time in the Crusader III, but Don Engen did.

As his work as a test pilot drew to a close, Whitey found himself involved in several truly interesting projects that would have made any aviator's mouth water. On the horizon were two particularly futuristic aircraft, the Martin P6M Seamaster, an all-jet flying boat meant for the maritime patrol mission but with the ability to carry nuclear weapons, and the Consolidated XF2Y Seadart, one of the few jet-powered flying boat fighters ever designed, let alone produced. The only other such aircraft to ever make it to reality—three were built—was the Saunders-Roe SR.A.1 of 1947 in England that used the ancient River Thames as its "runway."

But both these advanced aircraft, while certainly having their own eventual flight programs, were gone by the time Whitey was ready to be their project officer. Although he never flew either one, he did have an experience while flying chase on the graceful P6M while at Patuxent. The Seamaster was getting expensive, and its mission was being clouded by other developments such as the Polaris sea-launched intercontinental missile, which could be carried by a new class of nuclear submarine.

One day, Whitey was flying chase for a P6M south of Pax. The purpose of the flight was to demonstrate the flying boat's rolling pullout technique. The procedure was for the pilot to enter a high-speed dive and then pull out at the same time he rolled the big "boat." South of the small town of Waldorf, Whitey in an F4U watched as the Seamaster pilot started his dive from 22,000 feet. He was supposed to pull out at 15,000 feet.

As Whitey followed the P6M down, his Corsair's engine quit as the flying boat started its roll. The Corsair's prop stopped, just froze. There was not a lot Whitey could do to restart and he was thinking about bailing out. He looked around for an airfield, but the only fields around were Pax and Andrews AFB far to the north. Of course, he was much closer to Patuxent. He called to announce his problem and the P6M leveled out to follow the faltering chase plane.

Whitey was now thinking about when to jump. He knew he had to get out by at least one thousand feet, but if he could coax his F4U to stay in the air for another several minutes, he might make the field at Pax. At least his big four-bladed prop had stopped; if it had been windmilling, the drag would have been much too great and he wouldn't have been able to make much forward travel.

Finally, he could see the field, although the longest runway was downwind as opposed to the normal landing upwind. Whitey put down his landing gear, but suddenly he saw that he wasn't going to make it. The gear put too much additional drag on the Corsair. A thought came to him and he dove the big fighter to build up as much speed as he could as he kept heading for the runway. As he flew over the end of the strip, Whitey pulled back on the stick, making the Corsair balloon, and with the accompanying ground effect he was able to drop onto the runway, safe and sound. The P6M landed on the water without further incident.

The Seadart, four of which were built, although only three were flown, was a unique design that incorporated fuselage-mounted skis to land and take off from the water. The aircraft's performance was not that promising, certainly not for a fighter, but it was an interesting type that attracted attention. Unfortunately, a test pilot was killed on November 4, 1954, during an air show in San Diego, and during a redesign, the aircraft's dual skis were replaced by a single ski. For the next several months, the basic design of the Seadart was fiddled with and refined, but by 1957 the project was shelved mainly because of increased expense and the fact that the need for such an aircraft was gone. Thus, Whitey never had a chance to fly these interesting new types.

Whitey had a lot of time in the Douglas AD Skyraider, testing Ed Heinemann's last major reciprocating-engine prop attack aircraft. Produced at the end of World War II, it was too late to see action in the last stages of the Pacific War, but it certainly gave a good account of itself in Korea flying in both attack and fighter-designated carrier squadrons as well as a few shore-based Marine Corps units. It was a solid, highly capable, and powerful aircraft that would continue flying in the fleet well into the 1960s and even in certain special roles the 1970s.

In 1949, a young naval aviator had even taken off with his AD's huge wings folded. He barely managed to stagger back to the field before crashing, his only injury being a few slight burns from the resulting fire as he got out of his plane. Wings-folded flight was not unknown and several types managed to make different forms of it, including the F-8 and A-7 and F-4. Usually, the main damage was to the aviator's pride and reputation, and normally because of the aircraft involved, their powerful engines, and the fact that the folding wing portion was relatively small, they were able to maintain some sort of controllable flight sufficient enough for the pilot to regain the ground. But the wing of the AD (A-1 as it was redesignated in 1962) had a major portion of its wings capable of folding, leaving a small stub wing. Thus it was of some interest as to how these particular ADs were able to take off and fly. The Navy called on one of its most experienced aviators to investigate this phenomenon.

Whitey found he was indeed able to take off with his Skyraider's big wings folded, fairly easily. He was surprised to look over his head to see the huge wings now nearly vertical in the slipstream. One can only guess that although with the wings now vertical, their drag had been greatly reduced and the stub wings could now lift the big AD by themselves. Still, it was something he wouldn't recommend as regular part of the AD's flight regime.

Along with then Lt. Cdr. Don Engen, Whitey was also involved in making long, nonstop, unrefueled flights in Skyraiders, the longest being logged as an eighteen-hour low-level round trip from a carrier and return, flying a weapons delivery profile. Because of the Skyraider's important capability as an A-bomb carrier, many carrier attack squadrons had specific targets designated in the event of such a war, each individual pilot being regularly briefed on his target folder. There was little hope of AD drivers making it back from this mission, but then the stakes were admittedly high and they had to be included in the mix of assets available in whatever initial strikes would be launched.

The designated pilots routinely practiced their hops, flying long flights to imaginary points, normally taking anywhere up to twelve hours, a tribute to their skill, dedication, and endurance. But eighteen hours was something of considerable credibility. If anyone could do it, though, it would be Whitey Feightner. He also did the same sort of long-distance delivery flights with the McDonnell F2H Banshee, logging more than 2,800 miles in one flight. Testing the Banshee's A-bomb-toting abilities had been the main reason for the tragic trip out to the *Midway* in 1951 where George Duncan had had his near-fatal crash.

Another aspect of all this testing and development for nuclear delivery involved the curious practice of sealing an aircraft's radios, requiring pilots to go out and fly the delivery without any means of communications or navigational aids. Whitey placed the responsibility for this extreme ruling on Noel Gayler.

Another of Gayler's ideas was setting up exercises where all the defense units on the East Coast would try to intercept the ADs as they flew their nuclear profile.

After launching from a carrier, the AD pilots would attack various targets along the coast and inland. Sometimes the AD involved was a multiplace -3N or -4N with radar operators—this would be when the radios were not sealed. Sometimes the attacker was a Banshee. Often there would be rotating cycles where one group of strikers would launch at noon and recover at midnight, followed by another group of strikers that launched at midnight and recovered at noon.

The pattern was to launch and then immediately drop down to water level; the next time the pilot climbed was to begin his approach back to the ship twelve hours later. It was a real test of every pilot's stamina and flying and navigational skills. Whitey's eighteen-hour flight involved his leading a flight of ADs—the other two Skyraiders flown by Bud Gear and Bill Stewart—each with blue-painted Mark 76 practice bombs with small explosive charges, and hitting the target complex called Pine Castle near Jacksonville, Florida. Whitey and his flight arrived at their target in an area of low clouds. The ADs also carried three 300-gallon fuel tanks and extra oil. The AD was a known oil burner and a pilot had to be aware of his oil consumption after long flights. After twelve hours, they transferred two gallons of oil.

They performed a loft maneuver putting their weapons on target and departed. On another day, he and his friends flew the same mission, this time attacking Eglin AFB after they had launched from the *Midway*, now east of Guantanamo on Cuba. Again, they were successful on placing their bombs on target without ever being intercepted.[3]

Besides all the weapons testing, Whitey participated in testing the exciting new development of the angled carrier deck, which had come from England. Up to then, carrier decks were straight landing fields with the recovering aircraft landing in a straight line up the flight deck, hopefully trapping and stopping before the plane hit the forward deck area where many aircraft were usually tied down. Now, with an additional landing area angled to port away from the main deck, returning planes could safely launch and trap without interfering with the forward deck area. It was an important redesign that revamped the accepted form of the carrier that had been used for some forty years.

Along with the angled deck, a new development appeared that involved the catapults that launched planes. These "slingshot" devices were normally hydraulically operated, giving a real kick in the pants to the pilot sitting in the plane as it was booted off the deck. Now, with steam providing the power to launch from the cat, the ride was smoother and more dependable.

VX-3 got the job of testing the new catapult, with skipper Noel Gayler pushing for the incorporation of the steam cat into existing and new carriers. He had made the first steam cat launch in a Panther in December 1953, traveling to the Naval Air Material Center at Philadelphia, where the new device was installed.

With British crews showing the way, American sailors learned how to operate the steam cat. Whitey took an AD and followed his CO to formally inaugurate the new cat. On December 3, Gayler launched without any problem, and Whitey was next. Somehow things got a little confused, and the catapult crew did not change the pressure setting after launching Gayler's F9F.

When the cat was fired, Whitey's aircraft shot off, getting airborne half way down the track. But when the towing bridle that attached the plane to the cat let loose, it literally flung the big Skyraider almost straight up, much like a slingshot. Whitey could have done a loop with all the momentum he had, attaining a speed of 220 knots instead of the normal 95. But Whitey kept control and landed, and procedures were refined and the steam cat was authorized for use on board ship.

CHAPTER 11
BACK TO THE FLEET AND COMMAND

Nukes On Board Carriers and Command of the Rippers

The question of nuclear bombs on board carriers and the Navy's desire to have planes to deliver them developed soon after World War II. Although it was Army Air Force B-29s (albeit with Navy weaponeers who armed the bombs) that dropped the first and only A-bombs used in actual combat, the Navy perceived that it, too, could make a contribution in this new field of warfare. If carrier-based aircraft could deliver a nuclear bomb on Soviet or Chinese mainland targets, it would justify the construction of large "flattops"—the super carriers. The large *Forrestal*-class ships, the backbone of the U.S. carrier fleet during the Cold War, were built primarily to launch nuclear strike aircraft.

The AD Skyraider was soon equipped to carry a small 1,630-pound nuclear bomb. Skyraiders and their pilots practiced their techniques and highly classified routes and deliveries for more than ten years, even as the Navy fought the Air Force to retain its small but politically charged role as America's secondary but indispensable atomic force.

Whitey was involved in developing these lengthy bottom-busting flights, launching at low level and maintaining these low altitudes until reaching a predetermined pop-up point where the pilot would zoom to a higher altitude, "loft" his weapon, and make a rapid rolling maneuver to escape the bomb's blast. Frankly, no one really expected the AD pilot to survive, but there was always hope.

Another program of bringing nuclear weapons on board carriers revolved around operating a Lockheed P2V Neptune, a large twin-engine (later with twin jet engines in underwing pods) aircraft meant for the lengthy maritime patrol mission, but from a shore base, never an aircraft carrier. Because of the limited and specific flight-deck dimensions of a carrier that included the bulk of the island imposed on the starboard side of the deck, many people felt the big Neptune was not the answer.

A P2V had launched from the *Coral Sea* on April 28, 1948, after being craned on board ship the previous day in Norfolk. Cdr. Tom Davies made the takeoff, followed by another P2V flown by Cdr. John Wheatley, both helped along by eight JATO bottles. It was a major accomplishment.

Testing of the Neptunes continued through 1949, with Whitey making a long-distance flight in October 1949. Eventually, however, the mission of a large aircraft capable of delivering a nuclear bomb from an aircraft carrier evolved into the short-lived North American AJ Savage, a singularly unsuccessful aircraft that saw limited service, using two traditional reciprocating engines and a single turbojet in the tail.

The AD was replaced in its light attack mission and then its nuclear-delivery mission by another Douglas product, the A4D Skyhawk, again from the genius of Ed Heinemann. Whitey came to know the little jet bomber well, taking the first Skyhawk squadrons, Navy and Marine, on deployment in the *Essex* as the air group commander. While in VX-3, under the command of another Pacific ace, Cdr. (later Adm.) Noel Gayler, Whitey participated in a number of developmental missions, usually with Banshees. In one flight, three F2Hs flown by Gayler, Whitey, and Michael Ames launched from the *Midway* east of Cuba, then headed for their target on Lake Erie. After their simulated delivery, the pilots were to return to their carrier. Their opposition would be all the assets of the North American Air Defense Command (NORAD), an impressive adversary, even in an exercise.

Refueling from their Savage tankers and then flying at low level with meticulous planning, the Navy aircraft headed for their target, coming up on it as Air Force fighters circled at 20,000 feet. The Banshees lofted their "shapes"—bombs that simulated a small Mk. 7 A-bomb—and as the ersatz weapons exploded, the USAF interceptors wheeled over in hot pursuit of the fast-departing blue "enemy" fighters.

Maintaining their low-level dash, Whitey, Gayler, and Ames struck out over the East Coast. But as the Air Force came into view, the Banshee pilots began high-speed climbs to 50,000 feet, which proved too much for their pursuers. The Navy flight settled into a cruise mode, found another tanker, and, after more than eight hours in the air, trapped back on board the *Midway*.

Talking to his former boss and long-time friend, Vice Adm. Jerry Miller, Whitey commented:

> Low-level flying is a mind-set operation. You have to get people used to a different perspective, which means a lot of low-level flying. . . . From then on, it's relatively easy . . . Nobody thought we were going to be able to fly for twelve or more hours in the A-1 prop aircraft. But, after developing the technique and practicing a lot, everyone accepted the concept.[1]

The gold ring for most dedicated naval aviators is command of a front-line squadron. Whitey had given the first fourteen years of his naval career to tours in squadrons that saw intense combat in the Pacific and then to several units involved in testing and development, as well as the unique experience with the Blue Angels, which was not at the time a designated squadron. He had done well in all arenas, achieving the highly desirable status of fighter ace with appropriate awards, and then on to test-flying the Navy's newest aircraft, such as the F7U Cutlass, long before they went into fleet service.

His annual fitness reports consistently placed him in the top 10 percent or higher of his contemporaries in all areas, and he was well known as an affable, unflappable, highly capable aviator who was always considered a valuable asset to any commanding officer's roster. Now it was time to give him his own squadron. And not just any squadron.

In January 1955, now a commander, Whitey received orders to the Red Rippers of VF-11 as the CO. It was indeed a plum assignment. The Rippers flew the Navy's newest F2H-3 and -4 Banshees, with the combined roles of attack and fighter. The F2H-4, nicknamed the "Big Banjo" because it had "grown" from the earlier model Banshees of the Korean War, now featured night fighting and night bombing capabilities, including atomic weapons. This specific capability was a primary consideration for the Navy, immersed as it was in a battle with the Air Force as to who should have that responsibility.

The Rippers had several specific targets in the middle of Europe, and, like the earlier AD Skyraider nuclear missions, the missions were generally considered one-way, with the pilot having to choose the point at which he would have to abandon his aircraft and hope for the best. Although aerial tanking was being developed, there was little cross-training with the Air Force, and Navy tankers were just not to be depended on to make a rendezvous with outbound Navy strike aircraft.

There were several disadvantages to taking the Banshee that far into interior Europe, one of which was that its radar had not been designed for such deliveries. There was no terrain-clearance capabilities—something we take for granted today—and although there were considerations given to low-level attacks, the terrain was generally mountainous and existing radar altimeters would be of real concern.

Fortunately, the squadron had a bright operations officer and excellent pilot, Lt. John Stewart, who was also working on his PhD. Together with a highly experienced enlisted maintainer who had worked with the manufacturer and had special experience in altimeters, Stewart set to work fine-tuning the squadron's instruments and quickly getting the sensitive altimeters to be much more reliable. Lieutenant Stewart was certainly headed toward bigger things and had actually been selected for lieutenant commander when he died prematurely.

Another problem was the Banshee's nose gear. The aircraft did not have enough nose clearance at the takeoff point from a carrier. The squadron designed a unique extension of the nose strut that inflated just before takeoff, giving a useful 14-inch increase in the space between the deck and the nose.

VF-11 had a long history. It was established in 1927 as VF-5 in Norfolk, and after World War II it was redesignated VF-11 and equipped with the F8F Bearcat. By 1950, the squadron was flying the F2H-2, then the F3D Skyknight. But another change brought F2H-4s. With Whitey in the lead, the Rippers did well, receiving the "Battle E" after placing first in toss-bombing competition in 1956.

There was growing pressure for now CVG-10 (CV meaning carrier) to get going with its cruise. Its original operations area in the western Mediterranean was soon changed to the eastern Mediterranean as the 1956 Suez Crisis erupted into war in October. Whitey took his squadron on board the *Coral Sea* for a deployment to the Mediterranean. In August 1956, VF-11 deployed with CVG-10, and in October the 1956 Suez Crisis erupted, with the new state of Israel fighting its second major war with its Arab neighbors. France and Great Britain quickly became involved in the brief but bloody conflict. Meanwhile, the American carrier group watched from the sidelines, ready to evacuate U.S. citizens if required. At times there were minor conflicts between U.S. and British carrier groups, which were admittedly operating in a confined area. The British seemed to be annoyed with the crowded air space and let people know it.

There was a great need for night fighters, and Whitey's VF-11 was fed into the mix with British and French squadrons. The Rippers kept up nightly patrols off Cyprus, often around the clock. The pilots could see British and French planes as they headed toward the war zone. Identifying unknown intruders was hard because the Israelis and the Egyptians often flew the same general type of aircraft. The British and French marked their aircraft with yellow-and-black "invasion stripes," similar to those used in 1944, but positive identification was still difficult.

Vice Admiral D. F. Durnford-Slater (Royal Navy), commanding the Anglo-French Task Force, complained to the Admiralty that the U.S. Sixth Fleet "are an embarrassment in my neighborhood. We have already twice intercepted U.S. aircraft and there is a constant danger of an incident. Have been continually menaced during the past eight hours by U.S. aircraft approaching low down as close as 4,000 yards and on two occasions flying over ships."[2]

Some British pilots shared the admiral's view and complained that encounters with U.S. aircraft led to less-than-favorable hand-signal conversations, beginning with the British asking who their new friends were. When the Americans did not give a satisfactory reply, the British signaled in strong language for the Americans to go away. Whitey remembered these occasional confrontations with their erstwhile allies. It was a touchy situation. The British were fighting a war, and their American cohorts were standing off to make sure their country's citizens were not in harm's way. Unfortunately, the British often overflew the American task force without notice, and this lack of long-established etiquette could not be ignored even for old friends. Predictably, the admiral's sentiments were not totally shared by those in the cockpits. Royal Navy Venom pilot Squadron Leader J. R. Maitland reported that although he had been intercepted by U.S. Navy aircraft, they had never come up on the British fighters in the war zone and had normally just joined up for a moment, waved, and left.

Whitey and the squadron concentrated on their night flying missions. He knew that such a demanding mission always brought the best from pilots as they strove to meet its requirements. He would schedule night flights at lower altitudes, below

15,000 feet, sometimes on one engine—the Banshee had two—to extend their flight time. He saw to it that everyone qualified for an instrument green card, which allowed the holder to make his own decisions about when to take off or what he could do once airborne. The card was usually required of senior section and division leaders, and instructors who had acquired sufficient experience to lead formations, but having every man holding a green card indicated the high level of expertise in VF-11. In addition to the green card, Whitey's aviators also qualified for an efficiency "E," something not always accomplished in every squadron.

Whitey's CAG was Cdr. Douglas A. Clark, a Hellcat pilot from World War II and the recipient of the Navy Cross and three Distinguished Flying Crosses. He had worked in several postwar development programs and knew what flying was about in the Navy. He and Whitey got along well, which usually made for a good cruise for everyone. As the squadron CO's direct reporting senior, keeping the CAG happy was priority one for any skipper. CAG Clark responded to VF-11's successes by giving Whitey the highest marks on his fitness report, saying in part, "Cdr. Feightner has done an outstanding job . . . and is recommended for rapid advancement." When Clark finished his CAG tour, he had to fill out another report on all his COs. He repeated his earlier assessment of the Red Rippers' skipper, writing that Whitey was "an outstanding [squadron] commander." Whitey reciprocated with the feeling that Clark "was ideal for the job [of CAG] because he understood the mission and really helped us in getting the right facilities on the ship." Whitey was talking about dedicated spaces for handling atomic weapons. The Banshees had a lot of special electronic gear required for aiming and preparing the A-bombs. No other carrier aircraft had such exotic equipment.

The targets for the F2Hs were developed and assigned by the Joint Strategic Targets Group, a Navy group, which coordinated designations and scheduling to prevent Navy and Air Force strikers from arriving over the targets at the same time. U.S. Navy pilots in the Mediterranean were scheduled to take out most of the communist airfields as well as dispose of any interceptors waiting to attack the incoming bombers from bases in the United States. Often the enemy airfields were actually undeveloped grass strips, seemingly a waste of expensive and powerful A-bombs, but the Soviets were well known for producing rugged aircraft able to take off from equally rugged bases.

It should be remembered that this was before all the sophisticated reconnaissance satellites we take for granted some sixty years later, a span of years that covered a seemingly myriad number of wars, conflicts, and confrontations that regularly threatened the very existence or at least the well-being of the planet and its struggling population.

Sometimes, the struggle was between the United States and the communist monolith spreading its tentacles across the globe, much like that of the earlier Japanese/German octopus and eagle of the late 1930s and early 1940s. The contest for world domination hadn't gone away or even diminished with the end of World

War II and the deaths of the Axis dictators. It simply changed species. Now it was the Russian bear stalking the American eagle. Each had its own family of minions that obtained intelligence for their master. For the United States, it was coveys of long-range intelligence-gathering aircraft like the P2V Neptune and other related peacetime maritime patrol types.

The British and Taiwanese (displaced mainland Chinese after the 1949 revolution that brought the communists to power over the world's most populous nation) had their own programs, each pointed toward listening in on their enemies' activities in Eurasia. All these allied aircrews and their planes faced the real danger of being intercepted and shot down by determined Soviet and Red Chinese fighters. The United States lost several reconnaissance aircraft from the later 1940s to the late 1960s, and the British and especially the Chinese also suffered quite a few losses. The Soviet bloc seemed immune to these terrible numbers and also seemed content to remain behind their Iron Curtain, letting the confounded Western powers spend their planes and crews in the fatal practice.

CAG-10 had a good deal. Most of its squadrons were located at Cecil Field near Jacksonville, Florida. The Fury and Cougar fighter squadrons shared the flight line with the ADs, AJs, and F2Hs. No squadron had to come from another field and everyone worked at getting the wing ready for deployment. Whitey was fortunate to have lots of talent in both his officer and enlisted ranks, especially in the area of delivery of their atomic weapons. Normally, the Banshee pilot made a 110-degree dive, releasing his bomb as he began an Immelmann, a half-loop ending when the pilot rolled from an inverted position to upright and wings level heading in the opposite direction from where he started the maneuver.[3]

One of Whitey's young aviators wondered if it would be better to complete the loop and continue on the original heading, thereby saving time and gaining a little more distance when lofting the bomb. It would be good to have a way of automatically releasing the bomb at the 110-degree point, lofting it toward the target. Lt. Bill Stewart, Lt. Merle Rice, and Lt. Dick Gordon helped with the design of the black box that would launch the bomb. With Lieutenant Gordon, Whitey finally went out to try the new system. As Whitey went inverted at the top of the loop and launched his weapon, Gordon called that the skipper was on fire.

Whitey rolled upright and shut down his port engine because he was getting a fire light for that engine. But Gordon called that he was still on fire. Whitey remembered an abandoned field about five miles away and headed for it. As he set up for landing, he could see the old concrete runway covered with weeds. Undaunted, he lowered his gear and landed.

He jumped out and could see that his aircraft was still burning. He took out his survival knife, dug up dirt, and threw it on the fire until it was out. It was a gutsy move considering the Banshee still had fuel and could have exploded at any time. Later, the fried F2H was placed on a flatbed truck and taken back to Cecil and eventually repaired. A subsequent investigation revealed that a break in the fuel line had started the fire.

Still, the Banshees kept their nuclear strike mission for which they had spent so many hours preparing. Whitey and six senior pilots even attended a survival course offered by U.S. Army Rangers at Fort Bragg, North Carolina. Some might think this precursor to the Vietnam-era camp at Warner Springs, California, was for wimps, but Whitey would certainly argue the point.

After three days of jungle survival training, they went through a survival, escape, and evasion (SERE) course, which culminated in a prisoner-of-war (POW) episode. Whitey was the senior officer in the group. The "enemy" guards tried everything to get Whitey to separate his men for various work details, promising "special treatment" for cooperation. There were also intense interrogation sessions, complete with loud music and firecrackers thrown into the POW compound. At one point, as they were being trucked to another area, Whitey's POWs were accosted by an individual who jumped on the truck's running boards wielding a knife, or so it seemed. It was a rescue hijacking. This action precipitated another phase of survival that even included butchering a chicken and calf.

OINC in Kansas

The flatlands of Kansas are not exciting examples of terra firma. Farms and wide prairies make up large percentages of the land and only occasional centers of populations like Topeka and Wichita offer relief from the otherwise desert-like landscape. Perfect for dependable year-round flying.

A center of military life in the Midwest was the naval air station at Olathe, some forty miles west of Kansas City. Originally, when the Navy was interested in establishing a base for its Naval Reserve aviation activities, a location was considered at the Kansas City airport. That choice was less than ideal, though, because of the growing air traffic in the area and the fog that often developed off the Kansas River and Missouri River.

A second choice was another field used by TWA as an emergency airport near Olathe. Free from fog, it was also outside the busy traffic area of Kansas City. The Navy bought the land and built its air station a thousand miles away from any ocean. Olathe became a busy training field during World War II, and in 1951 its runways were lengthened to accommodate jets and heavier transports.

Eventually, there were several reserve squadrons at the centrally located base, as well as the Navy's main air traffic control training facility where people who manned airfield towers learned their important work. It was the only place where ground control approach (GCA) was taught, an important part of any large base's all-weather operation.

Whitey's former skipper Jimmy Flatley, now a captain, had served a tour from 1950 to 1952 as the commanding officer of NAS Olathe, which had been established in October 1942 as a large training base. By the time of Flatley's arrival, there was also a Marine Corps training detachment and two Air Force units. The reservists came from surrounding communities in Nebraska, Missouri, and Kansas and had been part of the huge U.S. military establishment that had fought World War II only five years before. Olathe was also a major recruiting center for the Navy, gathering naval aviation hopefuls into a cadet program that helped the various pilot and crewman pipelines maintain their constant replenishment of the fleet communities.

When Whitey got orders to Olathe in March 1957 it was as the officer-in-charge (OINC) of the Jet Transitional Training Unit (JTTU), a self-supporting activity some seven hundred miles from its parent command, CNAVANTRA, the Naval Air Advanced Training Command. JTTU had been established in 1955 and its mission was to help experienced aviators who flew props to move over to jets before entering fleet jet squadrons or going to ships that operated jets. It wasn't a bad set of orders following a squadron command. There would be plenty of flying in an atmosphere conducive to daily flights, and it was a chance to show his leadership skills beyond the squadron as he helped groom experienced aviators as they moved to a new community.

The JTTU's course was barely two months long. Another course, of only two weeks, was designed for oncoming COs of carriers. It gave these captains a chance to focus purely on flying, almost like when they were newly winged ensigns and had nothing to do but fly and fight. They went away delighted and ready to assume their new command refreshed.

There were more serious intentions, such as taking the big new Douglas A3D Skywarrior on board. Still the largest aircraft to ever regularly operate from a carrier, the A3D, nicknamed the "Whale," was originally intended to be the Navy's carrier-based nuclear bomber. It was a handful coming on board even the larger *Forrestal*-class carriers then entering service in the mid-1950s, but especially the smaller World War II–era *Essex*-class ships, several of which continued serving into the mid-1970s through the Vietnam War.

Whitey recalled, "To try to operate day and night with an A3D off [the *Essex*-class ships was] a pretty demanding job . . . a lot of these pilots were sent [to JTTU]. . . . I got a message from a heavy attack wing commander saying that, 'I want a demanding course set up where the pilot has to keep his head out of the cockpit and not fly by instruments all the time.' Many multi-engine pilots weren't tactical pilots at all. They got in and they put their heads down and flew instruments."[4]

The senior course was well-received and often included simulated encounters with "MiGs," portrayed by Whitey and other instructors. These engagements were intended to show the older aviators the advantages of keeping one's head out of the cockpit and to keep looking around like tactical jet pilots were trained to do. The JTTU was flying single-seat F9F-6 Cougars, swept-wing developments of the Panther. Marginally supersonic, especially in a dive, the Cougar enjoyed a long, productive career in front-line Navy and Marine Corps squadrons, then later as advanced trainers.

One day Whitey was returning from a "MiG" hop. He was alone and happened to look to his left, where he saw four Cougars locked in a tight formation and in a loop! As he flew nearer to investigate, he recognized his four students, all senior captains, having a good time following each other in tight formation aerobatics. Men like Edward C. "Eddie" Outlaw and William F. "Bush" Bringle would all make flag, yet here they were behaving like newly winged ensigns out having a great time once again, free of the responsibilities of command, wringing out their new jet fighters. Outlaw was an ace with six kills. Bringle would retire with four stars.

Whitey led the four wayward aviators back home and they all quickly apologized for their group transgressions. But it was obvious they had gained a lot of confidence flying their new planes, and that, of course, was the mission of the course. The senior aviators loved flying the latest technology, and Whitey and his staff, aware of the great careers many of their senior "students" had, considered the course a great chance to indoctrinate and educate these leaders in the new aircraft that were entering the fleet and operating concerns associated with them. Whitey even went so far as to paint each captain's name on the Cougar he flew while at Olathe. Whitey was fortunate in having good instructors. As word of the courses at JTTU went through the Navy, he found he had only to ask for a particular individual and his orders were quickly cut. It was something like the Fighter Weapons School—Topgun—some years later.

At one point, Whitey's boss was the renowned Joe Clifton, a colorful pilot of World War II whose capabilities and outgoing personality personified the makeup of the classic fighter pilot, with kills over a Mitsubishi Sally bomber and a Zero in November 1943. Now a rear admiral with the nickname of "Jumpin' Joe," Clifton was the head of the Advanced Training Command, and since JTTU was part of that organization, Clifton was Whitey's reporting senior. Aggressive and tough, Clifton was not an easy man to please, but he wrote Whitey glowing fitness reports calling him "an outstanding Naval officer and aviator in every respect." He made special note of Whitey's senior officer course. "He deserves especial [sic] commendation for his tactful and pleasant manner in his association with the senior officers who undergo jet training . . . [he is] a temperate young man and is respected and admired by every officer and man in his unit."

Of course, Whitey has his own memories of Joe Clifton. Clifton took the initiative of getting checked out in the Cougar, even joining students as they "bounced" in preparation for carrier qualifications and often taking it upon himself to brief the group of neophyte aviators, many of whom were going out for their first traps in a first-line fleet fighter.

"He was always a great one for the troops," Whitey recalled, saying that Clifton liked the Kansas City area and also what the JTTU was doing. So he visited Whitey and his unit often. He would get everyone together in a hangar and jump up on one of the work benches. "If you never had a Joe Clifton briefing, this was worth the price of admission. He'd get up there and he'd preach Rocks and Shoals.[5] He'd get so excited tears would run down his cheeks. And the crew would have gone out and died for him right there. He was an absolute spellbinder."

One night Clifton and Whitey went in to Kansas City, first for a great KC steak and then to see the major league baseball game, which fit both men well as both were great athletes and Whitey at one time had been considering a career in baseball.

After a big steak dinner, Whitey watched as his boss finished off a whole pint of ice cream. Leaving the restaurant, Clifton sought out a cigar store while Whitey brought the car around. They got to the stadium, where they endured a major rainstorm. Undaunted, the two aviators sat in the pouring rain through the complete game. Joe was having a good time.

Whitey knew he could count on support from Clifton whenever he needed it, but he also found that he had to keep a good selection of tires because his boss was prone to blowing them. Apparently, Joe never quite got the hang of landing the new type of plane. He was used to putting down his Corsair or Hellcat with a decidedly heavy hand, but a jet required a slightly lighter touch or the brakes would lock at the high speed Joe used on landing, resulting in blown tires. To be prepared, Whitey maintained a stock of tires in the general areas where Clifton might be at any one time. The admiral's aide would call Whitey to let him know the boss's schedule and where to bring extra tires.

Stories of Joe Clifton were all around the Navy. He was simply one of the great characters the service, especially naval aviation, fostered. Unfortunately, he developed many health problems and suffered quite a few operations that involved amputations. He died in 1967 of circulatory problems at the young age of fifty-nine.

Running the JTTU had an unforeseen, though positive effect on Whitey's career. His appreciative senior students all rose to command carriers as well as other important units. Thus, when Whitey had to deal with them later on, they were predisposed toward a pleasant working relationship. When he later took CAG-10 on board the *Essex*, the CO of the ship, Capt. Tom South, wasn't a stranger. It also didn't hurt that the members of future promotion boards were also more than familiar with Whitey Feightner's accomplishments and personality. He had become more well-known than some of his contemporaries, and where a few of these equals were not promoted, he was, perhaps because the board members knew him better than others in the zone.

Whitey also had a good time flying, often adding sixty to eighty hours to his logbook every month. An odd aspect of JTTU's makeup was that there were no administrative types, no yeoman or personnelmen to handle the daily paperwork. Instructors filled in where needed as well as the regular maintenance troops and chiefs. There were quite a few chiefs, and many of these highly experienced senior enlisted leaders were doing a lot of work themselves. Whitey solved this problem by telling them they had to wear dress uniforms and instruct junior members rather than do the work themselves.

As good as the flying was, weather could also be a problem in the geographic center of the United States. The flat, often hot, then cold atmosphere could spawn deadly meteorological tantrums: tornadoes. Once, Whitey and a student were trying to get back to the field ahead of an advancing storm. They were on final, gear and flaps down, when the first lightning strike hit between the two Cougars and the runway. They landed and managed to get off the runway just as it began to pour. A deluge followed the two blue fighters as they taxied to the JTTU ramp. It was raining so hard that no one could come out from the hangar to direct them into their spot on the line. So the two pilots waited for an hour as more than eight inches of rain pelted them. The wheels of the Cougars were almost under water.

Out to the Mediterranean and CAG-10, or Whitey Briefly "Joins" the USAF

Finally, the time came for Whitey to join his air group, which was in the Mediterranean. During his brief duty at Jacksonville, he sampled several of the aircraft that equipped his air group, including the Douglas F4D Skyray, the current "hot rod" of American naval aviation, and the first A4D Skyhawks in fleet service, as well as his old friend the Douglas AD Skyraider. Then he prepared to head out to his new command.

Unfortunately, there was a political storm brewing. Commander, Naval Air Force Atlantic (AirLant), the Bureau of Naval Personnel (BuPers), and Sixth Fleet were embroiled in a contest of authority. BuPers—the Navy's personnel command—had ruled that CAGs should change whenever their tours ended, whether during deployment or ashore, at home. The tour was usually eighteen months but could involve training time as well as administrative and predeployment exercises, and therefore a new CAG might assume command perhaps four to six months before he actually took his air group to sea.

Rear Adm. Charles R. "Cat" Brown was commander of the Sixth Fleet. He had commanded two carriers in the Pacific during World War II and eventually rose to full admiral before retiring. Cat Brown did not agree with BuPers and demanded that CAGs finish their tours, return to home port, and then change. Commander Feightner could not relieve the current CAG-10, Capt. Al Morton, until the air wing and the carrier *Forrestal* returned to the United States.

Back at Jacksonville on February 13, 1959, Whitey was finishing an A4D hop when then Capt. (later Vice Adm.) Jerry Miller, who was operations officer for Rear Adm. Wendell G. Switzer, Commander, Fleet Air, Jacksonville, told him to pack his gear and get on board a twin-engine C-131 headed for Charleston, South Carolina. He would than take an Air Force C-121 Constellation that was going to the Mediterranean. Of course, Whitey had been ready for a long time and quickly got to the plane going to Charleston.

The Connie trundled to the runup area where it stopped. Two military policemen boarded the plane and asked for Whitey. He dutifully held up his hand and the two MPs showed him orders that would take him off this plane and place him in another transport as a special secret courier. He told the two enlisted men that he had orders to CAG-10 and that they couldn't do this to him. They quickly produced another paper that said yes they could and would.

Soon, the erstwhile prospective CAG-10 was on another aircraft, an Air Force C-124 Globemaster,[6] this time to play nursemaid to some badly needed equipment, apparently ten thousand pounds of top secret Navy electronics gear (he never did learn just what it was). Whitey was now a designated top-secret courier equipped with a .45-caliber pistol, and he was a passenger in one of the military's most awkward, certainly one of the most unappealing aircraft. It was one hell of a way for a Navy fighter pilot, an ace no less, to make his way over to take command of a front-line carrier air group.

Installed in the back end of the huge transport, sitting on a little bucket seat, his trusty .45 strapped to his waist, now courier Feightner resigned himself to his current though hopefully temporary situation as the C-124 made its way to the runway. It was 5:30 in the afternoon. It was going to be a long flight.

This flight was also going to be a check ride for a new Air Force squadron commander and his new operations officer, a new major who would eventually take over the squadron. There was also a major on board who had just finished C-124 school. The plane commander was an Air Force Reserve captain who was also the check pilot on his last flight before retiring as soon as they returned to the United States. In addition, there was the normal aircraft crew.

This being a check ride, the natural thing as far as the examining pilot was concerned was to chop an engine on takeoff. The big four-engine transport came to a screeching halt on the runway as the power came back. As Whitey held on, the lights returned. The crew had mishandled the dead engine and had turned the 124 into the mud alongside the runway. It was raining and now the big silver aircraft was at dead stop and slowly settling into the mud.

It wasn't until midnight that the ground crew could pull the Globemaster out of its ignominious position off the runway. Eventually, the plane was back on the runway and towed to the hangar, where the crew washed off the mud from the landing gear and inspected the transport for any damage. Everything was fine and the crew prepared once more for takeoff. This time, there would be no chopped engine!

The takeoff was uneventful and the course was set for the Azores. En route, however, another problem reared its head: the crew had run out of time. They had to get their rest. Air Force rule! They stopped at Bermuda for the night. They didn't forget about the Navy commander in the aft end. He was relieved of his duty and all the officers made their way to the bachelor officers quarters, where they all got a good night's sleep after deciding to take off somewhere around two o'clock the next afternoon. When they awoke, it was time for breakfast at the British-run Officers Club even though it was now the afternoon of the new day. Whitey didn't care for the menu, though, Hungarian goulash. He decided on an omelet with ham and bacon. It would later prove to be one of the best decisions he would make during the entire flight. Everyone else chowed down on the goulash.

After their meal, the travelers made their way to their aircraft. As they took off in the late afternoon, there was a loud bang and the crew shut down the number 3 engine, the inboard engine on the starboard wing. Back at his station in the aft end, Whitey was listening intently and figured that the check pilot was up to his previous shenanigans. But what had happened was that the exhaust stacks on that engine had come off and struck the cowling.

As the crew circled the base on Bermuda, they tried to decide on their course of action. They were too heavy with gas to return to the field, so they decided to circle to burn off fuel to get down to their max landing weight. After orbiting for twenty minutes, the stalwart crew decided they were close enough to Europe that they only needed three engines, so they exited the pattern and headed east, plodding along on three of their four engines.

The light was fading, and eventually the crew chief made his way aft to ask his Navy passenger if he would come up to the flight deck as per the plane commander's request. Delighted to leave his cold, cramped seat, Whitey got up and headed forward. He was not prepared for what awaited him. The captain check pilot was prone in his bunk, the victim of food poisoning; his color was actually blue. The major was on the radio talking to a doctor somewhere on the ground.

Meanwhile, the lieutenant colonel asked Whitey if he wouldn't mind flying the plane for a while because he wanted to go with the crew chief to check the engine that had been shut down. It turned out that they now figured they could use the extra engine. The C-124's wings were big enough to have a limited internal walkway that allowed the crew to check engines in flight. This unusual design would now come in handy. Whitey took his place in the left seat and was suddenly alone, flying this lumbering behemoth of an airplane. Of course, he was no stranger to big aircraft and was glad to help. He held the plane on autopilot at nine thousand feet and just simply flew along watching the myriad dials and gauges in front of him.

But now, the major took ill as the effects of the goulash got him too. Whitey had been at the controls for an hour, and it was now raining and the air was getting a little bumpy. The lieutenant colonel from somewhere in the starboard wing called Whitey to see if he could "crank up number 3." They went over the prestart checklist and Whitey dutifully went through the motions, watching as the oil pressure came up. They now had four engines. Just in time, too, as the rain began to intensify.

Just as Whitey was settling back into the routine of flying the Globemaster, the instrument panel in front of him began to shake. The air outside was getting fairly choppy and was giving the C-124 a chance to show why its nickname was "Old

Shakey." Calling on his vast amount of instrument time, Whitey kept the aircraft on course. A young naval officer appeared behind him and told Whitey he was the navigator. He had just received a weather report that said the bad weather was all around them and actually reached to the Azores, which they had just left. The young man was actually a j.g. from a destroyer, a black shoe, not an aviator, and he had been "loaned" to the Air Force for cross-training for some reason. Whitey asked him where everyone was.

The j.g. reported, "Well, the skipper's blind." When Whitey asked for more information, it turned out that the plane commander had been in the nacelle when Whitey cranked up No. 3 engine. A warning plaque that said not to be in the nacelle in flight because of carbon monoxide dangers was apparently ignored. The skipper got a really bad dose of the poisonous gas and had lost his sight. So a Navy commander aviator and lieutenant junior grade ship driver were in charge of a huge, four-engine Air Force transport over the Atlantic.

The crew chief finally came up to the flight deck and Whitey asked him to show him how to run the fuel system. The crew chief responded that they had plenty of fuel and that should not be a concern right now. At this time, a call came in that a B-17—there were still a few of these ancient World War II bombers flying as life savers and shepherds—was being sent out to find the wayward C-124 and guide it over to a field. The B-17 had all sorts of radar and once it found the transport, it could lead it to safety.

The controller asked Whitey, "Who are you?"

Whitey replied he was a Navy fighter pilot. Dead silence followed. Finally, Whitey realized he had better give them more information and said, "I am also a Pax River test pilot and I've flown a lot of big airplanes."

"Keep it coming," the controller finally answered.

Then the controller advised that he thought Whitey could fly out of the storm and make his destination, which was only twenty to thirty miles away. To add to the pressure, the doctor on the ground indicated that the lieutenant colonel had to be on the ground soon or he wouldn't survive the flight. After some discussion, Whitey asked if the airport had a GCA (ground-controlled approach) facility. The controller replied that the trouble was a strong crosswind and there was only one runway. In true fighter pilot fashion, Whitey replied, "Well, if you have a GCA, just pick us up and we'll get it on the ground some way." So here he was flying a large aircraft in which he had no time, in a storm, hoping to land at night on a restricted runway with a heavy crosswind. The next few minutes would prove interesting.

Whitey told the j.g. to go back to the major. The major gradually came up to the flight deck and got into the right seat. Whitey explained to him that because he knew the aircraft, it would be better if he could bring himself to make the landing at least. At first the major declined, questioning whether he could remain conscious long enough to get on the ground. Whitey replied that he would take over if he had to.

By this time the GCA controller had them and Whitey was now under his control. The major said he thought he could do it and he took the controls from Whitey and landed the airplane. As they rolled out, he told Whitey to get ready to take back the controls. But the Air Force pilot held on until they stopped, two days after Whitey first got his orders.

As soon as the C-124 stopped it was surrounded by trucks and people, all anxious to remove the sick people. The lieutenant colonel and the captain were rushed to sick bay. The rest of the crew and passengers remained overnight, and the next morning, a new crew flew the airplane—with Whitey still on board—to Rabat in Morocco. The word about the patients was they were doing well, which was not entirely true. The lieutenant colonel's illness was bad enough that he lost his command and had to medically retire from the Air Force. The captain, on the other hand, recovered from his food poisoning, as did the major and others passengers.

When the transport landed at Rabat, Whitey finally delivered his secret gear. Al Morton, the man he would relieve, was standing by with an A3D. He had flown from the carrier. Whitey got in and his next stop was the ship. Over the years, he thought about the entire incident. A courier had to have qualifications, and unfortunately for Whitey, he was in the right place at the wrong time, but he had all the requirements to be designated a courier.

For all his effort during the "Old Shakey" incident, Whitey never received so much as a thank you from the Air Force. Certainly nothing like an Air Medal or perhaps a Distinguished Flying Cross. In typical fighter pilot fashion, Whitey laconically entered in his logbook, "C-124 491024/4.2 hours/Bermuda Lages." Over time, if and when he retold the story to a friend or at an Officers Club bar, the tale got spun up beyond what had actually happened, which generated anger from the blue-suit crowd on the other side of the Pentagon. At one point, when both men were at the Fort Myer Officers Club one evening, the USAF chief of staff accosted him, asking for details and mumbling that the story just couldn't be true. But it was, in its purest form. The general listened as Whitey told him the story, nodded and seemed satisfied, though obviously annoyed, probably with his own people. He and Whitey were well-acquainted and the general knew there was absolutely no reason to doubt his Navy friend. Understandably embarrassed, the Air Force never offered any form of appreciation to the Navy commander for his stellar performance in helping to save a valuable transport and its crew.

To add a little salt to the wound, when he stepped onto the *Forrestal*'s flight deck any thoughts he might have had about finally taking over the air group were quickly blown away. The admiral commanding the Sixth Fleet had prevailed; Al Morton could not be relieved by Commander Feightner until they were all back in the States, or at least until the carrier had started its return trip back home, which meant there was another month to go. During that time, Whitey took advantage of his status as just another pilot and flew as many of his prospective group's aircraft as he could. It was a good chance to get to know the squadrons and their people. He also got the opportunity to check out as officer of the deck (OOD) under way. It was usually a requirement for more junior officers, but the commander wanted his more senior types to also have the knowledge and skill. It was a good chance to gain ship-handling skills, which would come in handy at a later, but soon to come, time.

Whitey understood and gained as much education as he could. If things went right for him, he would certainly have command of such a large ship in the coming future. The CO of the carrier, Capt. Allen M. Shinn (later Vice Admiral), was an excellent ship driver and he did his best to impart some of his knowledge to his senior officers. He showed them how to go alongside and refuel from other ships, and how to conduct a replenishment at sea. He commented, "I want to see these approaches made smartly and correctly up here."

Eventually, the ship made it home and Whitey relieved Captain Morton and assumed command of CAG-10.

Command of a Group and Disappointment

Whitey was looking forward to operating from the big *Forrestal*. Her large flight deck and the fact that she was a new class of carrier offered a great opportunity to fly the latest generation of naval aircraft from a major advance in carrier aviation. At the head of the pack was the Douglas F4D Skyray. With its unique (for the Navy) delta-wing shape, the F4D, or "Ford" as it was almost inevitably called, was a real hot rod with tremendous climb capability. Its major drawbacks were its limited range and its touchiness around the ship. Additional fuel tanks cured part of the duration problem, but its handling characteristics remained a problem for inexperienced aviators. It had, as Whitey put it, "beautiful radar," but "landing that airplane aboard at night [was] a real handful. And in fact, if you lost the rudder boost you were fortunate to be able to land it on the carrier at all."[7]

One new fighter that was beginning to join the fleet was Vought's world beater F8U Crusader. Long and sleek with a gaping shark-like nose-mounted air intake, the Crusader enjoyed a long and successful career as both a fleet defense fighter and tactical reconnaissance platform that saw considerable action in Vietnam as well as during the 1962 Cuban Missile Crisis. But in the late 1950s, the F8U-1 and the F8U-1P (fighter and reconnaissance variants, respectively) were the shapes of coming naval tactical aviation. Where the troublesome F4D served a relatively short time, the last (albeit naval air reserve) Crusader squadrons were not decommissioned until 1984 and 1987. The French, however, kept flying their Crusaders into the 1990s.

Whitey loved the Crusader. And why not? It was a true fighter pilot's airplane. It was fast, maneuverable, good-looking, and had four 20-mm cannon, not the .50-caliber machine guns still being stuffed into a few jet fighters of the time. At first, he didn't consider the F8U a good mount for new aviators, and perhaps he was right. Certainly the Crusader's early mishap record seemed to bear this caution out.

The Crusader was a thoroughbred, but skittish. It had to be respected and handled properly or it would not forgive any ham-fisted handling, especially close in around the ship. Whitey would gain membership to the informal but exclusive "4-C Club." Members had to have logged time in the F4U Corsair, the F7U Cutlass, the F8U Crusader, and the A-7 Corsair II, all Vought/Chance Vought aircraft. He had flown nearly every plane in the *Forrestal*, which included the F-8 (F8U), and during his future assignments in the Pentagon, in Naval Air Systems Command, he tried the new A-7 Corsair II.

He thought that the community was fortunate that no one had to land a Crusader on a straight-deck carrier. By the time of the F8U's arrival all the carriers were now using the angle-deck design, which really helped the early Crusader's problem with hook-skip, where the tailhook would occasionally bounce over the arresting cable and spoil an otherwise good landing. For a time, Crusaders also flew from the larger ships, like the four new *Forrestal*-class ships, but the new fighter could prove troublesome on the smaller World War II–era *Essex*-class carriers. One late version of the popular Crusader flight-jacket patch had the holder claim, "I survived 27 Charlies!" The 27C was a modified *Essex* carrier late in its career. The deck space was considerably smaller than that of the larger *Forrestal*-class ships.

As Whitey prepared to deploy with his group, two weeks into his command word came that CVG-10 would deploy on board the *Essex*, not the *Forrestal*. The decision was a shock to everyone in the group. Not only was the World War II carrier much older than the *Forrestal*, its flight deck and other spaces were much smaller. It was hard enough making a six-month cruise in the cubicle laughingly called a stateroom—that was what the officers bunked in!—but the 1942 *Essex*'s flight deck was never as expansive as the *Forrestal*'s "roof." It would make handling some of the larger aircraft much more difficult. Besides the A3D, the F4D, albeit a single-engine, single-seat fighter, still required a more powerful catapult for a comfortable launch.

A special, redesigned air wing was going to make the deployment. There would be one night-fighter squadron, VF-13 flying the Skyray, and a day-fighter squadron, VF-62 equipped with North American FJ-3M Furys, a fine aircraft that carried missiles. There would be no Crusaders or A3Ds, both of which later proved over and over in Vietnam that they could, indeed, operate from *Essex*-class ships. The bombing duties would be handled by VA-176 with Douglas Skyraiders and two Skyhawk squadrons, both flying the A4D-2 (later A-4B), Navy VA-106 and the first Marine Corps jet attack unit to go on board with Skyhawks, VMA-225. A detachment of VAW-12 AD-5W Skyraiders and a detachment of Grumman F9F-8P Cougars from VFP-62 for photo reconnaissance rounded out the lineup, along with HU-2 and its two HUP-2 helicopters for plane guard. It was quite a full roster, with a lot of different types, some of them getting old.

Whitey was not looking forward to handling the demanding F4D. He knew, and was told by people who knew what they were talking about, that the *Essex*'s old H-8 hydraulic catapults delivered a real jolt in the rear end. To see for himself, Whitey scheduled time at Patuxent so he could experience a few shots in the Skyray. He was not disappointed. The land-mounted cat gave such a shot that his knees would jam against his shoulder as he jutted forward against his harness. After about nine shots, he certainly understood the trepidation of some of his friends. Why the force of the hydraulics was so hard was never explained, even though the Skyray's nose wheel had increased tension on it to keep the gear down. The shot made the holdback fitting shoot into the air, leaving the nose wheel to fly up into the air and bang down again on the track once, twice, three times before the aircraft left the track.

Even though a fellow pilot had warned Whitey about the effects of the shot, Whitey blew him off, saying he had had plenty of cat shots and was ready for anything. But even with as much time as he had, Whitey couldn't have been prepared for the terrific slap of the cat at Patuxent. He nearly passed out, and as it was, his head hit the headrest behind him. After several additional launches, Whitey and his team decided the problem lay with the "geometry of the bridle on that shuttle."

The cable that attached the F4D to the catapult shuttle was such that after the plane was put in tension, tightened down just before the shot, the long nose gear strut was pulled way down and out of alignment. The minute the holdback fitting broke, right after the firing of the cat, the nose wheel actually left the track and then would bang down again not once, but twice before the aircraft came to the end of the catapult. The effect was to throw the pilot around so hard that if he held onto the stick, he would be thrown forward, then back, forcing the F4D to overrotate, and as it left the flight deck the shuttle tore off the F4D's fuel drain valve. The Skyray left the deck on fire.

This unusual and dangerous situation had to be addressed. Whitey took eight catapult shots on the field at Pax River. At day's end they had some idea of what was happening, but they actually didn't know about the fire aspect until they had gone out to a ship for qualifications. With all the trials and experimentation, it was decided that the pilot had to let go of the stick on launch. The pilot's torso harness was also tightened even more than usual before the launch. It was not a good feeling for a pilot to know he had to let go of his main control device, especially at night in the rain.

Returning to Norfolk to meet with the squadron COs, Whitey told the assembled air group, "You know, this is a pretty marginal situation." Whitey joined VF-13 for a CQ on board the USS *Franklin D. Roosevelt* (CVA 42). The decision was made to install heavier arresting cables to accommodate the heavier loads now in the fleet. A tripod hook was also installed that relieved the problem of sway that bit into the hook and created the possibility of the hook parting from the assembly.

With all the new changes, Whitey and the squadron made their day landings and then started the night traps. Whitey got five night recoveries and stopped to refuel. He and his aircraft were then lifted back up to the flight deck, where he could remain on the elevator to observe the continuing landings. The lieutenant colonel XO of the Marine A-4 squadron trapped, but as he hit the deck, the cable parted on the port side of the deck, even with the new heavier cables. The pilot must have known he hadn't trapped safely and immediately applied full power to take off again. But the cable had not come out of the tailhook, and as he ran up the deck, the aircraft flipped over onto the deck, killing the pilot instantly. Operations were halted for a while until the XO and his aircraft were cleared from the landing area.

Later, when the group got on board the *Essex*, all the changes had been incorporated, but another problem was waiting. There was not enough catapult pressure to launch aircraft with a full tank or an extra fuel tank, so launches had to be made with internal fuel only, which permitted only thirty-five minutes of flight time. Afterburners were definitely required for launch and they used a lot of fuel. They were, after all, taking fuel injected directly into the afterburner itself. It was an expensive way to gain more speed.

Then the holdbacks weren't big enough. One of the younger aviators had his holdback fitting break prior to launch. He didn't have enough speed to leave the deck and he simply taxied off and into the water and was lost. Unfortunately, Whitey had been standing by his F4D and he had turned his head to watch the launch. He was not wearing his flight helmet. His plane captain was already up in the Ford's cockpit holding Whitey's helmet. Not wearing a flight helmet on the roof was common practice at the time because the headgear shielded too much of the noise from pilots, who wanted to hear everything as they walked to their aircraft.

When the holdback split on the catapult, one piece flew back and struck Whitey square in the forehead. If he had not had his head turned, it would have probably been fatal. As it was, his sinuses were smashed and he had a small skull fracture. He had to be quickly flown off by the C-1 COD (carrier onboard delivery) back to Norfolk and then transported to the naval hospital at Portsmouth. AirLant Vice Adm. William L. Rees rushed it all through. He had just come on board to observe the action.

Whitey was in the hospital in Portsmouth for a month, and only when he passed a test in the high-altitude pressure chamber was he cleared not only to remain on active duty and not medically retired, but to continue flying and retain his new command. He "rode" the chamber up to 43,000 feet, where the technician "dropped" him while the flight surgeon watched to see that he did not suffer any ill effects.

Instead of calling a halt to the flight operations, the captain continued the CQ. Over the next few weeks, a heavier holdback was designed and it seemed to solve the problem. After that tragic start, everyone in the group, including Whitey, finally qualified and the group and ship were ready to deploy.

For a time, CAG-10 cruised in the *Coral Sea*. In between the *Essex* class and the *Forrestal* class was the three-ship *Midway* class: *Midway, Franklin D. Roosevelt,* and *Coral Sea*, CVB 41, CVB 42, and CVB 43, respectively. For a brief time they were the largest ships in the world. One day on the trip home after deployment, Whitey was on the bridge. The weather was sunny, but there was lots of wind following a frontal passage. The sea was fairly rough as the big ship plowed its way home. There was a quartering sea from the starboard side, and it made for a rolling, uncomfortable ride, not to mention an awkward deck that rose from the stern, then settled. Not the best offering for recovering aviators.

The ship was running fairly fast, at twenty-five knots, and the deck crew was respotting the flight deck with a McDonnell F3H Demon, a large, single-engine, underpowered fighter whose pilots normally launched with an open cockpit canopy in case they had to eject on launch. Two sailors, normally young junior enlisted men, had the Demon out on the starboard, aft No. 3 elevator, having pulled the big fighter from the hangar bay below the flight deck. This procedure was normal and observers waited for the sailors to start the lift up to the flight deck.

Suddenly a freak wave, a big swell, caught the ship under that elevator, raising it halfway up to the flight deck then dropping it just as fast. The elevator never stopped. It hit bottom then stopped, snapping its cable. With all that weight having dropped that distance, the elevator, the Demon, and the two sailors and their tractor were bounced right off the ship into the roiling water below. Fortunately, what could have been a fatal mishap at least ended happily when the two waterlogged crewmen bobbed up to the surface, thankful for their lifejackets that everyone was required to wear on the flight deck.

When the *Essex* reached the Mediterranean another operational problem appeared, namely not having enough wind over the deck to launch an F4D with additional fuel tanks, usually a single centerline, but sometimes with one under each wing. The old ship just could not get up enough speed, even with a catapult launch. Thus, the Fords were launched on days when there was a lot of wind anyway and on special missions. The Skyrays would climb to 40,000 feet where they would make a couple of intercept runs before recovering behind whatever group was returning.

The Fords were not that welcome in the group or the carrier. They demanded a lot of attention and were not good for anything except getting to altitude fast. The Skyray's thirty-five-minute duration certainly didn't make it a favorite of the ship's captain. They required a fast cycle on the deck, which was trouble for the flight deck crew.

One night, the weather was not good, and only Whitey and VF-13's CO launched. There were several A3Ds known to be airborne from another ship about to in-chop to the Mediterranean. The A3Ds were looking to get a radar image of the *Essex*'s battle group. Whitey and the CO decided to try to intercept the Whales. Each F4D carried one external fuel tank.

Whitey went first, using his afterburner as standard procedure. He was no sooner airborne than the CO, Cdr. Norm Berree, called, "CAG, you're on fire!"[8] Later, the investigation determined that the tank had not been tightened sufficiently and fuel was being siphoned out of the tank and back into the afterburner, where it ignited.

After the call, Whitey turned around to see that the entire sky behind him was aglow. He came out of burner and the fire went out. There was nothing else and the plane was flying normally. By now the CO was airborne. Whitey jettisoned the tank and the two aviators managed to intercept one of the A3Ds before quickly returning to the ship.

Whitey was becoming disenchanted with the futuristic Skyray. Another hop added to his bad feeling about the delta-winged interceptor. One night, he was up late with a few junior aviators practicing intercepts. It was raining heavily on the recovery, at around three in the morning. As the leader, Whitey trapped first and watched the next recoveries.

The No. 3 pilot, another first-tour aviator, was having a lot of trouble making the approach to the deck. He missed trapping twice, and on the third try he slammed his aircraft down onto the deck, breaking his nose wheel assembly and without engaging a wire. So he was obliged to make yet another circuit. He was now low on fuel without any shore fields to go to.

Whitey ran up to Prifly, the ship's tower and observation station in the island structure, to find the air boss, who is usually the third senior officer on board a carrier and the man in charge of air operations. Whitey told him he should rig the barricade. This heavy net is usually the last chance for any pilot having trouble landing. The LSO out on the stern brought the young aviator down low and slow in the driving rain. Fortunately, he actually trapped and didn't need the barricade.

When everything had quieted down, the captain sent for Whitey. Whitey made his way up to the bridge to see Capt. Tom South, who asked his CAG why he wasn't consulted before the barricade was erected. Whitey said simply that there had not been enough time to get Captain South involved. Whether the CO was satisfied with that answer, no one ever knew. Whitey had given an honest answer, but he knew he had broken protocol by not at least telling the ship's skipper what he wanted to do.

Later, he confided that if time had been taken to inform Captain South, they probably would have either tried one more time to recover the youngster—he was nearly out of fuel—or perhaps have him eject close to the ship at night in a rain storm, or they might have lost him altogether. Anyway, it would have been a risky business for all concerned. No matter how such an emergency was handled, Whitey felt that the F4D didn't belong on a small deck.

CAG of the *Essex*

Whitey's experiences with the F4D gave him a lot of food for thought for the Douglas interceptor. On one hand it was fast, could climb like the proverbial "bat outa hell," and had a nice armament array consisting of four 20-mm cannon and later, a spread of the AIM-9 Sidewinder missiles beginning to make their appearance on American aircraft. On the downside, and perhaps more importantly, it was hard to handle in close quarters like around the carrier, even on takeoff from a wet runway with a full load. It was incredibly short-legged and offered little room for expansion, no room for further development. He summed it up neatly. "[It] was a lot of fun to fly but it was just limited [in its] usefulness . . . and it was phased out pretty rapidly."[1]

Meanwhile, the Marines of VMA-225 were eager to make the first carrier deployment of their new little bomber, the A4D Skyhawk. But like any new aircraft, the Skyhawk had its share of problems too. It was not a good airplane to fly on instruments, and the Marines were not anxious to fly at night or in bad weather. This reluctance, of course, limited their usefulness to the air group, and it was something Whitey had to deal with immediately.

He talked to Captain South, the *Essex* CO, who told his CAG that he had to convince the Marines they had to fly in all mission weather. Whitey spoke to the squadron CO, Lt. Col. Arthur R. Boag, and he agreed to a four-plane group, with Whitey in the lead, with the skipper, the operations officer, and the XO in the other three aircraft. The day wasn't that great. The carrier island's mast was in an overcast, but the four A4Ds launched anyway.

The tops of the overcast were at 40,000 feet. Whitey kept the formation beneath the clouds until the other three aviators were joined up with him. Then he started climbing, right up through the gray scud until they broke through. Whitey and his charges flew around for a while before breaking up to return to the *Essex*. It was a simple flight but it evidently had the desired effect because the Marines had learned they could fly their new jets in most any conditions.

One of the highlights of the cruise was having President Dwight D. Eisenhower on board for a while. The president was visiting Greece at the time and stayed with the *Essex* until she reached Naples.

Whitey was enjoying his job as CAG. For one thing, it gave him the chance to fly any aircraft he chose from any of the squadrons in his group. For the two or three hops a day, he could choose from the AD, the A4D, or the FJ, which he loved, especially at night. He thought the Fury had the best cockpit for comfort, particularly at night. Although it was basically a day fighter, it was a true pleasure to fly after sunset. The Fury also had a longer range than the dedicated night fighter F4D. He flew A4Ds with the Navy and the Marine squadrons, and was able to hold his own during any bombing missions. He even flew the cranky Ford to visit—cross deck—the British carrier HMS *Victorious*. The Skyray was "too much airplane for that ship," he recalled. He later returned in a Fury and it was a much better fit as he trapped without any problems. He was impressed with how the Royal Navy ran its operation.

Part of the *Essex* task force went into the Black Sea, leaving the other part at Istanbul, Turkey. The sortie into the Black Sea was meant as a political statement that the U.S. Sixth Fleet could and would go anywhere in the open sea and intended to keep doing so. The trip also helped reinforce the Turks, who had to always remember that though they were part of NATO, they were geographically up against the USSR. It was also a chance to gather fresh intelligence on Soviet fleet movements, but especially radar mapping.

Flying with radar at high altitudes inbound over friendly territory, Whitey's crews would then drop down as they approached the target areas, where they knew that in a real situation interceptors would be taking off to reach them. Eventually, the route would call for the Navy aircraft to climb back up to altitude. This was an important phase because with unpredictable winds at that height, having a radar checkpoint you could depend on certainly made things easier at night.

The period did not have the highly developed airborne electronic countermeasures (ECM) we take so much for granted in the twenty-first century. Still, one or two ADs had early equipment that could record the signatures of Soviet emitters. Signal intelligence (SIGINT) was best left to the local governments and to the U.S. Air Force, which was more involved in gathering such important intelligence data.

Another important aircraft was the big A3D, which Whitey had flown at Patuxent and on board the *Forrestal* occasionally, but not from the *Essex*. He considered it "a gentleman's airplane with no surprises." With long legs and good radar capabilities, the "Whale" was an important part of the lineup. But, although it did fly from several *Essex*-class carriers during Vietnam, it could prove a handful for inexperienced aviators.

There was always concern about violating foreign air space, so to offset this concern, CVG-10 made a lot of weather reconnaissance flights, often under the cover of darkness. Although the Soviets had good radar coverage, Whitey's squadrons flew almost stealth-like, knowing there was little the Russians could do about any inadvertent intrusions. And if, as happened one time, they sent up a couple of interceptors, the Americans' radar let them know of the threat in time for Whitey to bring his flight back over northern Italy, go into a dive, and break out over the overcast and head back to the ship, leaving their pursuers to drop away over Yugoslavia. It was serious but good fun that tested everyone's skills.

Occasionally, Soviet aircraft would also test the intercept abilities as well as the general watchfulness of the American task force by sending snooper aircraft, usually Tupolev Tu-16 or Tu-95 bombers to approach the fleet or actually overfly it at a low altitude. These flight also gained valuable visual intelligence for the Russians as the interlopers' crews took photographs of whatever aircraft were on the flight decks.

Obviously, these intrusions could not go unchallenged. Carriers had standing combat air patrols always airborne on station, ready to intercept the bombers with the red stars. There were certain guidelines, etiquette if you will, associated with these "exercises" that were useful for both sides.

Whitey remembered:

> We always intercepted the Russians with two aircraft, one in trail, while the other flew alongside the Soviet bomber. We used hand signals to direct them away from the ship. If they kept coming, we'd fire our guns. And, if they still kept coming—or if they opened their bomb bays—we could shoot them down, although, fortunately, things never went that far. We never knew what they were going to do, and didn't want to take any chances.[2]

Whitey was relieved, and after racking up his last flight hour and carrier landing in a VF-13 Ford (8,000-plus hours and 836 traps), he prepared for a brief assignment at the Naval War College (NWC) in Newport, Rhode Island. The NWC was considered a plumb set of orders, a reward for past successes. It is located on the naval station overlooking Narragansett Bay, in the picturesque colonial sailing town between Boston and New York. Students completed various courses designed to round out their already considerable naval experience. But before actually reporting to Newport, Whitey had a few months before he had to arrive and was therefore temporarily assigned to the staff of CVG-4 from February to July 1960 at NAS Norfolk, Virginia.

CVG-4 was a training group, involved in not only flight operations but development of programs. During this period, the Navy was concerned about sharply rising accident figures. Accidents—usually called mishaps—were a problem, and while safety was always given occasional attention between the wars, it slipped through fairly large cracks during World War II. After the war, and with the introduction of jets and helicopters that required new flying techniques, especially around carriers, erstwhile safety programs seemed to be getting out of hand. Something—a program, increased vigilance—had to come about.

Welcoming NATOPS and Enjoying the Social Life in Newport

One new far-reaching development was NATOPS—Naval Air Training and Operating Procedures Standardization. Normally, each aircraft had its own flight manual, a book that presented a specific aircraft's procedures and parameters, which was fine as far as it went. But the new NATOPS program also provided standardized boundaries and numbers that everyone could use, no matter what aircraft or environmental conditions.

In the early 1960s, NATOPS was gaining a foothold, and the huge, blue-covered manuals were becoming part of every aircrewman's kit, whether officer pilot or enlisted crewman. While at CVG-4, Whitey became involved with writing the first NATOPS manuals. Since he and his friends were fighter and attack pilots, they naturally decided to produce NATOPS books for those aircraft.

This was also the time of changes to advanced training organization. Replacement Air Groups (RAGs) were also under development, which contributed to the amount of standardization being incorporated into flight training. This was all designed to husband the vast amount of knowledge and skill and to reduce the terrible mishap rate plaguing naval aviation. There was no standardized way of making sure everyone knew all the eccentricities of a particular plane or the model they were flying at the moment. NATOPS provided that knowledge and ensured that no one could fly an aircraft without passing its specific NATOPS course.

Whitey and his group developed the methodology whereby pilots received a good cockpit checkout, then learned procedures for starting the engine followed by various systems such as fuel-control, avionics, and engine. The methodology then followed procedures encountered during the first twenty hours of flying that specific aircraft.

To some, the NATOPS course and its accompanying manual may have seemed like a "glorified instruction manual," and perhaps it was, but Whitey believed it all laid out a syllabus of familiarization for the all-important first twenty hours of operating a particular aircraft.

The authors of the NATOPS manuals were all experienced aviators, many former squadron COs with many hours in the planes they were writing about. Whitey wrote the book on the F4D, with which of course he was very familiar. He also chaired the group that decided the aircraft they would initially concern themselves with and bumped it up to the admiral at Naval Air Force Atlantic Command. Eventually, the newly organized RAGs had the NATOPS books in stock and ready for each new class of aviators.

Besides the Skyray, the Banshee was a specific type that required a pilot's constant attention. As good as it was, the F2H occasionally had structural problems that could result in its losing its wings if flown past its limit. Engines and fuel-control operation were also of great concern at this time, and a full-blown NATOPS program addressed this vital issue.

Various other safety programs throughout the Navy, especially in naval aviation, were under development, and they all ended up complementing NATOPS. The Navy Safety Center was incorporated with the separate Aviation Safety Center to become the Naval Safety Center, well known today by anyone who serves in any capacity in the Navy, Marine Corps, or Coast Guard. Whitey saw all these beneficial changes come about during his time, and he was right in the middle of it.

Whitey left CVG-4 and reported to the Naval War College in July 1960. For someone who had spent most of his career as an "operator," he was facing a new challenge of classroom work studying tactics and attending quality lectures in a variety of subjects. War gaming was also an important part of the syllabus.

The social life at Newport also became an enjoyable fixture of the experience, and Whitey and Vi took it all in. Unfortunately, this period also saw a lot of snowstorms, and for three months—December to February 1961—it seemed to snow every Thursday for four weeks in a row.

Whitey had to maintain his flying currency, and he took a ferry to the air station at Quonset Point, where he could put in time in T2V two-seat jet trainers, or the SNB, the twin-engine prop Beechcraft light transport. He also took advantage of the flying to make a lot of friends and contacts that would serve him well in the coming years. Networking is what we call it now.

Finishing the courses at Newport, Whitey found he had orders to Washington, D.C., to the Bureau of Aeronautics, called BuWeps at that time, working for Capt. (later Vice Adm.) Frederick L. Ashworth in the Aircraft Division. Ashworth had been the Navy weaponeer in the B-29 "Bockscar" when it dropped the second atomic bomb on Nagasaki on August 9, 1945, effectively ending World War II when the Japanese sued for peace a few days later. He had also flown a P2V Neptune from the USS *Midway* (CVB 41) off Norfolk, Virginia, on October 5, 1949, making a nonstop flight to the Panama Canal then to San Diego in twenty-five hours and forty minutes, a distance of 4,800 miles. It was a chance for Whitey to work for someone he greatly admired as well as with a group of people with an equally stellar reputation.

Whitey Meets the Phantom II

Whitey's new assignment was to the oncoming McDonnell F4H Phantom II, the latest product from the St. Louis manufacturer of the Navy's F2H Banshee and the Air Force's F-101 Voodoo strategic fighter. The F4H had started out as a single-seat design but had become a large, two-seat, radar-equipped aircraft envisioned as a fleet defense fighter equipped with the new AIM-7 Sparrow III air-to-air missile but also tasked with a variety of other missions including reconnaissance and strike. It had, in fact, recently beat out Chance Vought's redoubtable shark-like F8U-3 Crusader III, which many people even today, sixty years later, consider the ultimate jet fighter.

Whitey's first meeting with Captain Ashworth was most promising. The captain told his newly arrived commander there was work for everyone on the project. Whitey got to meet James S. McDonnell Jr., "Mr. Mac" as he was known by everyone in the company. From their first meeting Whitey knew that McDonnell was a patriot who wanted to build only the best aircraft for his country.

The initial F4Hs—six aircraft—had been built and flown with the Sparrow. The AIM-7 and later the close-in AIM-9 Sidewinder were the only air-to-air armament the Phantom would initially carry. It was a far cry from the heavily armed fighters of World War II, as well as the usual four 20-mm cannon that naval fighters were using in the late 1950s and early 1960s. The decision to use only missiles remains controversial even today, and it resulted in disappointing combat records early in the Vietnam War.

As powerful as the F4H was, it was loaded out with different bomb loads, once even hoisting twenty-two 500-pound bombs into the air, setting a world record. Lt. Col. (later Lt. Gen.) Thomas H. Miller (USMC) took the F4H up for the record flight. The Navy had to decide just what the Phantom's mission was, and they ultimately decided on an interceptor, although Mr. Mac wanted the Phantom to be considered an all-purpose type, which is what the new fighter actually became during its long career. Engine failure in the first twenty F4Hs caused concern, and several redesigns, especially around the air intakes, resulted in what Whitey called "a reasonably strong airplane that had a clear-cut mission and yet was flexible enough that we could use it for a lot of things."[3]

He had also come up with the idea of a "panic button," something that would let the pilot jettison his stores—rockets, bombs, fuel tanks, associated racks—if he needed to quickly divest his big fighter of its underwing load in an emergency such as combat damage or improper shot off a carrier's catapult. Time is life, and shooting off the flight deck without enough power to reach flying speed calls for split-second action. The panic button was installed in the armament panel of the pilot's cockpit, and it was used occasionally, particularly in Vietnam by shore-based Phantom crews and also by carrier-based F-4 crews.

In October 1962, the F4H-1 was redesignated as the F-4B. A major change in the designation system for all U.S. military aircraft resulted in an all-inclusive alphabet and simplification of the complex numbers and letters applied to aircraft, especially by the Navy. Some sources claimed the change came from then Secretary of Defense Robert S. McNamara's annoyance at the hard-to-understand designations.[4]

The F-4 began attracting worldwide attention as it set several high-performance records. Other countries wanted the Phantom in the inventories. McDonnell's hold in record-setting fighters would continue with the USAF's F-15 in the mid-1970s, and on into the 1980s with the arrival of the F/A-18 Hornet carrier fighter and fighter-bomber.

In the meantime, Whitey and his group came up with new ideas for record flights with the Phantom II, all meant to showcase the brutish fighter's capabilities at all altitudes, from low-level sand-blasting runs over deserts to the bone-numbing cold of high-altitude assaults on space-flight heights. In all cases, the F-4 delivered, proving itself to be one of the most powerful fighters ever built.

Whitey enjoyed flying the F-4, saying, "It was exactly what I wanted except that I did want a gun . . . the weight, about 5,000 pounds, was such that nobody wanted to pay the penalty, and we had the Gatling gun.[5] Later on, we put it in the F-4E, an Air Force model." Whitey considered the F-4 a fighter-to-fighter aircraft. Its Sparrow missiles were not meant for the close-in engagement of a dogfight. Therefore, the AIM-9 Sidewinder was added to the Phantom's armament as well as extra wing slats to enable the F-4 to increase its turn rate.

Rear Adm. (later Vice Adm.) Paul D. Stroop was head of the Bureau of Weapons (BuWeps), and he took Whitey to St. Louis, to be joined by a group of no fewer than *eleven* Air Force generals. The object of the meeting was to discuss the delivery of F-4s to the two services. Although the secretary of defense had ordered the reluctant USAF to begin flying the Navy's new fighter, it was still under the Navy's purview, and for the moment, decisions regarding the number of the Phantoms were apparently left to the Navy. Of course, history would show how happy the Air Force would be with the Phantom.

The generals wanted the current list of F-4s, but so did the Navy, of course. Admiral Stroop offered them twelve as a gesture of interservice cooperation, saying the new Phantoms could be flown by the USAF to foster their new training and transition programs. He only asked that when the USAF's allotment began arriving in service that the junior service return the fighters in the same condition in which they received them. Not unexpectedly, the generals declined. At which point, Stroop rose and, gesturing to Commander Feightner beside him, dryly remarked, "I give my commanders more authority than all of you flag officers in this room." Whitey had great respect for this particular admiral and had commented on what a great leader he was.

Stroop continued, "Isn't there anyone here that can stand up and accept the offer?" None did, and with the excuse that they had to return to the Air Board, the generals left.[6] Three months later, the Air Force changed its collective mind and accepted the Navy's deal. The USAF changed the F-4Bs to fit their requirements. They modified the landing gear, which after all, did not have to withstand the rigors of landing on board an aircraft carrier. They removed the tailhook—at least for the moment—and changed the J-79-GE-8 engines to GE-15s, which offered slightly higher power. With other internal modifications, the F-4B became the F-4C, which the Air Force used for a considerable time, especially in Vietnam.

All these machinations resulted, in effect, in two production lines and an increased per-unit cost, which over time was partly absorbed by international sales that saw the Phantom serve with eleven foreign countries from Spain to Israel and Japan. Japan built the Phantom under license, and besides its wartime service in the

U.S. Air Force, Navy, and Marines, it saw considerable combat with the air forces of Israel and Iran.

Whitey considered the F-4 "a very honest carrier airplane." It was strong and able to withstand operating from a ship (the British Royal Navy was the only foreign service to fly the Phantom from a carrier). He appreciated the addition of another crewman behind the pilot, the radar intercept officer (RIO).[7] The Air Force tried crewing their Phantoms with two pilots, equipping both cockpits with control sticks and flight instruments. The arrangement resulted in something of a class system that the Navy and Marine Corps avoided by sticking to an arrangement where each man had a specific, complementary role in successfully flying the Phantom's multiple missions. It was definitely a time of change or transition not only in equipment but in the basic makeup of a flight crew, something Whitey and other fighter pilots of his generation had not had to deal with. But he supported the changes because they came with the new designs that promised increased capabilities in his carrier navy.

CHAPTER 13
SENIOR COMMANDS

By May 1962 Whitey had been promoted to captain. It had been twenty years since he had been commissioned an ensign and received his gold wings as a naval aviator. Now, barely six months shy of his forty-third birthday, he had achieved senior rank and position commensurate with his capabilities and experience. Not all men can say that with conviction, but the man from Lima, Ohio, could. His quiet but confident and cheery demeanor, as well as his ability in the cockpit, had carried him far, but there was more to do.

Besides serving as the F4H project officer, he had also become the project officer for the joint Navy–Air Force TFX (tactical fighter experimental) fighter, which eventually became the F-111 swing-wing fighter-bomber. Admiral Ashworth had noted in Whitey's annual fitness report of June 1962 that Whitey had demonstrated a "fine sense of timing, an exceptional ability to resolve conflicting demands and the ability to inspire maximum cooperation and effort [by] a large number of military and civilian personnel." He was, the admiral continued, "an outstanding example of a professional Naval Aviator." Anyone who has been in the service could certainly understand and appreciate such high accolades from a high-ranking superior officer.

Whitey spent two years as the head of fighter design. In that billet he was deeply involved with late development of aircraft like the F-8 Crusader and the later models of the FJ Fury, especially the FJ-4, which could carry a small nuclear bomb. Other new types included the E-2 Hawkeye, which is still very much a part of the modern carrier air wing.

The Nuclear Admiral and the TFX: Two Different Problems in Navy Colors

Whitey had a chance to deal with the Navy's arguably most curmudgeonly, cantankerous personality, then Capt. Hyman Rickover, who had his own agenda of fostering the nuclear submarine and the application of nuclear technology overall. Dealing with Rickover was a unique education for Whitey, as it usually was for anyone who met the eccentric pioneer of nuclear power. Rickover was especially interested in micro-circuitry and the large amount of money the Navy had invested in its research and development. A special effort was being devoted to airborne early warning and the new E-2 Hawkeye from Grumman. Captain Rickover wanted in on the benefits, hoping to associate them with his nuclear submarines.

Whitey discovered, again as did most everyone else, that Rickover always knew more than anyone on a wide variety of subjects and always let them know it! Whitey remarked, "When you were talking to Rickover, you were a spectator and you listened while he talked. He dominated every conversation I ever had with him."[1] Later, Rickover was designated an honorary naval aviator, which, Whitey remembered, greatly pleased the old admiral.

Whitey's attention was soon focused on the TFX, a troublesome project that ultimately was canceled for the Navy, but ended up as the F-111 swing-wing, long-range attack/strike aircraft. The Air Force gained a measure of service from the F-111 in both the original bomber and later ECM roles, but the design proved too troublesome for carriers. Ironically, Australia took several in export and flew the "Aardvark" from 1973 to 2010, thirty-seven years of service.

The TFX originally began as a project for the Air Force and a replacement for the F-105 Thunderchief long-range nuclear strike fighter. Secretary of Defense Robert S. McNamara, however, got into the act and decided the new design should work for the Navy and the Marine Corps too. Nine aircraft companies came up with early design proposals, but by January 1962, Boeing and General Dynamics (GD), which had grown out of the old Convair firm, were the ones chosen to proceed with their designs. Five months later, however, both proposals had been rejected by the Air Force and Navy. While the Air Force liked the Boeing design, the Navy didn't.

McNamara ordered a runoff, and in this increasingly complicated and frustrating logjam, the Air Force's selection board and council approved the Boeing design. But McNamara approved the GD design in November 1962. This close monitoring and meddling was to typify McNamara's management style of defense programs and was to surface most strongly in the coming war in Southeast Asia.

One of the problems was that the two services required different aircraft, although the two planes were generally the same in conformation and overall design. The Navy required larger wings and a slower landing speed, necessary for carrier operations. Its F-111B would also include an advanced fire-control radar, which became the AWG-9 that eventually made up the heart of the F-14, along with the AIM-54 Phoenix, originally meant for the TFX.

The TFX had a lot of potential. It was capable of multiple roles and was designed with a triple-redundant, fly-by-wire system. But the internal, politically motivated meddling by Secretary McNamara soured the project for many of the service representatives, especially the Navy.[2] Eventually, as noted, the plane's radar and AIM-54 Phoenix found a home in the highly successful F-14 Tomcat. The radar and expensive missile might have worked on the Air Force's YF-12 interceptor version of the highly classified SR-71 high-speed, high-altitude reconnaissance aircraft that itself enjoyed a tremendously successful career, bringing back valuable high-resolution photography and frustrating "enemy" attempts to shoot it down at every turn. But the YF-12 was also stillborn. By the time the Navy retired its F-14 fleet in 2006, no U.S. Navy Tomcat had ever fired a Phoenix in successful combat, although it had come close over the Persian Gulf.[3] Yet the Iranians had depleted their store of AIM-54s and had achieved several successes with it during their protracted war with Iraq in 1980–1988.

There was a lot of board and congressional interaction as things got heated, and any real developments in deciding who would build the TFX were held up. The two main contractors vying for the job were Boeing and General Dynamics. The Navy said that although both designs were acceptable, it wanted to go with Boeing, but Texas-based GD got the nod in November 1962.

Whitey felt there had been infighting and since the Air Force was going to get the lion's share of whatever came off the production line, its choice was the one that was ultimately made. The Navy fought the TFX at almost every turn. The plane was just too big for carrier use, even with its swing wings that would facilitate below-flight deck stowage. There were too many things that could go wrong with its group of advanced systems, including its cockpit escape module, which was too heavy and unreliable, especially for use over water. The plane the Navy really wanted was the F-14, which would incorporate the AWG-9 radar and its AIM-54 Phoenix. Like so many projects developed for or jammed down the throats of many individual services, the TFX was too big, too complicated, and much too expensive to meet its design requirements. The Navy finally got its dedicated long-range fleet-defense interceptor, the Tomcat. And Whitey would be involved with that too.

In the end, the TFX was a debacle for the Navy. Whitey and a small group of senior aviators helped prepare CNO (Chief of Naval Operations) Adm. George W. Anderson Jr. to testify before the Armed Services Committee, along with Vice Adm. Thomas Connolly, then Deputy Chief of Naval Operations (Air, Op-05). Whitey and the other two "helpers," civilian George Spangenberg, the chief of design at the Naval Air System Command (NAVAIR), and Lt. Cdr. John T. Shepherd, were kept in the CNO's office in the Pentagon so they could be immediately available to answer questions from Admiral Anderson. Capt. (later Adm.) Isaac C. "Ike" Kidd, the CNO's chief of staff, stayed with them. Spangenberg was the typist and quickly typed out the answers to be dispatched to the admiral.

Anderson gave Congress an earful that laid out the Navy's case for rejecting the TFX. He said as forcibly as he could that the TFX was just too heavy, inflexible, and not the right plane for the Navy. Although Congress was impressed, maybe even sympathetic, Anderson was relieved by Secretary McNamara, with whom Anderson had had, not surprisingly, a combative relationship.[4] Actually, this confrontation might have just been the final straw for McNamara, who was widely known to have been put out with his CNO following the Cuban Missile Crisis the previous

October.[5] He and Admiral Anderson had butted heads from the moment the volatile situation had developed, and certainly during the tense week of October 24 when it seemed the fate of the entire world hung in the balance, the two men were constantly at odds. Following Anderson's retirement, President John F. Kennedy appointed him ambassador to Portugal.

Whitey also believed that a lot was done to get all the Navy players out of town. Besides forcing the CNO's retirement, the Navy sent Shepherd and Whitey out to far-flung deployments. There was little that could be done about George Spangenberg, however, as he had just received the Distinguished Navy Civilian Service Award in 1963. It was one of several such awards he would garner in the next forty years before his death in a car accident in 2000.

One other personality that figured in this administrative drama was Capt. Elmo Zumwalt (later CNO and admiral). He was in charge of the study that killed the Navy's TFX. While the Navy was desperately trying to distance itself from the TFX/F-111, it was also trying to foster interest in its new F-14 Tomcat fleet-defense fighter, which would replace the F-4 and F-8.

While all this was going on, as the project officer Whitey had the chance to actually fly the Navy's F-111B. He was particularly interested in the escape capsule design that did away with individual ejection seats and instead placed explosive prima cord around the breakaway points. When a crewman initiated ejection, the cockpit was simply cut from the main fuselage and launched as a complete capsule. Whitey appreciated the design although it took a lot of time to smooth it out. He noted that when the F-111 was deployed to Southeast Asia during the Vietnam War, several naval aviators were sent along. Two of them were actually killed in action.[6]

There were problems with the plane's terrain-avoidance radar, which placed the plane and its crew in a bad position when flying in bad weather. But Whitey liked the plane's low-level flying capabilities. He once took another pilot with him. The F-4 chase plane was flown by a former Marine Corps aviator, Lt. Col. Philip F. Oestricher, who had flown F4Ds with VMF(AW)-114 in the fleet and FJ Furys in the reserves, and had graduated from Test Pilot School as a civilian member of Class 44 (1966). Whitey flew a low-level mission west of Dallas, racing along at near Mach 1. It was a bumpy ride, and the chase plane's fuel tank lost its tip fairing. The General Dynamics test pilot in Whitey's right seat was along for the ride, and Whitey was happily demonstrating the plane's different capabilities while they flew below an eight-hundred-foot overcast.

Whitey headed toward a mesa, racing along at near the speed of sound at two hundred feet. The F-111 was under control of its terrain clearance system and should have cleared the mesa easily. But as the aircraft began to raise its nose to go above the big stone, Whitey caught a needle movement from the corner of his eye. It was the little dial that showed when the terrain clearance system was engaged. He gaped as the needle flipped down to zero, indicating that the terrain system was disengaged and now it was up to human skill to fly the plane over the mesa. He and the company test pilot began flailing around and quickly completely disconnected the system as the plane shot up into the air.

Rocketing up into the overcast, Whitey finally got everything settled down and flying level. "At those speeds," he said, "you just breathe on the stick and you're gaining 500 feet." After everyone's breathing returned to normal, Whitey indulged in some dogfighting, then went back to the field at Dallas to make four ground-controlled approaches (GCAs). He had plenty of fuel, noting, "The airplane had long legs."

Back to Sea

Following his tour at BuWeps, Whitey got orders to Carrier Division 2 as the operations officer in the USS *Enterprise* (CVAN 65), the world's first nuclear-powered aircraft carrier.[7] The *Enterprise* was already deployed to the Mediterranean, and Whitey was actually replacing an operations officer who had come down with medical problems. Whitey always believed, however, that Secretary McNamara was trying to get the people involved with the TFX mess out of Washington as payback for opposing his support of the trouble-ridden program.[8]

As it turned out, Whitey would be working for Capt. Frederick H. Michaelis and his boss, Rear Adm. Bill Martin, who had taken over Carrier Division 2 in May 1963. Both senior officers were Pacific War veterans. "Mike" Michaelis was an ace with five kills in Hellcats in VF-12, and Bill Martin was a TBF squadron skipper (VT-10) and TBMs while CAG-90. Both men had great combat experience and were highly respected throughout the Navy. Whitey remembered, "We called them 'two of the true leaders of naval aviation.' "

Martin had been one of the original and leading exponents of night flying for the carrier navy, and he then pushed the operation into all-weather flying as well. Whitey was delighted to see the two men and the feeling was mutual. In fact, Rear Admiral Martin told Whitey he had asked for him when he knew he had to replace the carrier's operations officer.

To his surprise, Whitey learned that he would be able to take his wife along on the trip over to the Mediterranean. It was an all-expenses-paid, ten-day sea tour in a Navy transport. Whitey and Vi detached from his tour in Washington in July 1963 and headed for their new assignment. It was a dream tour for Whitey, working with people he knew and enjoyed, as well as being back in the carrier navy.

The *Enterprise* was actually in Naples when the Feightners arrived in the Mediterranean, so Whitey reported immediately and began his new assignment. From the beginning, he liked his new job and considered it one of the best of his career. Besides the *Enterprise,* the carrier *Saratoga* (CVA 60) was also in the division. Capt. John Lacouture was the Sara's skipper. The *Saratoga* was part of the four-ship *Forrestal* class, all fossil-fueled, while the *Enterprise* and its division was something of a showcase because along with the carrier were two other nuclear-powered ships, the cruiser USS *Long Beach* (CGN 9) and the frigate USS *Bainbridge* (CGN 25). Along with these three trendsetting surface ships, the nuclear submarine USS *Seawolf* (SSN 575) occasionally operated with the divisions.

The deployment was actually nearly over. Both carriers were due back in the States in two months, with a quick replenishment and second deployment back to the Mediterranean. Whitey left Vi in Europe, which was fine with her as she used the time alone to travel and pick up several languages. She ended up learning enough French, Spanish, Italian, and German to make her way comfortably during any trip to these countries.

One of the little projects Whitey and his friends worked on was outfitting Admiral Martin's "barge"—his personal motor launch—which they considered inappropriate for their boss and friend. Captain Michaelis and Whitey got the barge into showcase shape, adding chrome and macramé to areas on the barge. They knew Admiral Martin enjoyed traveling around to different ports, making appropriate visits, and he was pleased with his new conveyance. Unfortunately, when Admiral Martin paid a call on Vice Adm. Bill Ellis, commander of the Sixth Fleet, they all were unprepared for Ellis taking such a shine to his two-star's barge. He told Admiral Martin that he would send his aide over the next morning to effect a swap. Not the smoothest of ways dealing with a subordinate, especially among flag officers, but the next morning that is exactly what happened!

Whitey and his coworkers enjoyed this time of exercises and testing each other's skill as well as those of their Soviet shadowers. The American task force could normally keep its speed up and maintain a reasonable distance from the Russian adversaries. One time, the Soviet intelligence ship that normally followed the carriers, trying to gather as much information as it could, was proving to be more than its usual annoyance. The task force was in the eastern Mediterranean, headed north to the Aegean Sea.

A message came in from LantFlt tasking Admiral Martin's force to find out what the Soviet ship's captain's true intentions were and where was he going. In turn, Whitey sent a message to the *Bainbridge* tasking the frigate's captain to follow the intelligence ship. Accordingly, the frigate turned 90 degrees and headed for the trawler. The *Bainbridge* was gone for a month. It was a flexible situation. The frigate had its provisions and didn't have to be concerned about refueling. Apparently, now having the tables turned and having acquired its own trailer, the Soviet ship eventually entered the Black Sea via the Aegean Sea and the Dardanelles to seek the safety of a nearby port and lose its unwanted American company.

There were a few disadvantages to nuclear power. While the new technology allowed uninhibited movement, it also meant longer deployments or diversionary trips. Shore leave and port visits and their morale-boosting remedies to lengthy at-sea periods became less frequent occurrences, permitting crew morale to plummet. It was plain that Admiral Rickover in Washington wanted the task force to make a longer round-the-world cruise, unrefueled, nonstop with its destination back at Norfolk. Admiral Martin did not agree with this plan, and he fought it with a lot of messages, all to no avail. The *Enterprise* returned to Norfolk on September 5, 1963.

For the next few months, her crew went through the normal postcruise activities of refitting their ship and beginning preparations for her next deployment in 1964, which would be that round-the-world cruise under nuclear power, named Operation Sea Orbit. Planning for this ambitious cruise began right after the new year. The Navy's three nuclear-powered surface ships—*Enterprise, Long Beach,* and *Bainbridge*—would traverse the globe without refueling. It was to be an important demonstration of nuclear power in general and more specifically the United States' command of the seas.

The only major interruption occurred during the week of October 20, courtesy of hurricane Ginny, which marched up the East Coast with what seemed to be a dead eye on the Tidewater area, including Norfolk and its huge nest of ships. Its wind gusts were up to ninety-five knots and it was dropping copious amounts of rain. But this storm couldn't seem to make up its mind as to exactly where it was going. For nearly a week it meandered around off the North Carolina coast, looping and tying itself into a progression of meteorological knots before straightening out and making a more direct line north. During this time warnings went out, including one to the Norfolk area on October 20. These warnings are actually advisories, usually suggesting the recipients head for the open sea to ride out the storm instead of having their boats slam against their piers, which could result in heavy hull damage.

After returning from the 1963 deployment, Whitey had the chance to take care of a double hernia that had been repaired before but was now still giving him trouble. He went over to the Portsmouth Naval Hospital for the operation, after which he was returned to the ship but prohibited from going ashore. He couldn't walk any stairs or climb ladders, and thus he was a prime candidate for a long period of standing watch in port. He understood and accepted the daily responsibility.

That Sunday afternoon, though, with things fairly quiet and being the senior officer on board, he found himself responding to the hurricane alert, requiring the *Enterprise* to get under way, a standard procedure to keep a ship from being pounded against her pier in the storm. It was safer to ride it out at sea. Suddenly, the commander aviator became the CO of the Navy's newest and most powerful ship. He may have been attached to the Carrier Division staff, but he *was* the duty officer—the CO's representative with considerable authority—*and* the senior officer on board. There was no time to waste, even though Captain Michaelis as well as the XO and Admiral Martin were all ashore. It was up to Commander Feightner. Helped by his top-notch crew, the carrier was soon moving out toward the Virginia Capes and relative safety as the hurricane advanced toward Hampton Roads. Whitey sent helicopters ashore to find Michaelis and Martin. They found the two senior officers but could only get Captain Michaelis back on board. A lot of shore-leave sailors were also left on the beach, but the carrier made it out in time and safely. As it turned out, Ginny eventually turned northeast, heading out into the Atlantic, barely brushing the remaining U.S. coast.

Later, Whitey mused over what he had experienced: functioning, in effect, as CO of the Navy's—indeed the world's—newest and biggest, most powerful warship, and under way, too. Later, he thought how different was the military life from that of a civilian. Training and understanding of established procedures went a long way in preparing one for emergencies that many people could never face.

The *Enterprise* departed Pier 12 on February 8, 1964, crossing the Atlantic, in-chopping to the Sixth Fleet on February 19, and entering the Mediterranean on February 22. The carrier quickly began a series of exercises and by April was designated the flagship for Task Force 60. Throughout these long months, preparations for Sea Orbit were well under way. By May, Admiral Martin was relieved by Rear Adm. Bernard M. Strean, always known as "Smoke" to his contemporaries. "Smoke" Strean was a former skipper of VF-1 and a veteran of the air campaigns of the Marianas and the Philippine Sea. Strean was also given another "hat" as Commander TF 1, the world's first nuclear-powered task force.

The *Enterprise* rendezvoused with the *Long Beach* and the *Bainbridge* on May 13, and the three nuclear ships again went through long periods of tests and exercises before the history-making Sea Orbit cruise. Whitey was in on all the meticulous planning, all of which would stand him in good stead throughout the coming months and later in his career.

A series of port calls throughout the Mediterranean allowed for a lot of interesting liberty beloved by all sailors. There were, however, the inevitable unexpected events. A young aviation boatswain's mate, ABH3 J. M. Davis, was blown overboard from the *Enterprise* on the evening of July 20. The crew of the ship's Kaman H-2 helicopter retrieved the young sailor within two minutes.

Later, Admiral Strean wrote, "The purposes of Operation Sea Orbit were: To test the capability of these nuclear powered ships to maintain high speeds for indefinite periods over long distances in all environments of weather, seas, and seasons, without refueling or replenishment of any kind . . . [and] to enhance the military and political image of the United States."[9] The cruise would dispense with the normal underway replenishments to test the nuclear ships' ability to survive and keep going in the face of a global nuclear war with the Soviet Union. The cruise route would involve going down the western coastline of Africa, around the notorious Cape of Good Hope, across the Indian Ocean and Pacific Ocean, and around Cape Horn at the bottom of South America, and then up along the eastern coast of the United States back to Norfolk.

Admiral Strean took Carrier Division 2 around the Cape of Good Hope, and from the tip of Africa he headed for India and Australia, then Rio de Janeiro in Brazil. It was an impressive display of American sea and air power that amply demonstrated to the world that the United States could bring its considerable muscle to any part of the world whenever and wherever it wanted.

Once they got to Africa, the task group moved along the coast, giving occasional air power demonstrations, or inviting kings and dignitaries out to see American naval aviation close up. The air shows were impressive, even the C-1 CODs (the carrier-on-board delivery cargo planes) participated, flying four in to the country to bring out the king and his ministers. Two RA-5s would come from dead ahead, five miles right on the water at Mach 1. As they aimed right for the *Enterprise*, they would split, left and right, as they made the ship's island, resulting in a big sonic boom. And that was only the beginning.

Some sixty airplanes were airborne for each of these shows. An aerobatic team of four A-4s would fly by in formation, then break to perform various maneuvers. The cruiser *Long Beach* would run out its anti-aircraft missiles, while a Crusader came in at 12,000 to 14,000 feet, dead ahead of the ship. F-4s would be coming in from astern, heading straight for the lone F-8. Only when everyone got to the island did the Phantoms pull straight up into individual Immelmann (a standard aerobatic tactical maneuver attributed to World War I German aviator Max Immelmann) turns, ending up behind the Crusader to simulate firing missiles in a dramatic demonstration of an intercept.

The finale came as the *Bainbridge*, five miles ahead, would turn directly and head for the *Enterprise*, with all ships making thirty-two knots. Just as the bows would have crossed, the *Bainbridge* would go right full rudder, into the carrier, and at only three or four hundred yards off to starboard. The frigate would seem to stand still, dead in the water, rolling as its missiles came to bear on the huge nuclear carrier. But the show wasn't finished.

An AD Skyraider would run across the whole force, dropping flares, while the Crusader and Phantoms came up the port side, firing their Sidewinders as they came to the bow. The ADs would then demonstrate their loft bombing techniques to close the demonstration. Admiral Strean was not impressed and called to move the Skyraiders closer, which resulted in shrapnel coming on board the *Enterprise*! Today, with all the emphasis on aviation and ship safety, such an all-out show of force would never be allowed. Shrapnel hitting the carrier?! And high-speed maneuvers over another fast-moving fighter? But, times were, indeed, different in the early 1960s.

The task force put on twenty-eight of these power shows as it went around the world from Africa to India and onward, all the way home. The stop at Capetown, South Africa, proved especially interesting. The sea was rough, heaving up and down with twenty- to thirty-foot waves. It was, after all, the monsoon season. The little South African navy destroyer *Simon van der Stel* (D 237), carrying its chief of naval operations Rear Admiral Hugo H. Biermann, could not make the rendezvous, so the *Enterprise* went in to meet it. The rain was coming down in buckets and the little ship was struggling between the massive waves. Yet a small band stood in the deluge to play honors as their admiral lifted off in a tiny Westland helicopter not much bigger than a bubble-top Bell from one of the gun mounts. The CNO enjoyed lunch on board the big American nuclear carrier with Admiral Strean. Finishing his meal, the big Dutch admiral thanked Strean and said, "And now, I'll go back to get ready for your return." Strean turned white but said only, "Very good." The two admirals boarded the little helicopter and flew over to the destroyer so that the American could "enjoy" a cup of coffee with his South African hosts.

As the task force moved along the coast and through the Mozambique Channel into the Indian Ocean, the task force now headed toward their next important stops, Kenya and Pakistan. This portion included the excitement of the crash of an H-2 off the carrier's bow after losing power. Fortunately, all four helicopter crewmen were rescued. The little helo floated upside down and a motor whaleboat from the *Bainbridge* had to tow it back but the cable parted as a crane tried hoisting it out of the water, and the H-2 sank in forty fathoms.

The task force then participated in an exercise with three Pakistani ships, which then escorted the Americans to Karachi, West Pakistan, for a port visit. Rough weather conditions, including six- to eight-foot swells, prohibited any but the smaller *Bainbridge* from entering port. The *Enterprise* and *Long Beach* had to anchor several miles out. But the distance didn't keep the task force from launching an impressive air show for their hosts before continuing down the west coast of India.

The Americans participated in an exercise with the Indian navy. In the middle of the games, one of the Indians' new Soviet-made Kamov helicopters had one of its engines fail. The big helicopter dropped into the sea and capsized, trapping the crew and passengers. The helo's flotation bags deployed, however, and Captain Michaelis decided to try to rescue the people inside the helicopter. There were several SEAL teams on board the *Enterprise,* and they went to help the recovery effort.

Coming alongside the overturned aircraft, sailors could see brown shapes moving in the water. They were sea snakes, common in that part of the world, three to four feet long and highly venomous. The SEALs did their best to shoo the snakes away by splashing. Fortunately, the sluggish snakes proved not to be a real problem, and the SEALs and their partners in the rescue teams got everyone out of the helicopter, which was eventually brought on board the *Enterprise.*

As things calmed down, the task force began its final legs home, visiting Indonesia and then Australia, always a welcome break for American ships. The welcoming Aussies overextended themselves for their fondly remembered World War II comrades-in-arms. The air show on September 4 was considered one of the best in the entire cruise, and it was viewed by what was estimated to be some 100,000 enthusiastic citizens of Sydney. A visit to New Zealand was met with the same enthusiasm as in Australia.

The task force next made the normally hazardous trip around Cape Horn, keeping between two weather fronts and avoiding the terrible weather that characterized such voyages. Most of the ships made it without incident, but the *Long Beach* was slow making a turn and got caught in the trough between two huge waves. The big cruiser rolled twice, the first to 40 degrees, the second time its mast hitting the angry water. It looked like the ship was about to go under, then it righted itself as the CO poured on the power and pulled his ship upright. Watching from the bridge of the *Enterprise*, Whitey had thought the *Long Beach* was lost.

Traveling through Cape Horn signified the task force was finally on its way home, with visits to several South American ports. Now, with the task force headed up the east coast of South America, Admiral Strean called Whitey to the bridge one day. Whitey had been working on messages for Rio de Janeiro indicating their projected arrival time at the Brazilian city.

It was early, just before sunrise. As the men on the bridge stared, the entire ocean around them was covered with leaping tuna. The incredible display lasted for thirty to forty minutes as the task force entered into Rio's harbor. It was the beginning of Mardi Gras. The *Enterprise* steamed into the harbor, which was a little close for the big carrier. The rocks seemed to be close enough to touch, but the water was clear enough to see below the waterline. The Brazilian navy's sole carrier, the former British HMS *Vengeance*, now the *Minas Gerais*, was a neighbor, complete with aircraft, including a squadron of A-4s.

Later, after all the shore-leave sailors were reclaimed and on board, the Americans left Rio and headed north toward Norfolk, Virginia. Sea Orbit ended on Sunday, October 3, 1964, as the *Enterprise* and *Long Beach* returned to Norfolk and the *Bainbridge* to Charleston, South Carolina. These ships and crews had steamed 30,565 miles. The *Enterprise* and its cohorts returned with surplus fuel and ammunition and food, vindicating nuclear power.

Too soon, the *Enterprise* and her ships began their second cruise workup period. Word came that Admiral Rickover was coming down from Washington and would be joined later by a group of influential Congressmen. The officer of the deck woke Whitey when Rickover arrived at the brow at Pier 12. It was 3 a.m. The old admiral came on board in wash khakis and Whitey greeted him, saying that Admiral Strean would join them presently.

"I don't want to see him," Rickover grumbled. "I want a haircut."

After waking the poor barber, who gave his famous and inconsiderate customer his trim, Whitey asked if the admiral wouldn't like breakfast in the flag cabin. It was now 5 a.m. Things continued to take on an Alice-in-Wonderland feeling as during the meal, Rickover tugged at Strean's sleeve.

"I want this task force under way at 10:30 this morning," Rickover said. Of course, Strean was no fool and probably checked with the CNO two hundred miles to the north to make sure that he was supposed to follow the engineering admiral's demands. "I have a group of Congressmen coming down," Rickover continued, "and we've got to convince them of the efficacy of nuclear power. We have to give them a demonstration."

His command triggered a mass exercise and flurried activity, but the task force, including the three nuclear ships, was under way heading for the training area of the Virginia Capes, or VaCapes as it is universally known throughout the fleet.

Still in demand mode, Rickover now said, "I want them line abreast." After the three nuclear ships were in position, incredibly, he now called for each ship's saluting cannon to fire and start what amounted to a drag race! Rickover took the Congressmen out to the fantail and began describing the proceedings.

As crazy as it all was, there was some sort of method to Rickover's madness. The immense power of their nuclear power plants really made the ships dig in their sterns as their screws took large gulps of the Atlantic and threw them out more like twenty-five-foot speed boats than multithousand-ton warships. At eighteen to twenty knots, there were rooster tails behind the carrier and its two companions. As Whitey later recalled, the event had to be seen to be believed.

The *Bainbridge* quickly took the lead as the ragged formation reached thirty-three knots. Suddenly, Rickover ordered, "All stop!" The *Bainbridge* "squashed" in the water, simply stopping almost on the proverbial dime. The other two larger ships' momentum carried them ahead of their smaller companion. Rickover's congressional visitors were duly impressed. For all his faults in personality and relationship to people around him, Rickover enjoyed the rare ability to carry Congress in his pocket. There were people who worked closely with the unpredictable engineer who liked him, indeed got along with him, after a fashion.

As the task force prepared for another deployment to the Mediterranean, Admiral Martin received his third star as Sixth Fleet commander. Whitey jokingly maintained that Martin simply wanted his special barge back. Admiral Strean started out with his task force but became sick and remained in his quarters for most of the deployment.

Whitey loved the *Enterprise,* successor to his wartime CV 6. So did others. The nuclear carrier had many visitors during port visits. It seemed to take everything in stride, except for one day in the Bay of Biscay, off France's west coast, an area known for its rolling seas. This time, the ocean impeded the carrier's speed. There was also a fair wind from the west, which further hindered progress. As the ship tried making a turn to port, it got hung up and began a 17-degree roll, the flight deck nearly touching the water.

The overall tour in the *Enterprise*, and especially how he had handled the emergency departure in the face of an advancing storm, would help Whitey in the last years of his colorful career.

CHAPTER 14
DRIVING HIS OWN SHIP

Whitey's next assignment, about midway through his time as a captain, was a big step: command of a ship, something even beyond leading a squadron or air wing. Following the normal sequence, he was assigned to a smaller "deep draft" ship, in this case a fleet oiler, the USS *Chikaskia* (AO 54), an older twin-screw but good size ship that carried two million barrels of fuel, a fairly large amount. Fleet oilers are important commands. They deploy with their task force and are in constant demand. After they "give" their load of oil and fuel, they have to be replenished by other ships and so are important middlemen during any time at sea. After such a command, one usually moves up to a larger ship, usually a carrier (for an aviator, since carriers always had to have a naval aviator in command). In the task force, the AO's role is important, although less glamorous.

The *Chikaskia* was in overhaul at the Portsmouth Naval Ship Yard across the river from Norfolk, so Whitey had some time. He went to the "toot and whistle school" to gain some education in driving a ship. He had none, other than what he had picked up in the *Enterprise* under Mike Michaelis's tutelage. No one had ever asked him if he knew how to do it. For a few days, along with other classmates, he played with ship models in a large tank taking turns moving them around. It wasn't much, but at least he gained a feel for moving ships.

He then went to the dry dock and took command of the oiler, which was undergoing repair to her boilers. Orders unexpectedly arrived directing him to take the *Chikaskia* out of dry dock and lay her alongside a pier and load her up. Then he was to proceed toward Jacksonville, Florida, form Task Group 28.3, pick up eleven destroyers, and head to the Mediterranean. Suddenly, Whitey was a task force commander!

Checking who he had on his bridge crew, he found an ensign fresh out of navigation school, along with twelve other officers. The XO had carried over from the previous CO, and he had one lieutenant. Everyone else was new, including the engineering officer and the first lieutenant. It was going to be interesting.

Whitey had been told that after the oiler, he would take command of the USS *Forrestal* (CVA 59), one of the Navy's new super carriers. Finally, after getting things in order, the *Chikaskia* made her way down the channel and out to Chesapeake Bay, heading toward Jacksonville and its role as TG 28.3, eleven destroyers and an aging fleet oiler.

Whitey hosted a brief visit by the destroyer squadron commodore, who told the new captain, "We'll form on you." The crossing went well, and Whitey turned over the destroyers to the Sixth Fleet and turned around for the return voyage to Norfolk.

Time didn't stand still, and after a week of tooling around the Tidewater area, the *Chikaskia* was ordered to Puerto Rico as the duty oiler for Operation Springboard. Whitey's ship had been recently equipped with a probe-and-drogue system for transferring oil, similar to the aerial refueling apparatus then being installed in military aircraft. The receiver ship would come alongside the tanker, which would then fire a probe and shotline over. The receiver's crew would then draw the probe over and insert it into the receptacle and refueling would begin. The new innovation was fast and relatively neat.

After Springboard, Whitey headed for the Mediterranean and a new deployment. Once there, Whitey joined the task force with the carrier USS *Franklin D. Roosevelt* (CVA 42), skippered by Capt. (later Vice Adm.) Malcom W. "Chris" Cagle. Whitey enjoyed watching how other COs worked their ships. It was good training for him; some people were aggressive while others were more timid. This observation was especially true during close-in maneuvering during refueling operations with Whitey's oiler. Cagle's technique was tentative, probably because Cagle did not want to be involved in a repeat of a collision some days earlier between another ship and an oiler. The Sixth Fleet commander had been particularly hard on the two skippers involved, and Cagle was bound and determined not to place himself in that position. Accordingly, he eventually placed his carrier at the extreme length of the hose, about as far as it would go, according to Whitey.

Between refueling and resupply operations, Whitey and his crew enjoyed themselves visiting many European ports. As the senior officer afloat during these port calls, Whitey had the responsibility of hosting various visits from port officials. He also struck up good relations with other tanker skippers, who often gave Whitey the benefit of their long years of ship handling, which he was always glad to soak up. Once during the mistrals that plague that part of the world with high winds and seas, Whitey took advantage of what one old Norwegian captain had told him.

He dropped one anchor on either side of his ship while keeping the screws turning at low rpm. This setup prevented the *Chikaskia* from dragging with the running seas. The time in the Mediterranean enabled the fighter ace to learn how to handle big ships, and Whitey put it to good use as well in qualifying a number of his officers as OODs under way, no small achievement. Certainly his crew appreciated their captain's methods as well as his concern for their careers.

Whitey's crew was mainly made up of black shoes (ship drivers). The officers were from the Newport OCS (Officer Candidate School). One of them—the engineer—was a mustang (a former enlisted man), while the second—the electronics officer—came from the U.S. Naval Academy. The crew also included several top-notch chiefs, always a highly desirable commodity for any skipper. He also had the skills of a gem of a chief boatswain's mate. The twenty-two-year-old ship was well set up for her new commanding officer.

One night, the *Chikaskia* would rendezvous with the task force. Whitey was in his at-sea cabin, just aft of the bridge. It was the captain's stateroom where he could take a break in quiet times when at sea but still be readily available to the bridge. Twenty miles from the rendezvous point, the OOD called to say the task force was coming head-on instead of approaching from abeam or astern. Whitey went back to the bridge in time to see the *Franklin D. Roosevelt* indeed bearing down on his position. The carrier turned to port, and the OOD froze, leaving Whitey to take command. He ordered, "Left full rudder, and all ahead full." It was close. The two large ships slid by each other with barely enough room to spare.

His navigator needed little time to "snap in." He had been in destroyers and thus had experience, which helped while steaming in formation. He became one of the old reliables. The XO was six foot four, built like a football player, and was already a standout. He had been on board the oiler two and a half years and knew the old ship stem to stern. The XO is usually the disciplinarian on board ship, but in this case discipline was a little lax. Apparently, the former CO had not been well liked and made no secret of being unhappy with his assignment, which translated to an unhappy crew.

Not surprisingly, the chiefs approached Whitey to suggest sprucing up the ship. The subsequent attention paid off when, while alongside the spanking new *Enterprise*, the flag lieutenant, who knew Whitey from his previous tour on board the nuclear carrier, asked how he had been so lucky to get a new ship. The *Chikaskia* did shine with new paint and polish. Whitey had given his crew all the leeway they needed to redo their old ship top to bottom, stem to stern.

In actuality, the *Chikaskia* had gone through a predeployment inspection by Capt. M. P. Refo III, Commander Service Squadron 2, and had *failed*. However, as Captain Refo noted in Whitey's departure fitness report, "the dedicated efforts of Captain Feightner and his ship's company . . . corrected all discrepancies and developed a high state of readiness."

Whitey's positive manner worked its way down through the crew. Besides making their ship shine, the men also found their CO cared about them and their careers. Somehow, the *Chikaskia* included a Hobie Cat—a recreational catamaran—among its equipment. When time and conditions allowed, Whitey permitted swim call and the sailors would dive off their ship or use the Hobie to sail. There was also a man with a rifle positioned so he could watch the swimmers and ward off any sharks or other uninvited visitors who might try to crash the swim party. And, in fact, during one swim fest off Genoa, an inquisitive whale shark—the world's largest fish—put in an appearance.

The sailors scrambled out of the water and onto their ship, from which they could look down and observe the mammoth creature. Whitey estimated its length at thirty-five to forty feet and its girth at fifteen feet as it swam around occasionally, seeming to raise its head so it could watch them. At one point, it began bumping the *Chikaskia*, perhaps as a greeting or a test to see if this object was worth a meal. But the fish evidently decided it wasn't and swam away.

Whitey also called one of his chiefs aside and noted that several sailors were coming up for promotion. He asked the chief to organize a group of tutors to help the sailors pass exams and make their advancements. Again, the results were more promotions and a happy crew.

Another area was communications between families. In these days of e-mail and cell phones, it's hard to realize how hard it was to keep in touch with loved ones using only letters and occasional shore-based telephones. Ports and sailing times made it all the more difficult and costly. Whitey did his best to give his people as much shore time as he could. Vi kept a small apartment on a hill overlooking the harbor in San Juan, Puerto Rico, and Whitey could watch the ship and also take a little time ashore himself.

There *were* occasional problems. Once while returning to the harbor, the pilot nearly steered the ship onto rocks. Whitey quickly relieved him, which did not sit well with the base commander. But Whitey replied that at least they had not run aground.

Later, while on deployment in the Mediterranean, Whitey and his crew found themselves averaging thirty replenishments a week, four a day. Destroyers one day, then the larger cruisers and carrier on the following days. It was good training for everyone and Whitey was able to qualify several junior officers as OODs, and thus avail himself of a good night's sleep every so often.

Liberty in the Mediterranean was good, too: Naples, Barcelona, Majorca, southern France. Discipline was good among the crew. Once while in Cannes, the French gave the *Chikaskia* crew a lingerie show, after which the sailors could buy "special" gifts for home. It was all great fun and helped dissuade Whitey from a long-held opinion that when he could no longer fly, he would leave the Navy. He laughed, "I hate to admit it to my aviator friends, but I really enjoyed driving a ship. It's one of the things I never had any problem with. If you've done a lot of formation flying, the relative motion is so natural that it was easy, so long as you plan ahead."[1]

Whitey would find, however, as he later commanded a larger, more mission-oriented ship that the relative freedom he enjoyed as CO of an oiler would disappear, especially since he had a task force commodore on board most of the time and would be part of almost daily exercises with the overall group instead of waiting to replenish a thirsty ship. In the meantime, he enjoyed getting attaboys from appreciative skippers such as the CO of the cruiser USS *Springfield* (CLG 7), who sent him a message asking if they could break the refueling record the next day using the *Chikaskia*'s probe apparatus that had helped the oiler do so well.

Whitey was up to the challenge, and using the course and speed the other captain gave, Whitey set up going twelve knots and was ready as the cruiser slid right up alongside. There was no need to shoot the probe over; Whitey's men simply heaved it over to their customer separated by only the large fenders hung over both ships' sides. In seventy-four seconds the *Chikaskia* was pumping oil. The cruiser moved out barely twenty-five yards, enjoying the quick service and calm seas. Everyone was impressed, including the admiral commanding the Sixth Fleet.

When Whitey's time in the oiler was coming to an end, he and four other COs were summoned to the office of Vice Adm. B. J. Semmes, the chief of naval personnel, commonly called BuPers. It was the department that dealt with matters relating to the administration and assignment of everyone in a Navy uniform. Admiral Semmes told the captains that a new ruling by the Navy had made LPHs (landing platform, helicopter) major commands and that all five of the captains would be getting command of an LPH. It was a disappointment for aviators like Whitey, who had been in aviation all his career and had in fact been promised command of one of the Navy's newest carriers.

In reality, there was more to it than that. A ruling from the late 1920s had stipulated that only aviators would command aviation ships, which at that time meant only aircraft carriers with traditional fixed-wing fighters, dive bombers, and torpedo bombers. With the development of the so-called helicopter carriers in the 1950s, however, many black shoes looked at the new types as merely surface ships that happened to carry—occasionally—helicopters, not fixed-wing aircraft. They felt that the new ships were surface ships and should be skippered by regular surface warfare officers.

Not so fast, the aviators said. They began fighting the contentious new opinions that were demanding 1100s—the surface warfare designator—as the captains of the new LPHs and other amphibious warfare aviation ships. Thus, Whitey and his friends were in a new generation that were pioneers in a new form of aviation warfare.

Finally, while all the other deputy CNOs were housed in the Pentagon, BuPers had his headquarters in the Navy Annex, overlooking the Pentagon from a prominent hill to the southwest. The chief of naval personnel also had a smaller office in the Pentagon, and while in that second office, Admiral Semmes, who had been a destroyer skipper in World War II and had been awarded the Navy Cross for action off Okinawa in May 1945, had taken the opportunity to visit Whitey and give him more specific information about his new command. Normally, admirals do not go to captains, but in this case and for whatever real personal reasons Semmes might have had, he took a stroll to visit his newest LPH skipper.

Whitey felt that the admiral's tone as well as the quirky little leer he gave him just added more salt to the news of the new assignment. Semmes acknowledged Whitey and his group's collective dismay but tried to sweeten the bitter pill by offering him the chance to go down to Pensacola to go through an abbreviated helicopter training course. Capt. Al Morton and Whitey snapped up the admiral's invitation. Soon Whitey was a designated rotary wing aviator, broadening his resume and adding to the already impressive list of aircraft he had flown. He would have his own Huey helicopter and he would also check out in the Kaman H-2 and Boeing Vertol CH-46, as well as the H-34, all of which enjoyed long productive careers in the fleet and the Marine Corps Fleet Marine Force. He even investigated the AH-1 Cobra gunship.

Actually, during his time at Patuxent in flight test, Whitey had had the good fortune to be checked out in helicopters by one of the Marines' first helo pilots, Marion Carl, but since he would be more officially involved with helicopters, the course at Pensacola was definitely an advantage. He also came to appreciate the helicopter's role in antisubmarine warfare (ASW), especially at night.

Whitey attended the Amphibious Force Command and Staff Indoctrination Course at Little Creek, Virginia Beach. Although Whitey took a while to get over his disappointment of losing the *Forrestal*, his natural exuberance helped him develop anticipation for his upcoming new assignment as captain of the USS *Okinawa* (LPH 3), a new ship, commissioned in April 1962. The *Okinawa* was a single-screw design, not the best for control, especially with the large sail area created by her island.

Whitey would be only her fifth captain and she would enjoy a thirty-year career. Whitey found himself with an excellent crew, including a good XO and operations officer. He took command on February 23, 1966, relieving Capt. J. L. Evans while the ship was in the Philadelphia Navy Yard, and he brought her to her home port of Norfolk, Virginia. That initial cruise was a learning experience, particularly in maneuvering and getting the ship alongside the pier. Getting people on and off the *Okinawa* was a major, almost continuous operation. In an operational exercise, with troops now gone, the concern was to establish a medical reception facility with triage and doctors ready to recover the wounded.

After spending four months in the Caribbean, Whitey accepted a volunteer assignment to sail the *Okinawa* to Vietnam, which meant getting over to the Pacific by transiting the Panama Canal and steaming up to San Diego before heading west. Unfortunately, by the time he arrived in the Southern California port on February 8, 1967 (he had left Norfolk on January 24) Whitey's brief command tour was up and he had to turn over the LPH to Capt. William H. Alexander II in March 1967.

By Whitey's estimate, the *Okinawa* registered a third more flight hours than any other LPH during that period, with only one mishap. One Marine H-34 had a landing mishap in which three Marines died when the aircraft went over the side. On a usual day, the ship conducted some three hundred cycles in a constant stream, with one helicopter launching while another landed. There were medical exercises, which would help later when she arrived off Vietnam, lifted troops into combat, and often brought their wounded back for life-saving care.

To keep his knowledge and understanding of operations current, Whitey qualified in a Marine CH-46 Seaknight, then the Corps' primary transport and airlift helicopter. His flying skills were still with him and he found flying the twin-rotor aircraft "a piece of cake," even at night. Training was constant, whether off Little Creek, Panama, in the Caribbean or in the Mediterranean. The commodore of the amphibious group was Rear Adm. Robert S. Salzer, an old destroyer man who later rose to vice admiral and saw a lot of command service in Vietnam.

Whitey and Salzer enjoyed a good working relationship. Whitey thought him congenial, knowledgeable, and practical. Throughout his career, Whitey always kept a positive outlook and tried to appreciate every person he met, even when it was obvious the individual had professional and personal problems.

Whitey appreciated any specific person, enlisted or officer, junior or senior, who exhibited that spark of intelligent, skillful capability that lifted him above the group and helped the greater cause. It may sound simple, but it is not always readily apparent or available. It was this ability to work with people that always helped Whitey stand out in a crowd.

Rear Adm. (later Vice Adm.) William P. Mack, commander of Amphibious Group 2, wrote Whitey's departing fitness report, noting that Whitey was "an extremely able, skillful and conscientious commanding officer." Mack also noted that Whitey paid particular attention to crew morale and that the *Okinawa* had received the prestigious Flatley Award for aviation safety during Whitey's tenure.

Whitey even worked with Rear Adm. (later Vice Adm.) John Bulkeley, who had won fame and the Medal of Honor taking Gen. Douglas MacArthur out of the Philippines in the dark days following Pearl Harbor. After several weeks of intensive predeployment training involving a shipload of young Marines, Bulkeley, then the CO of the Guantanamo Bay Naval Base, Cuba, asked Whitey if he could take the families of the Marines and ship's crew to Jamaica for a weekend. Without the Marines on board, there was plenty of room and the families could be easily accommodated.

Heading for the island, the *Okinawa's* crew hosted their guests with a movie and food. The plan was to make their destination in the morning, but an emergency developed when a crewman took a wrong turn and fell overboard right into a place where the islanders threw their garbage, which attracted many ravenous sharks. Whitey quickly brought the big ship to a halt and ordered lights on the water. But all efforts were in vain and the hapless young sailor was never found.

Whitey and Bulkeley got along well. Whitey visited his home for dinner several times, which allowed Bulkeley to tell his war stories. Bulkeley could be very demanding, and although he and Whitey worked well, he could be hard on other captains; he had quite a lot of authority and was not afraid to wield it.

One petty officer stopped Whitey's nephew, Jim, who had come on board so that his uncle could swear him into the Navy. Jim eventually became an F-8 pilot. The petty officer asked if Jim was Whitey's son or nephew. "He's a great CO," the enlisted man offered. It was an endorsement any skipper would prize.

Whitey did have occasional concerns on board the *Okinawa,* which he characteristically negotiated in his affable but directly focused manner. The heart of the ship's mission was that of the Marines who regularly came on board, including the dedicated aircraft group comprising several individual squadrons of CH-46s, Hueys, and H-34s. Other Navy captains could not always depend on such an easygoing atmosphere dealing with the headstrong Marine COs who wanted to do things their way and did not always combine their efforts to join the Navy-Marine team.

Whitey, though, had always appreciated the Marines, from his earliest days in VF-10 serving on Guadalcanal with Marion Carl, John Smith, Bob Galer, Dick Mangrum, and all the high-spirited, courageous members of their Wildcat and Dauntless squadrons. During his command tour, Whitey went out of his way to work with the Marines while expecting them to return the favor, which they did. Admiral Salzer contributed to the effort. Whitey felt he made the Marines feel part of the ship.

With all the work and effort, it was no wonder that Whitey felt incomplete when he had to leave before bringing the *Okinawa* and its crew and Marines to Vietnam, where they would be quickly involved in combat operations. The fighter ace was only too ready to lead in the fight, but it was not to be. The senior folks back in Washington had been watching him for some time, and now the time had come for Whitey to serve in the Pentagon, away from the intense pace of operations in the fleet.

CHAPTER 15
A SENIOR TOUR

Most aviators try to keep from serving in Washington, especially the Pentagon. They would much rather fly as long as they can see and hear and their reflexes respond to any danger or impulse. "Flying a desk" is not an assignment that a gung-ho type will actively seek or accept. And the Pentagon? Well, it may be a nice place to visit for a few days or even a few weeks, but no gold-winged driver worth his flight pay wants to "live" there.

But, unfortunately, the facts of military life are you have to pay your dues, and for every great set of flight orders to a tip-of-the-spear squadron, the payback is at least one, maybe two, correspondingly dull, even politically dangerous orders back in the real world in the five-sided puzzle palace. Whitey had certainly put in his time in the late 1950s at NAVAIR, working as the desk officer responsible for a number of new fighter programs. He had performed well and had left a satisfied feeling in Op-05, the Navy aviation directorate. It was a two-edged sword: do well and you may get a nice set of orders back to the fleet, but you also may leave with the feeling that they want to see you back, in a more senior position.

New aircraft and their programs were just starting up and they needed a highly experienced aviator like Capt. Whitey Feightner. Vice Adm. Tom Connolly was in charge of 05, and Rear Adm. Jerry Miller, an old acquaintance of Whitey's, was Op-50, plans officer. Miller had asked for Whitey personally, and Whitey had accepted the friendly summons with eager anticipation. His billet would be head of aircraft programs, and all their managers would work for him in Op-506, carrier division.

When Whitey arrived, Rear Adm. Noel Gayler was now deputy chief of naval operations (DCNO) for research and development, which included everything concerning aviation and associated weapons. He asked Whitey to come to a meeting of eight admirals. Whitey found the group of flag officers arguing about how many individual aircraft would be assigned to the F-4 program. Whitey had been the Phantom program manager, and here, several years later, he found senior officers still debating how test aircraft should be used.

And now the Grumman F-14 Tomcat had put in an appearance as the new fleet defense fighter, projected for the last quarter of the twentieth century. A swing-wing fighter, the F-14 had been the Navy's dream in the early confrontational days surrounding the Air Force's swing-wing TFX, later to emerge as the troubled F-111. Capt. Mac Snowden was the F-111 program conductor, and other programs fought for time and money, including the Grumman A-6 Intruder, a carrier-based, twin-engine, two-seat medium bomber and the replacement for the A-4 Skyhawk, and the Vought A-7 Corsair II, which was a much different approach to the role of light attack.

With this troika—F-14, A-7, and A-6—the U.S. Navy would have a fine trio of carrier strikers that would enjoy thirty-year careers in war and peace, ultimately placing American naval air power in the forefront of world military operations time and again. No other nation—not even Britain with its redoubtable Royal Navy—could emulate the U.S. Navy's flexible capability. It was, indeed, a good time to be in the Navy Pentagon.

After the time spent in his earlier tour dealing with the ill-conceived TFX, Whitey had walked into another design beset with problems, not the least of which was the choice of the Pratt & Whitney TF-30 turbofan, which left a lot to be desired, and the rising cost of the big fighter, which nearly killed the proposal altogether. Many of the senior aviators also thought the day of the gun-armed fighter, equipped only with cannon, was over, and they wanted the F-14 to be armed solely with missiles that could go after the Tomcat's main prey, the bomber. They weren't thinking about how the F-14 might deal with the close-in situation of the traditional dogfight. With all his combat expertise, and the nine kills to prove it, Whitey knew instinctively this was a dead end.

In Vietnam, the Navy's F-4, which used only the Sidewinder and Sparrow air-to-air missiles, did not always get a kill. This lack of what should have been more confirmed kills should have warned the leadership of the dangers of depriving the new fighter of an internal gun. Even the Air Force was incorporating a nose cannon in its Phantoms (the F-4E) and had also used the stopgap measure of carrying wing-mounted pods with one or two cannon, which had in fact gained several kills for Air Force Phantom crews.

One day, Whitey asked Admiral Connolly, "Why is it when every fighter pilot in the world and all the operational people want a gun, we can't have a gun in the F-14?" Surprised, the feisty three-star looked up at the bold captain and laughed.

Then, he said, "Because I'm a mean old bastard. Now get out of my office!"

Actually, it was more than that, and Whitey knew it. Connolly was too tough and dedicated a man. In reality, he was trying to hold down the F-14's burgeoning weight, which was now well over 70,000 pounds for a combat mission. The underpowered TF-30 was not up to the task of pushing that heavy a load. Installed, a gun would add another 5,000 pounds.

Connolly fought like a tiger for the F-14, but it cost him his job and possibly another star. Congress remembered another time in March 1968 when the admiral had appeared before the Armed Services Committee deeply engaged in checking out the wayward TFX project. When the committee chairman, Senator John Stennis, asked Connolly about how heavy the Navy's version had grown and the problem of finding a suitable engine, he declared, "Mr. Chairman, all the thrust in Christendom couldn't make a Navy fighter out of that airplane!" It was a shot heard throughout the halls of the Pentagon, and it effectively canceled the TFX. Unfortunately, it also ended the career of one of the Navy's most effective and capable aviator admirals of that period. In gratitude for Adm. Tom Connolly's support and his colorful personality, the Navy decided to name the F-14 the Tomcat. It fit anyway, and it preserved the long-standing tradition of labeling Grumman fighters with "cat" names.

Another flag officer Whitey got to work for was then Rear Adm. William D. Houser, a highly experienced and well-liked aviator with combat experience in World War II and Korea, as well as deployments to Vietnam as the CO of the carrier USS *Constellation* (CVA 64). In 1968, Bill Houser was director of Aviation Plans Division of Op-05, which was responsible for the war plans for the Joint Chiefs of Staff. He was also responsible for the development of the new aircraft coming in. Tall and lean, Bill Houser was always the gentleman with a smile that came to endear him to the men he worked with and who worked for him, including Whitey Feightner.

Perhaps Connolly might have been CNO, displacing the men who came later, like Elmo Zumwalt. There have not been a lot of aviator CNOs. Connolly had friends in Congress, even in the Marine Corps, but he retired from Op-05, which Whitey, among others, considered a loss for the Navy.

At the time, the Vought A-7 was under development just before entering fleet service. The little A-4 had served well, but a replacement in the uniquely Navy role of light attack was needed, and soon. By the early 1970s, the A-4 deployed only in the World War II–era *Essex*-class carriers USS *Hancock* (CVA 19) and USS *Oriskany* (CVA 34), although the latter ship was slated to get A-7s for its air wing soon.

Working with Admiral Zumwalt

Admiral Miller called Whitey into his office. "The fighter study's going on," Miller said. "Zumwalt's going to do it, but we have to have input and furnish the manpower." Miller told Whitey he was going to work with Zumwalt on the study, something Whitey was not too anxious to do. Zumwalt had established the Systems Analysis Division, which got into everything regarding requirements and development of new weapons and related programs. Whitey and his group put out their usual effort, only to be confronted by Zumwalt one day.

Zumwalt was not an aviator and his commands were in the surface Navy, including the so-called brown water navy in Vietnam. One of his group had apparently convinced the admiral that the Navy should create a "hedge" of $96 million to keep the F-111 program going. In February 1968 Zumwalt told Captain Feightner that his work had indicated such a need, which surprised Whitey because his group's study had come up with exactly the opposite findings.

Whitey looked straight at Zumwalt and replied, "Admiral, that is not true. I am not going to be a party to this. I'm taking my troops and going back to Op-05."

Zumwalt dismissed everyone in the room before turning to Whitey and taking him out to the parking lot. The two men got into Zumwalt's car and drove to the Army-Navy Country Club. No words passed between them as they took Columbia Pike and then turned onto Glebe Road and finally arrived at their destination, where they found CNO Adm. Tom Moorer, together with Admiral Connolly and Admiral Miller enjoying a round of winter golf. A highly regarded, soft-spoken aviator from Alabama, Moorer listened as Zumwalt started. "We need a decision, Boss. We've come to an impasse," indicating Whitey. Zumwalt then proceeded to tell the CNO about the disagreement on getting the TFX.

Admiral Moorer absorbed Zumwalt's account and thought for a moment or two. Finally, he told Whitey that he had to side with "Bud," Admiral Zumwalt's nickname. Whitey caught a glimpse of Admiral Connolly, who looked like he was about to explode with anger. In fact, Admiral Miller had to restrain his friend, and he had to cover his own mouth in consternation.

Shortly afterward, Connolly had his famous session with the Armed Services Committee declaring the TFX a major mistake, effectively trashing the trouble-plagued aircraft, at least as far as the Navy was concerned. But the TFX program did not die just then and there. Interservice politics were still alive. Paul Nitze, the Secretary of the Navy, had met with Admiral Zumwalt and they had decided to buy a squadron of F-111Bs and stop all the hassles. In the end, the Navy did buy a few of the big swing-wing strikers but gave them to the Air Force, along with several highly trained TFX-experienced crewmen and ground troops, all to give the Air Force more depth as they deployed the new type to Vietnam. As noted earlier, two Navy aircrewmen were killed in action flying the F-111. Whitey watched from the sidelines. It was small satisfaction that his strong feelings about the F-111 had been borne out. It was definitely not right for the carrier navy.

Whitey next found himself with the VFAX, which slowly evolved into the McDonnell F/A-18 Hornet, two engines, twin-tailed, state-of-the-art avionics, a true fighter-bomber for the 1990s. The Hornet was able to do both missions, as dramatically demonstrated in January 1991 during Operation Desert Storm, when two Hornet pilots on a strike mission switched to the fighter mode and shot down two Iraqi MiG-21s. But the Hornet had terribly short legs.

Whitey did not care for Zumwalt's style. Frankly, he was not alone, particularly among the rank and file. He considered Zumwalt a "political animal . . . dishonest as the day is long."[1] Zumwalt was, in Whitey's estimation, always ready to play the game of politics, hoping to gain more advantage over his foes. He was definitely a liberal naval officer, something of a contradiction, who really didn't believe in traditional order and discipline.

154 / Chapter 15

It was probably a tough assessment, but Zumwalt's tenure as CNO (1970–1974) was marked by unrest and unfortunate displays of enlisted rebellion as well as officer relaxation of personal deportment. Whitey Feightner always tried to be honest with the admiral with the long sideburns, which had started a trend throughout the Navy; officers and men alike took advantage of the Zumwalt period of relaxation of hair-length requirements. Whitey knew Zumwalt generally appreciated his team's work, but he was not an aviator and his reputation in Vietnam had been made largely by commanding the brown water navy, the river war in South Vietnam.

Whitey felt that Zumwalt knew he didn't have many friends with brown shoes (aviators). In fact, he knew Tom Connolly in particular had it in for him, and Connolly's only protection was Secretary of the Navy Paul Nitze. A sorry state for a soon-to-be CNO. Zumwalt did not want the F-14, considering it too big, too expensive, and too difficult to maintain. He thought the F-111 was a better choice. Thus, Whitey and his study group were occasionally and generally hostile to the admiral, with *their* protector, Vice Admiral Connolly, backing them up.

Secretary Nitze was a smart, educated man, but Whitey had mixed feelings about him and never saw where Nitze's loyalties were. It was a busy time in Op-05. Besides finally burying the F-111 and finalizing the initial design and production of the Tomcat, concerns turned to the Ault report, from Capt. Frank Ault, late of the USS *Coral Sea*. It was an important study of why Navy fighter crews were not doing better against North Vietnamese MiGs. Another area was the initial design of the VFAX, soon to be known officially as the F/A-18.

The Ault report led to Topgun, the Navy Fighter Weapons School based at NAS Miramar, north of San Diego, and it highlighted problems with the Sidewinder and Sparrow air-to-air missiles. The Sparrow in particular was not dependable, and the Sidewinder's operating parameters were restrictive. In short, the all-missile-armed Navy F-4B and F-4J, and their rapidly retiring stablemate F-8 (which did carry four cannon and four Sidewinders) were not realizing their full potential. A lack of what many seasoned fighter aviators considered air-to-air training, something the Air Force was certainly experiencing as well, was another area of grave concern.

Another colorful fighter pilot who worked for Whitey during this time was Capt. Dick Bellinger, who is best remembered as the CO of VF-162 on board the *Oriskany* in 1966. He got the Navy's first kill over a MiG-21 in October 1966 after himself being shot down by a MiG-17 the previous July. A former B-25 instructor pilot at the end of World War II, Bellinger had switched to the Navy after the war and had made a name for himself over the years as a mercurial but talented aviator. He flew combat in the Banshee in Korea, and then met the Crusader, which seemed to be tailor-made for him. Thus, Dick Bellinger, or "Belly" as he came to be known, brought a lot to a tour in the Pentagon as desk officer for the Crusader.

However, Bellinger's raucous personality soon intensified, and it became obvious he had medical problems far beyond just being loud and extroverted. Sadly, he had to leave Whitey's group and eventually was medically retired with what was later diagnosed as Alzheimer's disease. His departure deprived Whitey and the Navy of a talent that might have brought a strong, knowledgeable individual to the study table.

Other new programs that were coming were the S-3, intended to replace the veteran S-2 for antisubmarine warfare work, and the EA-6B Prowler electronic countermeasures development of the A-6. Whitey had few budgetary problems, however. It was, after all, a much different, almost relaxed time. Even establishing a new far-reaching training program like Topgun was relatively simple. His study group also did major evaluations of the current MiGs in service, MiG-15 through the MiG-21. Information gained included the distinct lack of visibility from the cockpit, almost a hallmark of MiG jets, as well as problems with controllability and the maintenance attributes of the tough little Soviet fighters, which were eye openers.

Setting up Topgun simply involved moving money from one program to another, nowhere near as complicated as such action has become today. "It was one of the best things we ever did," Whitey recalled. "The timing was right. . . . We learned how to fight efficiently . . . and the kill ratio went up tremendously . . . the effect was almost immediate. The first few graduates that went out there started shooting down airplanes."[2]

The MiGs that Topgun students flew against were acquired from several sources, including Israel and occasionally defecting Soviet bloc pilots. Not surprisingly, Whitey got a chance to fly them all, from the MiG-15 to the MiG-21. He appreciated their turning abilities, which were decidedly better than American types, especially the larger, heavier F-4. "I was never in such a blind airplane in my life," he declared. "I was absolutely shocked the first flight in [the MiG-21] and looked out and found out I couldn't even see my own wingtip. [That's just] unheard of in a fighter airplane."[3]

Whitey and his friends discovered many more blind spots in a MiG-21, even though the airplane could turn better than its American opponents. In most circumstances, it was finally decided that the best action for an F-4 or F-8 pilot caught in a turning engagement was to split-S and make a right roll away from the MiG, which at high speed could not overcome the stick forces needed for the pilot to follow.

As can be imagined, Whitey found this period an exciting time of discovery as well as occasional confrontation. And all in all, his tour proved to be a good one.

CHAPTER 16
ENDING HIS CAREER: TIME TO MOVE ON

s the new decade of the 1970s dawned, Whitey Feightner could see the approach of the end of his naval career. He had achieved flag rank (rear admiral, lower half) in June 1970, and although at times he might have thought he could find another billet, it became obvious that the proverbial pyramid was getting too steep. At one point he was being considered for CNO, which would have given him four stars, but Whitey was never a political animal, didn't like playing that game, and knew that by not playing it he would never get to the top of the pyramid.

He had received the Navy Commendation Medal in September 1968 for "meritorious service from November 1967 to August 1968" for his work with the Navy Fighter Study, working for Rear Admiral Zumwalt. Whitey had several disagreements with Zumwalt, and the "NAVCOM" was an inappropriate award for an O-6, especially one of Whitey's experience and accomplishments. Two years later, in September 1970, Whitey received the first of two Legions of Merit, a much more appropriate award for a senior captain. This time, signed off by Navy secretary and former Rhode Island senator John H. Chafee, this medal noted Captain Feightner's "exceptionally meritorious service from June 1967 to August 1970" for his work on the very same project, the Navy Fighter Study. For once in his career, Whitey had fallen afoul of the political system when he had failed to play up to the *very* political Elmo Zumwalt.

In those years, Whitey's wife Vi had taken ill, and it was becoming harder to leave her or to consider any billet that would take them out of the country or that would require a lengthy sea tour. He had always been a good officer, always supportive of the Navy and its policies, and his fitness reports had always described his affable nature and ability to work with people, no matter their particular personality. His combat record was exemplary, even disregarding his status as an ace. He had dodged the Zeros and the flak. He had seen heavy action, had gone out on missions from which he almost didn't return. But return he did, through his own perseverance and flying skill.

After combat, he had kept that skill and courage as a test pilot, working on many of the Navy's earliest jet programs at the opening of a new age for naval aviation when experience in that arena was rare. Later, he again had proven his mettle as a senior commanding officer and had not let his disappointment at not getting command of a promised carrier keep him from giving his all in the command of another ship. His crews had always held him in high regard and were not afraid to tell people how they felt about their CO. So, all in all, Whitey Feightner was a seasoned, highly experienced combat aviator, leader, and overall exemplary naval officer. Although Whitey had not graduated from the Naval Academy, seemingly a stringent prerequisite to even being considered for CNO at the time (he was later unanimously made an honorary member of USNA class of 1942, which had provided so many successful leaders and naval aviators to the fleet during World War II), the office of CNO would have fit him well. But it was not to be. Another fighter study developed, this time in Op-50B under Rear Adm. Bill Houser. While the job may have sounded like the previous study with Zumwalt, Whitey was now the supervisor of the requirements branch.

Usually, after a shore tour in the Pentagon, Whitey could have been looking at a sea tour. In fact, he received orders to become COM 14, commander of the 14th Naval District, in Honolulu, Hawaii. The incumbent was Rear Adm. Charles C. "Red Dog" Davis. Whitey and Davis began talking, and Red Dog offered him several of his white uniforms. The billet required a lot of glad-handing, and a crisp, well-laundered uniform, especially white, was de rigeur almost every day. Whitey was glad to get some extra whites because as all naval officers know, this uniform doesn't hold up well when worn more than a day or two, especially in a warm climate.

Whitey was actually on the way out to his new assignment when his orders were changed to AIR-04, NAVAIR Logistics and Flight Support Group, at the Naval Air Systems Command in Virginia, at Bailey's Crossroads, just up the road a few miles from the Pentagon. The switch suited Whitey and Vi for a number of reasons. He wouldn't have to travel so far to get to his new assignment, and at least he didn't need all those whites! He also felt much more qualified for the job at AIR-04 (which involved supply and maintenance for *all* Navy units), which included a large pot of money as well as a considerable say as to where it went. Whitey had gained a lot of experience serving as the F-4 program manager and then with RA-5, the head of aircraft procurement of all the program managers in fighters. At AIR-04, Whitey had the advantage of people with experience in several different programs. He liked comparing the group to the Air Force, which did things "vertically," that is, keeping individuals in one aircraft program, limiting individual appeal and capabilities.

"You can get blinders on and you know it's hard not to push a program that you're connected with. And maybe it isn't the best thing. If you had more experience, you'd say, 'Hey, there is a better way to do this.'"[1]

He felt this lack of variation also contributed to stagnation in relationships with contractors and created a real detriment, including the vital area of supply and control. The stream of supply parts is an important aspect of maintaining aircraft. Foreign sales of aircraft were also a concern for Whitey's command. In the Foreign Military Sales Program, the A-4 was a premier example because of the large number of countries that also flew the little attack jet. The smaller foreign air forces, often with fewer than one hundred aircraft all told, required packages that included dedicated supplies to keep the planes flying. Naval air rework facilities (NARFs) were important to the effort, reworking and refurbishing aircraft for the U.S. fleet as well as preparing them for foreign customers. Whitey often visited NARFs. It was good to drop in and see the people in the local economies.

Weapons were also a concern. The AIM-9 Sidewinder had come a long way and had matured into a good, close-in missile, especially when combined with the F-14's impressive AWG-9 radar. The period was also the time of increased computer development, particularly in simulators and computer-generated imagery. So obviously there was a lot for Whitey to be involved with. It was like a changing of generations as technologies appeared with new requirements and demands, while Whitey and the people he worked with tried to meet them. The world of props and cloth helmets had definitely given way to jets and helmet-mounted weapon sighting systems.

Whitey even had the chance to fly the simulator for the highly controversial V-22 Osprey tilt-rotor, which was intended to replace the rapidly aging CH-46 medium-lift helicopter, now approaching its fifth decade of service in the Marine Corps. He was surprised at the simulator's incredible realism.

> Being an old helicopter driver, I thought "Well, this is a piece of cake." They launched me in the middle of the night to go to a platform out in the Gulf [of Mexico], and I'll tell you, I sweat [sic] just as much as if I had been there. That was realistic. It really looked like it. [I] went out there, the waves were lapping around, and all the lights and everything. It was about as realistic as it could get.[2]

Whitey was an early member of the prestigious Golden Eagles, a highly selective philanthropic group of respected naval aviators. A candidate has to have quite an enviable backlog just to be considered for nomination. During the Golden Eagles' annual convention, this time in Jacksonville, Florida, the members were treated to commercial game simulations that included programs for flying World War II fighters such as Spitfires, Hellcats, and Corsairs. For men like Whitey, it was like coming home.

Following the F-14 was the stubby A-7 light attack aircraft intended to replace the A-4. The A-7's successor was initially labeled the VFX and later the F/A-18. VFX planning included pricing, parts, programs, and a complete package to support it in the 1980s. Whitey's group was also involved in getting aircraft and munitions to Israel at the height of the 1973 Yom Kippur War, which had actually started badly for the Jewish state. The Israel Air Force (IAF) had lost many F-4s and A-4s and the United States had to dig into existing inventories to provide the desperately needed replacements.

In a round-the-clock operation, Whitey's teams got aircraft and bombs over to Israel to be quickly painted with the Israeli Star of David and loaded onto waiting planes and launched on another mission in less than twenty-four hours, a major logistics feat. Navy pilots flew from Norfolk to checkpoints and finally to the carrier USS *Franklin D. Roosevelt* (CV 42) for a final rest before launching on the final leg to an Israeli airfield, usually intercepted by IAF Mirages, often fresh from their own missions over Arab territory.

It was in the early stage of his assignment to AIR-04 that Whitey was promoted to rear admiral. He was frocked, a naval term for putting on the new insignia, in this case two stars, before an official date of rank and its corresponding increase in pay.[3] It is basically a courtesy that other services didn't follow, but it gives the new selectee increased horsepower. Many people supported Whitey's advancement, including Bill Houser, Jerry Miller, and Bill Shinn, who had been the CO of the *Forrestal*. The high-level interest was important at the time because making flag without having graduated from Annapolis was difficult.

Eventually, it was time for another change, and Whitey moved to NAVAIR to become head of all the Navy's aviation programs in AIR-01. He considered it changing from managing "hardware" to managing "people." It also included ensuring proper management of money. When a shortage of money threatened existing programs like the P-3 and the Tomahawk cruise missile—which would see so much service beginning with Desert Storm in 1991—it was up to Whitey to find the necessary funding, which was not an easy task. The AGM-84 Harpoon antishipping missile was another concern, and it was only because he had such good people working for him that Whitey was able to keep this important weapon a viable program.

The EA-6B Prowler ECM platform was also having funding problems. Congressional committee members never seemed to understand the growing importance of the ECM mission and the outstanding requirement to keep the big Prowler updated and ahead of Soviet radar advances. The growing cadre of senior aviators, most of whom had flown in Vietnam and had certainly appreciated the services of the "queer" types—vernacular for dedicated and often unusual-looking ECM aircraft such as the EA-1 and EF-10—later augmented by the appearance of the first Prowlers in June 1972, watched and sometimes participated in the discussion about ECM's value.

Whitey and his people testified at every opportunity before committees, anxious to plead their case. They usually found their congressional hosts very receptive and often willing to extend further funds where needed. They also knew when and whom to stroke. On one occasion Whitey and other admirals were to testify before Louisiana's Democratic congressman Felix E. Hebert's Armed Services Committee. Before calling the meeting to order, Hebert brought in Hyman Rickover so they could, with great flourish, promote the nuclear admiral. Rickover was still very much in charge of the Navy's nukes.

Along with other flags, Whitey would be summoned to have lunch with the irascible Rickover, if only to be educated on where the current pecking order stood regarding programs and money. The Navy offered Whitey an assignment in Iran, which was then still an important American ally. The shah of Iran was a big buyer of American arms and was looking at the F-14 for his country's next major fighter. But the political situation was deteriorating. Rebellion was in the wind, led by fundamentalist elements that didn't like the close ties between the shah and Washington. Whitey didn't like the prospects and decided it was time to retire. In truth, there was more to it, as mentioned earlier. The road to a third or even a fourth star seemed blocked, and Vi's worsening condition made it impossible for him to consider a permanent foreign billet. Actually, Whitey *had* gone to Iran on several occasions but only for a week or two.

The first time occurred because the shah was angry at being sent a mere lieutenant commander "black shoe," a ship driver with no knowledge of aviation matters. The shah made his displeasure known in no uncertain terms, reminding the Navy that he had just spent millions of dollars on top-of-the-line U.S. equipment and expected no less than a flag officer to be assigned as the liaison. Accordingly, Whitey was dispatched to address the irate Iranian leader's concerns. At one point, while in Iran, the shah called Whitey and told him he was in Italy where he had just bought ninety Italian helicopters. "When I return," the shah declared, "you will tell me what to do with them." Whitey and his aide thought fast and had the answer when the shah came back: Use the new helicopters for border patrol. The shah did so.

Later, after he had retired, Whitey made another couple of trips to Iran, this time as a company rep for United Technologies and its subsidiary, Pratt & Whitney, manufacturer of the F-14's engines, which were giving all early users of the Tomcat problems.

There was also the shadow cast by Admiral Zumwalt, now CNO, who was trying to bring in younger admirals. Now fifty-four and with thirty-three years of naval service, Whitey was still energetic and active, but he knew he couldn't fight changing policies regarding senior positions. After making the decision, Whitey didn't have much trouble keeping to it. And the Navy didn't expend much energy in trying to make him stay. On February 25, 1974, Vice Adm. David H. Bagley, in charge of BuPers, wrote a nice and proper letter to Whitey, saying in part:

> Recognizing the great wealth of talent and experience possessed
> by our flag officers, Admiral Zumwalt has suggested that those

who are retiring may wish to help us maintain an open line of communications. . . . We wish you fair winds in all of your future endeavors.

On the neatly typed letter, the admiral handwrote "Best of luck! Dave."

It was a less than stellar farewell, and something of a weak sop to include Admiral Zumwalt's name. Whitey also received a Gold Star to note the second award of the Legion of Merit, dated April 2, 1974, and like the first one in 1970, this citation was also signed by Secretary of the Navy John Chafee. The text noted Whitey's service as deputy commander for logistics/fleet support and as deputy commander for plans and programs in the Naval Air Systems Command from September 1970 through June 1974. Mention was made of Whitey's "inspirational leadership, superb business acumen, extraordinary managerial skill and sound judgment," as well as his "exemplary professional competence, resourcefulness and dedication to duty."

His final fitness report, dated September 11, 1974, also expounded the departing admiral's amazing qualifications and dedication to the Navy and his country. "His performance in this international capacity fully demonstrated his outstanding capability as a naval officer." The "international" reference was to Whitey's work with the shah of Iran. Ironically, the report was signed by Vice Adm. Kent L. Lee, now commander of Naval Air Systems Command and at one time one of Whitey's competitors for senior billets.

After he retired, Whitey occasionally found work as a consultant, helping to lead several groups like the American Fighter Aces Association (AFAA) and the Golden Eagles, and appearing at various seminars and gatherings. He was inducted into the Carrier Test Pilot Hall of Fame in October 1998. The author attended the 1987 Fighter Fling at NAS Oceana, and there were several well-known combat personalities, including Whitey and retired Brig. Gen. Robin Olds (USAF). A colorful personality, Olds was the only aviator to have kills in World War II and Vietnam. He had just missed becoming the first American ace of the war with four MiG kills. Other personalities attending were World War II P-47 fighter ace Robert S. Johnson and Vietnam MiG killer Cdr. John Nichols.

Outgoing and someone whose advice was still worth listening to, Olds drew Whitey away to the simulator building up the street from the auditorium, where a discussion of tactics had held the attention of the audience of young fighter crews. The building had two F-14 simulators and the two senior officers happily got into them after securing the services of two technicians to set them up.

The engagements were over fairly quickly. General Olds had lost none of his aggressiveness, while it had been some time since Whitey had flown a high-performance jet, even in a simulator. He was just happy to be holding onto a stick and throttle and throwing his simulated fighter all over the simulated sky. After an hour or so, the two aces got out of their seats eminently satisfied, each beaming with a happiness of long-sleeping memories once more awakened.

Later that night, at a formal dinner, Whitey and Robin wore their mess dress uniforms—Whitey in a white waistcoat and gold shoulder boards, and Robin in a blue waistcoat—each aglitter with miniature medals that actually jingled because there were so many. It was a happy sight to see these two warriors once more in the uniform of their country's military services.

At this writing, Whitey, at ninety-four, is still energetic and involved. He and Vi recently moved back to Ohio after closing his Arlington, Virginia, consulting office for FMS, Inc. Up to that time, he had participated in various activities related to his Navy experiences.[4] He did not fight in the Battle of Midway in June 1942, but often participated in the ongoing observances by the Midway Memorial Foundation of the pivotal battle, as well as maintained his house in the Georgetown section of Washington, D.C., with the help of his nephew Jim McBride, himself a former F-8 aviator, and also looked after his wife Vi. Having no children of their own, Whitey and Vi found satisfaction in helping rear the son of Whitey's youngest sister Eleanor, whose husband had been killed in France in November 1944 during World War II. He had barely stepped off the transport plane when a sniper's bullet found him. Jim and his wife Deb, and their two sons and one daughter, filled a void in the Feightners' lives and in return they have helped Whitey and Vi in their senior years.

Whitey Feightner, as mentioned in the introduction, is a supreme example of what writer and TV reporter Tom Brokaw called "the Greatest Generation," a group of Americans, fast leaving us, who stood up when called to defend their country and the free world when it was at its greatest peril. While we have thousands of Americans now in service who have echoed Whitey's historic, patriotic fraternity, the men and women who fought in World War II remain something truly special in this country's story. When the last goes, there will be a hole in America's tapestry that will never be repaired, and perhaps that is as it should be.

◆—➤ ACKNOWLEDGMENTS

Many people helped with various aspects of this account, from confirming historical facts and dates to photographic research. Each contributed in his or her own way and in amount of time and effort, so I am listing them alphabetically. They all helped, and thanks.

Dick Atkins, Vought History Group; Nancy Buchanan (NOAA); Mario De Luca, National Naval Aviation Museum; Archie Difante (U.S. Air Force Historical Center, Maxwell AFB); Dennis Feltgen (National Hurricane Center Miami); Steve Ginter; Joe Gordon, Naval History and Heritage Command; Dr. Richard P. Hallion; Glenn Helm and Randall Fortson of the Navy Department Library, Washington Navy Yard; Col. Denis J. Kiely, USMC (Ret.) (Senior Editor, Naval Aviation Museum Foundation); MC1 Mike Lindsey (Blue Angels); Jim and Deb McBride; Vice Adm. Jerry Miller, USN (Ret.); Frank Olynyk, PhD; Norman Polmar; Capt. Rosario Rausa, USNR (Ret.); Mari Rondeau, Patuxent River Naval Air Museum Association; Dave Seeman; Joe Stamm; Paul Stillwell; Jim Sullivan; Nicholas Thrasher (Managing Editor, *Foundation Magazine*, Naval Aviation Museum Foundation); Barrett Tillman. And an especially grateful thanks to Rick Russell, director of the Naval Institute Press, for his interest and help.

REAR ADM. E. L. FEIGHTNER'S ASSIGNMENTS

1. June–July 1941: Flight student, Grosse Ile, Michigan
2. July 1941–June 1942: Aviation cadet, NAS Corpus Christi, Texas
3. June–August 1942: Carrier qualifications
4. August–October 1942: Fighter pilot, VF-3 (assistant engineering officer)
5. October 1942–May 1943: Fighter pilot, VF-10 (assistant engineering officer)
6. May 1943–December 1944: Fighter pilot, VF-8 (engineering officer)
7. December 1944–May 1946: Fighter instructor, VF-98 (engineering and gunnery officer)
8. May–October 1946: Fighter instructor, VF-21 (engineering and gunnery officer)
9. October 1946–January 1948: Flag lieutenant and aide, Commander, Carrier Division 3 (assistant air ops.)
10. January–October 1948: Flag lieutenant and aide, Commander, Carrier Division 2 (assistant air ops.)
11. October 1948–June 1949: Test pilot training, student
12. June 1949–January 1952: Test pilot, Flight Test, NAS Patuxent River
13. January–July 1952: Pilot, Blue Angels
14. July–September 1952: Test pilot, NAS Patuxent River
15. September 1952–January 1955: Project pilot, VX-3 (development officer)
16. January 1955–March 1957: Commanding officer, VF-11
17. March 1957–October 1958: Commanding officer, Jet Transition and Training Unit
18. October 1958–February 1960: Commander, Carrier Air Group 10
19. February–July 1960: Standardization officer, Carrier Replacement Air Group 4
20. July 1960–July 1961: U.S. Naval War College, Student
21. July 1961–July 1963: Fighter design officer, BuWeps, Washington, D.C.
22. July 1963–November 1964: Staff operations officer, Commander, Carrier Division 2

23. November 1964–November 1965: Commanding officer, USS *Chikaskia* (AO 54)

24. February 1966–February 1967: Commanding officer, USS *Okinawa* (LPH 3)

25. April–July 1967: Defense Weapons Systems Management Center, Student

26. July–October 1967: Branch head, CNO (Op-506)

27. October 1967–October 1968: Branch head, Navy Fighter Study project officer, CNO (Op-506)

28. October 1968–October 1969: Director, Air Weapons Analysis (Op-05W) and director, Southeast Asia Analysis Group, CNO (Op-03Z)

29. October 1969–September 1970: Deputy director, Aviation Plans and Requirements Division, CNO (Op-50B)

30. September 1970–June 1974: Assistant commander for Logistics and Flight Support Group, NAVAIRSYSCOM (Air-04)

31. June 30, 1974: Retired

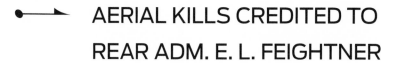

AERIAL KILLS CREDITED TO REAR ADM. E. L. FEIGHTNER

VF-10

| OCTOBER 26, 1942 | — | 1 Aichi 99 (Val) dive bomber |
| JANUARY 30, 1943 | — | 3 Mitsubishi G4M (Betty) bombers |

VF-8

MARCH 30, 1944	—	1 Mitsubishi A6M Zero-sen (Zeke) fighter
APRIL 29, 1944	—	1 Mitsubishi A6M Zero-sen (Zeke) fighter
OCTOBER 12, 1944	—	3 Mitsubishi A6M Zero-sen (Zeke) fighters

ACRONYMS AND ABBREVIATIONS

AAA	Anti-aircraft artillery
AFB	Air Force base
AVD	Seaplane tender
BuPers	Bureau of Naval Personnel
CAG	Commander Air Group
CAP	Combat air patrol
CarDiv	Carrier Division
CIC	Combat Information Center
ComNavAirLant	Commander, Naval Air Forces Atlantic
CNO	Chief of Naval Operations
CO	Commanding officer
CQ	Carrier qualifications
CV	Aircraft carrier
CVL	Light aircraft carrier
DD	Destroyer
FCLP	Fleet landing carrier practice
FDO	Fighter direction officer
IFR	Instrument flight rules
LantFlt	Commander Atlantic Fleet
LSO	Landing signal officer
LST	Landing ship, tank
NAS	Naval air station
OINC	Officer-in-charge
VF	Navy fighter squadron
VFR	Visual flight rules
VMF	Marine fighter squadron
VS	Scouting squadron
XO	Executive officer

Chapter 1. Growing Up in Ohio

1. After Mike had flown it, he sold the Bucker to famed aerobatic pilot Beverly "Bevo" Howard (1914–1971), who used it to win the 1946 and 1947 American Aerobatic Championships. He was killed in the little trainer in October 1971 while performing at an air show in North Carolina, but his estate paid to have the plane restored and donated to the Smithsonian in 1973.

   Murphy himself had a wartime career in keeping with his colorful prewar exploits. He found his way into the growing glider program as a lieutenant colonel. At 3 a.m. on June 6, 1944, he was in the thick of the historic invasion of Europe as the lead pilot of a CG-4A troop glider assault into landing zone Echo, just west of the town of Sainte-Marie-du-Mont. Riding behind him was Brig. Gen. Don F. Pratt (USA), assistant commander of the crack 101st Airborne Division. Although Murphy landed successfully, his glider was badly damaged when it overran the landing zone and skidded into a hedgerow of forty-foot-tall trees. The general and his aide were killed—making him the highest-ranking Allied officer killed during the landing phase of the D-day assault. Murphy also sustained severe injuries, including breaking both legs. Other officers in the glider were also killed. Mike Murphy passed away from natural causes in 1981.

2. Rear Adm. E. L. Feightner, USN (Ret.), Oral History, U.S. Naval Institute, Annapolis, Md., January 1990.

3. Ibid.

4. Red Hall got his gold wings and entered the Marine Corps. He flew F4U Corsairs with VMF-213 and became an ace with six kills. He passed away in December 2012.

5. Unless otherwise noted, all direct quotations are from Rear Adm. E. L. Feightner, USN (Ret.), Oral History, U.S. Naval Institute, 1990 and 2002.

Chapter 2. Flying the Navy Way

1. Rear Adm. E. L. Feightner, USN (Ret.), Oral History, U.S. Naval Institute, Annapolis, Md., January 1990. The F8F, the final Grumman prop fighter, was too late to see combat during World War II. Very fast, the little Bearcat flew with a few fleet squadrons after the war and with the Naval Air Reserve until many were sent to Indo-China to help the hard-pressed French.

2. Ibid.

Chapter 3. Training with Butch and Into the Fight

1. Rear Adm. E. L. Feightner, USN (Ret.), Oral History, U.S. Naval Institute, Annapolis, Md., January 1990.
2. Ibid.
3. Ibid.
4. Ibid.

Chapter 4. Fighting in the Solomons

1. Rear Adm. E. L. Feightner, USN (Ret.), Oral History, U.S. Naval Institute, Annapolis, Md., January 1990.
2. Ibid.
3. Barrett Tillman, *The Wildcat in World War II* (Annapolis, Md.: Nautical Aviation Publishing Co., 1982).
4. Rear Adm. E. L. Feightner, USN (Ret.), Oral History, U.S. Naval Institute, Annapolis, Md., January 1990.
5. Thanks to author Ted Edwards for helping clarify the traditionally clouded story of Swede Vejtasa's hectic engagement at Santa Cruz. At the time of writing, Ted is writing Swede's biography, helped by many lengthy interviews with Swede, then ninety-eight but still retaining sharp recall of those momentous days.
6. Peter Mersky, *The Grim Reapers: Fighting Squadron Ten in World War II* (Mesa, Ariz.: Champlin Museum Press, 1986).
7. Rear Adm. E. L. Feightner, USN (Ret.), Oral History, U.S. Naval Institute, Annapolis, Md., January 1990.
8. John B. Lundstrom, *The First Team and the Guadalcanal Campaign: Naval Fighter Combat from August to November 1942* (Annapolis, Md.: Naval Institute Press, 1994). It is impossible to praise author John Lundstrom's work too highly. His incredibly detailed and *fresh* research has set new standards for work in the subject of Pacific War aviation historical reporting.
9. Mersky, *The Grim Reapers*.

Chapter 5. With the Cactus Marines

1. Rear Adm. E. L. Feightner, USN (Ret.), Oral History, U.S. Naval Institute, Annapolis, Md., 1990.
2. Mersky, *The Grim Reapers*.
3. Ibid.
4. Mersky, *The Grim Reapers*; Lundstrom, *The First Team and the Guadalcanal Campaign*.
5. Steve Ewing, *Reaper Leader: The Life of Jimmy Flatley* (Annapolis, Md.: Naval Institute Press, 2002). Actually, the CO of the *Enterprise* was apparently so impressed with the young ensign's performance that he endorsed a submission

for a Navy Cross for the combined actions at Santa Cruz and Rennell Island. Eventually, Whitey received the Distinguished Flying Cross.

6. Mersky, *The Grim Reapers.*

Chapter 6. A New Squadron and a New Fighter

1. Max Brand, *Fighter Squadron at Guadalcanal* (Annapolis, Md.: Naval Institute Press, 1996).
2. There is a question of whether Bauer's final total was ten or eleven. His claim on October 3, 1942, for a Zero, which was seen to be smoking, was judged at the time as confirmed. But well-respected "aceologist" Dr. Frank Olynyk credits the claim as a probable, which at the time were usually judged destroyed. Bottom line: Bauer's official final score is eleven confirmed.
3. Rear Adm. E. L. Feightner, USN (Ret.), Oral History, U.S. Naval Institute, Annapolis, Md., December 1992.
4. Rear Adm. E. L. Feightner, USN (Ret.), Oral History, U.S. Naval Institute, Annapolis, Md., 1990.
5. For an excellent, more detailed account of Butch O'Hare's last flight as well as his Medal of Honor mission, see Steve Ewing and John B. Lundstrom, *Fateful Rendezvous: The Life of Butch O'Hare* (Annapolis, Md.: Naval Institute Press, 1997).

Chapter 7. *Bunker Hill* Action and Final Kills

1. There are currently 371 officially accredited U.S. Navy aces from World War II. The list has fluctuated over the years as research has changed an individual's status regarding specific kill claims. There was one U.S. Navy ace in World War I, one in Korea, and one USN *pilot* ace in Vietnam. The American Fighter Aces Association (AFAA) officially recognizes only pilot claims, not those of other crewmen such as F-4 Phantom radar intercept officers (RIOs). The two Vietnam USAF weapons systems officers (WSOs) and one Navy RIO are, however, AFAA honorees.
2. Rear Adm. E. L. Feightner, USN (Ret.), Oral History, U.S. Naval Institute, Annapolis, Md., 1990. Whitey had a chance to fly the Zero recovered in Alaska in June 1942. Its pilot, participating in operations in the Aleutians, had to make an emergency landing in a bog. His plane had flipped over, trapping him and probably breaking his neck and killing him. His A6M2 was recovered as the war's most valuable prize up to that time, brought back to the United States, and restored to flying condition. Several Navy aces flew it, including Lt. William Leonard, Lt. Swede Vejtasa, and Whitey Feightner. Whitey got the chance in 1943 when the Zero, which had been stationed at Patuxent, was brought up to Norfolk.
3. Ibid. The April 29 raid on Truk could be labeled Truk II after the big strike in mid-February.

4. Official citation.

5. Estimates of the number of aircraft lost on both sides vary and the number will probably never be confirmed to everyone's satisfaction. The Japanese did lose a considerable number, between around 300 to more than 400, which should include land-based aircraft destroyed by American fighters. The American losses are also often in question, with a number of as low as 30 and as high as 130 aircraft. Most of these were during the return from the combat area to the carriers now sailing in the dark, and because of the U.S. Navy aircraft quickly reaching the end of their endurance, resulting in numerous ditchings and in some cases outright disappearances. It wasn't until four days later, on June 23, that the last two-man crew from a ditched SB2C was found and retrieved.

Chapter 8. Testing Jets

1. Rear Adm. E. L. Feightner, USN (Ret.), Oral History, U.S. Naval Institute, Annapolis, Md., 1990.

2. Ewing and Lundstrom, *Fateful Rendezvous: The Life of Butch O'Hare.*

3. Rear Adm. E. L. Feightner, USN (Ret.), Oral History, U.S. Naval Institute, Annapolis, Md., 1990.

4. Ibid.

5. Ibid.

6. *Naval Aviation News*, September–October 1994.

Chapter 9. The Radical, Dangerous Cutlass

1. Whitey Feightner, interview with the author, 1988, Washington, D.C.

2. Ibid.

3. Ibid.

4. *Approach, the Navy and Marine Corps Aviation Safety Magazine*, July 1955.

Chapter 10. More Testing at New Commands

1. Rear Adm. E. L. Feightner, USN (Ret.), Oral History, U.S. Naval Institute, Annapolis, Md., 1990.

2. The author was at Dulles on that day. It was hard to see exactly what was happening as the USAF F-4s left the area, but as one of the Phantoms left the team and headed for what must have been a designated emergency bailout area to the west of the field, one parachute did appear, but it soon began drifting toward the blue-gray column of smoke from the crash. And later, another fatal mishap occurred when an ultra-light sport plane flying in front of the viewing area seemed to literally fold up in midair as the pilot could be heard to exclaim, "Oh, no!" The flimsy little plane fell to earth, killing the pilot right in front of the horrified crowd.

3. Over the years, the report of Whitey's eighteen-hour stint in a Skyraider has met with some skepticism, often from other highly experienced AD pilots who certainly have their own long-distance flight stories to back them up. There is no doubt that sitting on a hard, uncomfortable, poorly padded seat, in a big single-man aircraft droning along at low level, concentrating on the mission was highly fatiguing. It took extremely capable, dedicated aviators to do it right. The average hop was between nine and twelve hours, and to claim a third more time left people shaking their heads. To this day, however, Admiral Feightner affirms the logged time and the mission.

Chapter 11. Back to the Fleet and Command

1. Jerry Miller, *Nuclear Weapons and Aircraft Carriers: How the Bomb Saved Naval Aviation* (Washington, D.C.: Smithsonian Institution Press, 2001); from a taped interview with Rear Admiral Feightner.
2. Brian Cull, with David Nicolle and Shlomo Aloni, *Wings over Suez* (London: Grub Street, 1996).
3. The Immelmann turn was named for one of Imperial Germany's first aces, Max Immelmann, who is generally credited with performing the turn early in World War I. It was a quick way of reversing one's disadvantaged position out of a dogfight, and it quickly began part of any decent pilot's repertoire.
4. Rear Adm. E. L. Feightner, USN (Ret.), Oral History, U.S. Naval Institute, Annapolis, Md., 1993.
5. Rocks and Shoals was the predecessor of the Navy justice system's current set of legal rules (Code of Military Conduct) going up through the Korean War. The Code of Conduct was more specific and allowed for greater latitude in how an American prisoner of war could and should conduct himself in captivity. Its greatest test came quickly during the Vietnam War and has more recently been measured by Desert Storm in 1991 and Operation Iraqi Freedom and Operation Enduring Freedom following the attacks of September 11, 2001. American servicemen *and* servicewomen have still found proper conduct difficult to maintain under highly intense and torturous treatment by cultures usually diametrically opposed to that of the United States, harking back to inhuman treatment by the Japanese and German Gestapo of World War II.
6. The C-124 Globemaster II was a development of the C-74 Globemaster I, a large postwar design for a theater transport, able to airlift large pieces of equipment. Fourteen were built out of an original contract for fifty. The greatly redesigned Globemaster II entered service in 1950 and served for another twenty-five years in the Air Force and Air Force Reserve throughout the world. The James Stewart 1955 movie *Strategic Air Command* has several sequences showing C-124s decked out in highly colorful markings of the time, showing the portly Globemaster II to its best advantage. Not to be missed.

7. Rear Adm. E. L. Feightner, USN (Ret.), Oral History, U.S. Naval Institute, Annapolis, Md., 1993.
8. Commander Berree scored nine kills in the Pacific with VF-15 flying Hellcats and received four Distinguished Flying Crosses. He made captain having flown from thirteen carriers. He died in 2006.

Chapter 12. Out to the Mediterranean then Back to Shore-Based Developments

1. Rear Adm. E. L. Feightner, USN (Ret.), Oral History, U.S. Naval Institute, Annapolis, Md., 1993.
2. Whitey Feightner, interview with the author, 1988.
3. Rear Adm. E. L. Feightner, USN (Ret.), Oral History, U.S. Naval Institute, Annapolis, Md., 1993.
4. Larry Booda, "DOD to Standardize Aircraft Designations," *Aviation Week and Space Technology*, June 11, 1962.
5. The Gatling gun was a modern arrangement based on the late nineteenth-century predecessor of the machine gun that used a series of rotating gun barrels motivated by a hand crank. The result was a devastating field of rapid fire that usually came as a nasty surprise to enemy troops unfortunate enough to run into the gun's lawn-mower fire. The gun was resurrected to take 20-mm cannon shells and was placed in several U.S. fighters of the period. Its basic design has remained to the present day and forms the heart of the armament of many military aircraft.
6. The generals were probably part of what today might be called the Air Force Council, made up of representatives from Air Force Systems Command and Logistics Command, with perhaps a selection from the Air Defense Command and tactical Air Command. Although Whitey remembered at least one three-star across the table from him and Admiral Stroop, none of these senior officers had the power to make the call and probably had to brief the vice chief of staff (a four-star) and deputy chiefs of staff (three-stars) for acquisition, planning, and operations. This was also the period Strategic Air Command (SAC) was in control and therefore was more interested in bombers and missiles than a new fighter. Finally, it was also probable that the Department of Defense—meaning Secretary McNamara—had to be part of the process. Thanks to Dr. Richard P. Hallion, former historian of the Air Force (1991–2002), for his help in distilling this complicated situation.
7. RIOs were part of the overall group of naval flight officers (NFOs). They were highly trained, commissioned officers who were responsible for operating the F-4's radar system. For a time, the RIO was second to the pilot, and during that time there were occasional clashes between the two groups. By 1968, however, NFOs were finally given chances to command squadrons and other organizations within the Navy and Marine Corps. With the retirement of

the F-14 Tomcat and A-6 Intruder by the turn of the twenty-first century, the NFO community has been greatly reduced, with only maritime patrol (P-3 and oncoming P-8), electronic surveillance (EA-18G), medium attack (FA-18D, FA-18F), and airborne control (E-2C/D) still requiring nonpilot officers.

Chapter 13. Senior Commands

1. Rear Adm. E. L. Feightner, USN (Ret.), Oral History, U.S. Naval Institute, Annapolis, Md., 1993.
2. H. R. McMaster, *Dereliction of Duty: Lyndon Johnson, Robert McNamara, the Joint Chiefs of Staff, and the Lies That Led to Vietnam* (New York: HarperCollins, 1997), 162–64.
3. On January 5, 1999, two VF-213 F-14Ds engaged several Iraqi MiG-25s in the so-called No-Fly Zone, and on September 9, 1999, an F-14D from VF-2 shot a single AIM-54C at an Iraqi MiG-23. All three shots were at extreme range and without success.
4. Adm. George W. Anderson Jr., "The Reminiscences of Admiral George W. Anderson, Jr., U.S. Navy (Retired)," Volume 2, Oral History, U.S. Naval Institute, Annapolis, Md., 1983, pp. 495, 544, 558–59.
5. Whitey had an unusual experience during the crisis, and this might be the first time it has been described. He had been involved in practice drops of small nuclear weapons using a "shape" with an electronic simulator that produced a mushroom cloud. During the crisis in 1962, a Soviet freighter was known to be carrying thirteen nuclear bombs toward Cuba. When its captain refused to leave, the U.S. Navy was told to *blow it up*. Whitey remembered being flown out to the *Enterprise* and manning a specially armed Banshee, under the direct guidance of Cdr. (later Vice Adm.) Frederick L. Ashworth, who had armed the A-bomb dropped on Nagasaki on August 9, 1945. Before that mission, he had commanded VT-11, flying TBF Avengers in the Pacific. Ashworth told Whitey that when so ordered, he would launch, drop his weapon on the freighter, and bank hard to get away. He also told Whitey to turn off his radio after launch as there would definitely be no recall. It was a lot to absorb, but Whitey was ready. It was only when the time to launch approached that word came that the Soviet captain had turned his ship around and had defused the rapidly growing tension on the flight deck of the *Enterprise*.
6. In March 1968, the USAF's 428th TFS sent a detachment of six F-111As to Thailand as part of Operation Combat Lancer. Although the new plane did well in its fifty-five missions against North Vietnam, three were lost in operational mishaps, along with four of the six crewmen, two in each aircraft.
7. At the time of writing, the *Enterprise* was recently retired after a fifty-year career in peace and war, an enviable and proper successor to the Navy's most decorated ship of World War II, CV 6.

8. Rear Adm. E. L. Feightner, USN (Ret.), Oral History, U.S. Naval Institute, Arlington, Va., 2000.
9. Naval History Blog, U.S. Naval Institute, August 1, 2012. Operation Sea Orbit by Rear Adm. Bernard M. Strean, USN, Commander Task Force One.

Chapter 14. Driving His Own Ship

1. Rear Adm. E. L. Feightner, USN (Ret.), Oral History, U.S. Naval Institute, Arlington, Va., 2002.

Chapter 15. A Senior Tour

1. Rear Adm. E. L. Feightner, USN (Ret.), Oral History, U.S. Naval Institute, Arlington, Va., 2002.
2. Ibid.
3. Ibid.

Chapter 16. Ending His Career: Time to Move On

1. Rear Adm. E. L. Feightner, USN (Ret.), Oral History, U.S. Naval Institute, Arlington, Va., November 2002.
2. Ibid.
3. The Navy had an odd arrangement of allowing the new flag officer to wear two stars but actually only affording him the status of a one-star, or, as it was referred to, the "lower half." He still had to, when the time was right, be selected for another star or "upper half," while still retaining the rank of rear admiral. The other services occasionally objected to the misleading insignia, and finally in the early 1980s the Navy stipulated that the new one star would be called "commodore," another previously misleading term that applied to captains leading surface squadrons. The change lasted for a short time, and by the 1990s, "rear admiral" was again in use although denoted by the curious abbreviation of "RDML" for the lower half and the traditional RADM for the upper half.
4. Originally coined to indicate Foreign Military Sales during his time in the Pentagon. After retirement, Whitey and a couple of other retired Navy men formed a company to service other countries' requirements. "FMS" was still in use, but, keeping the letters, they named their new firm the Federal Management System. Other, unrelated organizations also carry the same initials, so there was occasional confusion, which kept corporate life interesting.

SELECTED BIBLIOGRAPHY

Armstrong, Jim. *From POW to Blue Angel: The Story of Commander Dusty Rhodes.* Norman: University of Oklahoma Press, 2006.

Cull, Brian, with David Nicolle and Shlomo Aloni. *Wings over Suez.* London: Grub Street, 1996.

Drummond, Anthony. *United States Naval Test Pilot School 1945 to 1983, Second Edition.* Annapolis, Md.: Fishergate Publishing Co., Inc., 1984.

Ewing, Steve. *Reaper Leader: The Life of Jimmy Flatley.* Annapolis, Md.: Naval Institute Press, 2002.

———. *Thach Weave: The Life of Jimmie Thach.* Annapolis, Md.: Naval Institute Press, 2004.

Ewing, Steve, and John B. Lundstrom. *Fateful Rendezvous: The Life of Butch O'Hare.* Annapolis, Md.: Naval Institute Press, 1997.

Francillon, Rene J. *McDonnell Douglas Aircraft since 1920, Volume I.* Annapolis, Md.: Naval Institute Press, 1979.

———. *McDonnell Douglas Aircraft since 1920, Volume II.* Annapolis, Md.: Naval Institute Press, 1979.

Ginter, Steve. *Chance Vought F7U Cutlass, Naval Fighters Number Six.* Simi Valley, Calif.: Steve Ginter Books, 1982.

———. *McDonnell Banshee, F2H-1,-2,-B,-N,-P,3,4.* Simi Valley, Calif.: Steve Ginter Books, 1980.

———. *McDonnell F2H-3/4, "Big Banjo."* Simi Valley, Calif.: Steve Ginter Books, 2011.

Lawson, Robert L. *Carrier Air Group Commanders, the Men and Their Machines.* Atglen, Pa.: Schiffer Military History, 2000.

Lundstrom, John B. *The First Team, Pacific Naval Air Combat from Pearl Harbor to Midway.* Annapolis, Md.: Naval Institute Press, 1984.

———. *The First Team and the Guadalcanal Campaign, Naval Fighter Combat from August to November 1942.* Annapolis, Md.: Naval Institute Press, 1994.

Mersky, Peter B. *The Grim Reapers: Fighting Squadron Ten in WWII.* Mesa, Ariz.: Champlin Museum Press, 1986.

———. *Time of the Aces: Marine Pilots in the Solomons, 1942–1944.* Washington, D.C.: Marine Corps Historical Center, 1993.

Miller, Jerry. *Nuclear Weapons and Aircraft Carriers: How the Bomb Saved Naval Aviation.* Washington, D.C.: Smithsonian Institution, 2001.

Polmar, Norman. *Aircraft Carriers: A History of Carrier Aviation and Its Influence on World Events, Vol. I, 1909–1945*. Washington, D.C.: Potomac Books, Inc. 2006.

———. *Aircraft Carriers: A History of Carrier Aviation and Its Influence on World Events, Vol. II, 1946–2006*. Washington, D.C.: Potomac Books, Inc. 2008.

Swanborough, Gordon, and Peter M. Bowers. *United States Navy Aircraft since 1911*. Annapolis, Md.: Naval Institute Press, 1976, 1990.

Tagaya, Osamu. *Aichi 99 Kanbaku "Val" Units, 1937–42*. London: Osprey Publishing Co., 2011.

———. *Mitsubishi Type 1 Rikko "Betty" Units of World War 2*. London: Osprey Publishing Co., 2001.

Thomason, Tommy H. *Chance Vought F7U-1 Cutlass, Naval Fighters Number Ninety-Four*. Simi Valley, Calif.: Steve Ginter Books, 2012.

Tillman, Barrett. *Enterprise, America's Fightingest Ship and the Men Who Helped Win World War II*. New York: Simon & Schuster, 2012.

———. *Hellcat Aces of World War 2*. London: Osprey Publishing Co., 1996.

———. *U.S. Navy Fighter Squadrons in World War II*. North Branch, Minn.: Specialty Press, 1997.

———. *Wildcat Aces of World War 2*. London: Osprey Publishing Co., 1995.

Wilcox, Robert K. *First Blue: The Story of World War II Ace Butch Voris and the Creation of the Blue Angels*. New York: Thomas Dunne Books/St. Martin's Press, 2004.

Williams, Nick, and Steve Ginter. *Douglas F4D Skyray, Naval Fighters Number Thirteen*. Simi Valley, Calif.: Steve Ginter Books, 1986.

INDEX

Yamato, 59
Zuiho, 26
Zuikaku, 29
Smith, Colonel John L., USMC ace
 at Guadalcanal, Medal of
 Honor recipient, 41
Spangenberg, G. A.
 civilian analyst, 77
 involvement with TFX, 132–133
Strean, Vice Admiral B. M., 137, 139
Stroop, Vice Admiral P. D., 128

T
Thach, John "Jimmie," 14
Trapnell, Vice Admiral F. M., CO of
 NAS Patuxent River, flying
 the AD, 74–75

V
VB-10, at Santa Cruz, 26
Vejtasa, Captain S. W. "Swede"
 at the Battle of Santa Cruz, 26,
 29, 30
 flies new F4U, 42–43
 at Guadalcanal, 34, 37–38

VF-8, 43, 44, 50
VF-10, 20, 25, 30–32
 at Guadalcanal, 33
 orders to Pearl Harbor and transi-
 tion to the F6F, 43
VF-11, "Red Rippers," 103–104
 night flying at Suez, 1956, 105
Von Tempsky Zabriskie, Countess
 Alexa, 18, 19
Voris, Captain Butch, 36
 CO of the Blue Angels, 81
VX-3, testing new catapults, 99–100

W
Wickindoll, Ensign Maurice "Wick,"
 VF-10 pilot, 25, 28

Z
Zumwalt, Admiral Elmo
 CNO, 152–153
 against the F-14, 154
 involvement with TFX, 133
 in Rickover's shadow, 160
 systems analysis group, 154
 Whitey's assessment of Zumwalt,
 153, 156

●————➤ ABOUT THE AUTHOR

Peter B. Mersky graduated from the Rhode Island School of Design in 1967 and was commissioned through the Navy's Aviation Officer Candidate School in 1968. He served in various assignments on active duty and in the Naval Reserve, retiring as a commander in 1992. After working as a government illustrator in the Washington, D.C., area, he was the assistant editor and then editor of *Approach*, the Navy and Marine Corps aviation safety magazine. He has written sixteen books and a hundred magazine articles and has reviewed more than seven hundred books in his regular column for *Naval Aviation News* and other periodicals.